About the Author

Although retired from working as an emergency nurse practitioner in the NHS Sarah Lewis remains a registered nurse, now mainly working on seasonal projects, as well as volunteering in her local community.

She was born in Harlow, Essex, where she still lives today.

Sarah appreciates the simple things in life, like a cup of tea, her vast family and friends, a flutter on the races, dressing up, swimming and make-up.

There are two things that categorise Sarah — her ability to enjoy life with a sense of adventure, and her ability to care for others.

In truth her life has always been dedicated to helping other people, she supposed, but now it was time to take a year out.

This is her story.

Just Him and Me

Sarah Lewis

Just Him and Me

Olympia Publishers
London

www.olympiapublishers.com

OLYMPIA PAPERBACK EDITION

A CIP catalogue record for this title is
available from the British Library.

ISBN: 978-1-80074-236-9

First Published in 2022

Olympia Publishers
Tallis House
2 Tallis Street
London
EC4Y 0AB
Printed in Great Britain

Dedication

to 'Auntie Pat'

Acknowledgements

Of course I wish to thank my wonderful mum and dad, beautiful family and fabulous friends for their constant love and support, but there are two special people in my life, without whom this dream would never have come true.

My dear Lou, we have been together since teenagers, and married for over thirty-five years (who would have thought?). You have the gift of patience and understanding. You are loving and kind. You look after me, are my protector, and I always feel safe with you beside me.
You are thoughtful and romantic.
I thank you; I love you, always and forever.

My remarkable son Dale — you are the most unparalleled and resplendent individual in the entire universe. You are handsome and smart. You are extraordinary and inspiring. You are supportive, loving and extremely generous.
You make me so proud every day.
You are my joy, my happiness, my everything.
I thank you; I love you so very much.

Prologue

Well, where shall I start? We met at secondary school in 1977 when I was just fourteen years old, Lou was sixteen. We used to frequent the local youth club called The Grove.

Betty was the youth worker there, she knew Lou fancied me, so one Valentine's Day she hatched up a secret plan with him, hid a red rose and a silver heart necklace in her old grey filing cabinet, called me in to the office where Lou was waiting for me to ask me to be his Valentine! I said yes!

Our relationship grew, Lou had just started to work as a butcher, and I was going to be a nurse. We would get married, live a normal life, have children etc.

At the age of sixteen, I gave birth to the most beautiful baby I had ever seen... our son, Dale, and our future had begun.

In the early days we lived with my mum and dad, we later moved to a small flat, but were lucky enough to do a council exchange into a three-bedroom house.

Margaret Thatcher gave us the opportunity of 'the right to buy' our house from the local council, so five years after the birth of our son we got married and began paying a mortgage.

I started my nurse training in 1987, Mum and Dad helped out so much, as did the rest of our family and friends.

We scrimped and saved, worked hard, brought up our gorgeous son, and before we knew it, and as we had talked/dreamt and planned, we had paid our mortgage off by the time I was fifty.

I had worked on the front line of the NHS for twenty-six years now, and was eligible for early retirement with full pension at the age of fifty-five. Only five years' time!

We talked about travelling, I could take retirement and my full NHS pension, and we could have a 'gap year'

We started to plan our dream trip, our son was now a man with a career and a home of his own that he shared with his darling partner Ed. We decided that life was too short to wait; we would take time out and go for it.

I retired from my work in October 2018, after thirty-one years' service, we planned to leave the UK in May 2019 after sorting out the house.

Our niece, Jess, would move into the house, as we really did not want to rent it out, or leave it empty. It suited her well, as she had not long been back from living in Australia. She was keen to have some independence and save for a deposit for a home of her own.

We had a rough itinerary, but would just book places as we went along, for two reasons really, in-case we needed to come home at short notice, and if we liked a place — stay longer, didn't like a place — move on.

As our departure date drew nearer a family tragedy occurred.

On 31st March, Mother's Day 2019, at 06:05 in the morning, I had a phone call from my distraught sister Ju to say that her husband, our brother-in-law Jeff, had collapsed at home.

I rushed round to find the paramedics attempting to resuscitate him. He had had a respiratory arrest, which led to cardiac arrest, and although the crew had managed to get return of spontaneous circulation with chest compressions, they were unable to intubate at the home. Jeff was taken to the local hospital where they managed to pass a breathing tube; he was transferred to the intensive care unit where he remained for the next five days.

On the 4th April my sister was told that efforts were futile, and that Jeff was unable to make any meaningful recovery.

Ju decided on making an organ donation, it was something that they had spoken about only two weeks prior to his collapse.

Both his kidneys, as well as his heart valves, were suitable.

Jeff died on 5th April, with Ju by his side.

The next few weeks were very emotional, as you can imagine.

Lou and I were in two minds about delaying our trip.

My sister was adamant that we should go as planned; she said Jeff wouldn't have wanted us to postpone.

Life really does turn on a sixpence.

Of course I had witnessed many family tragedies over the years in my line of work, and I have always been a believer of what I call 'OK, Sarah, Sarah' (whatever will be will be).

Our lives are generally mapped out for us but we can choose different pathways at the junctions we meet on the way.

Our son was very supportive; he would look after my sister while we were away. As would the rest of our wonderful family and friends.

Life is a gift, death is a given.

This is my personal account.

Welcome to our trip.

Chapter One
Morocco

May 7th

At 16:10 Dale dropped us off at Stansted Airport with a one-way flight ticket to Agadir... Eeekkk.

Of course there were lots of emotions whirling around in our heads.

We checked in and excitedly made our way straight to the champagne bar for a glass of fizz before boarding.

Our flight was on time, we swiftly passed through customs, although I was stopped and searched, nothing new for me, it seems to happen to me all the time. We stepped onto the plane to begin our trip of a lifetime.

The flight was smooth and we arrived in Agadir as scheduled, an hour in front of UK GMT, and 2,435km from home.

We changed up some money into dirham — Morocco had a closed currency which means you cannot get it until you are in the country, and headed to the hotel.

We had booked an 'all inclusive' for the first week so as to ease ourselves in, and arrived, at 20:15 local time to hear the sound of rapturous applause coming from the crowds in the hotel bar. Lou ran off immediately, Liverpool (his team) were playing for a place in the Champions League final, they had just scored and were winning 4:0.

I checked us in and we watched the end of the game, before heading into the buffet restaurant for dinner.

After dinner we sat in the bar and had some drinks, quite a few to be honest.

We sat and talked excitedly about our trip... ... ... Lou kept thinking he could see 'white rats' running along the window ledge outside??

May 8th

Up early, so we went down to breakfast. Lots to choose from as you would expect from buffet-style food, lovely and fresh.

We decided to go for a walk so ventured off along the seaside promenade and very wide crescent beach into town.

We couldn't understand why there were so few people around, all the cafes and restaurants seemed to be shut.

Ramadan.

Sunday 5th May-Tuesday 4th June.

THE most sacred month in Islamic culture based on the lunar calendar.

Muslims believe that Ramadan teaches them self-discipline, self-control, sacrifice and to empathise with those less fortunate than they are. A time for celebration and joy.

Amongst other sacrifices they fast from dawn until sunset.

Our first schoolboy error!

Couldn't believe that we had booked the start of our trip in a Muslim country at the start of Ramadan. Hence the reason the streets are empty and everything was shut.

We walked 6.4 miles according to my Apple watch which I was given as a retirement gift (amongst many other gifts) from my lovely colleagues at Princess Alexandra Hospital. I shall miss my work family.

May 9th

Spent most of the afternoon in the hotel and around the pool planning our next move, not quite believing that we had actually gone ahead with our plan.

We went for a ride around town on the Petit Train (tuktuk) and it seemed apparent there is not much more to do in Agadir other that walk along the lovely beach and promenade which was fine, that suited us.

Agadir is very deliberately developed and devoid of any culture since its destruction following an earthquake in 1960.

Everywhere is pretty modern and clean, the sea is cold though, as are the evenings.

Lou contemplated trying to get tickets for the Champions League Final in Madrid seeing as Liverpool got through, but prices are extortionate and the hotels, even hostels are £800 per person per night.

We did find out what the 'white rats' Lou saw on the first night were though.... It turns out that we had been sitting on a raised level looking out to sea on the first night, it was dark and what he actually saw were the tops of the heads of people walking by. We laughed out loud. It was so easy to see in the daylight, and when sober, it was so funny.

We walked to see the port, and to find the fish market. On the way, and completely out of nowhere, we were accosted by a local who followed us in a menacing way trying to show us to the market; he wanted money!

May 10th

Up early to go to the bus station and get tickets for our

onward journey and again we were accosted on the way by a local who was trying to get us to follow him to the local market... Like yesterday, it felt intimidating and he wanted money from us.

Eventually found the bus station and purchased our tickets for the next destination — we would be travelling north up the west coast to Essaouira.

We walked 6.2 miles in total.

May 11th

Had breakfast al fresco today.

Again, we went for a walk — 4.5 miles, then back to the hotel for a swim in the pool.

I joined in with the water aerobics.

We spoke to Dale on the phone, called Mum and Dad for a chat, and also spoke to Ju.

I miss them all, already.

May 12th

Not a very good sleep, the chants for morning prayer woke me at 04:00.

During Ramadan the salat (daily prayer) takes on an increased significance, both because the holy month is considered a time of reflection and purification and also because they shape the hours of the fast.

Every day during Ramadan, Muslims eat a pre-fast meal called the *sahūr*, which is taken before sunrise and culminates with the day's first prayer, the fajr.

The fast isn't broken until the sun sets. This is called the *iftar* meal and precedes the maghrib, the fourth prayer of the day.

Praying five times a day is obligatory for Muslims; they are spread throughout the day so that worshippers are able to continually maintain their connection to God.

Sat around the pool most of day, just relaxing and reading, it is nice sometimes to have nothing to do, isn't it?

Lou managed to watch some premiership football and I booked myself into the spa for a manicure and nail polish.

Lou spoke to his best friend, Bunny, and was delighted when he heard that he had come third in the super-six that they play together with a whole group of friends. He won £115.

May 13th

It's our last day in Agadir and, unfortunately, very cloudy and quite cold too.

Didn't do much at all, except pack and get ready for our move the following day.

May 14th

Up early by alarm.

A one-way ticket to Essaouira, a port city on Morocco's Atlantic coast famous for its riads.

Aka the Windy city, it is very popular with kite surfers.

It is a UNESCO world heritage site because its Medina is well preserved and maintains the integrity in architecture that it has had for centuries.

Apparently, it was also very popular for hippies, in the 60/70s too and several famous artists like Cat Stevens and Jimi Hendrix lived here.

We were looking forward to staying in a riad. I've seen them many times of course, on TV and in magazines and they always look so magical, like little palaces with their own courtyard and interior gardens.

Originally, they would have been stately homes of the wealthy. They are traditionally inward focused allowing for the Islamic notions family privacy, hijab for women and protection for all.

One hundred and twenty-three km and three and a half hours later we arrived in Essaouira.

The place was buzzing, a porter immediately took our backpacks and flung them onto the back of a trolley cart, and before we knew it, he's weaving in and out of the crowds, through the narrow winding alleys and lanes of the bazaar with the sounds of bartering sellers trying to get our attention, wafts of tagines and pungent spices, as well as the smell of leather, fish, fruit and flowers.

We paid twenty dirham (around £2) and were very grateful, as we would have never of found Riad Jade Mogador.

It suddenly felt like real Morocco.

The riad was quaint, with very narrow stairs, a central courtyard and a roof terrace.

We would have to take note of landmarks when out exploring or we would never find this place on our own.

We decided to walk to the famous harbour, once Morocco's main port for the entire country, and the most important trading port between Africa, Europe and the Americas.

It's an impressive place, packed with young men cleaning their vessels, fishermen landing their haul onto the dock surrounded by locals waiting to pounce. There are stalls along the dock crammed with fresh fish, and gulls hovering hungrily above, your feet sliding on the gutted discarded entrails.

After spending a few hours at the port we decided to go to the supermarket to try and get some wine.

One local chap told us to try the local Carrefour supermarket, as he said the smaller shops would definitely not have any.

Five point three miles later finally found the supermarket... and guess what? No wine, what were we thinking?

We now had to walk 5.3 miles back to the riad empty handed.

We had dinner at a local restaurant.

Stray cats and dogs are everywhere here, crying, fighting, barking and howling.

Very noisy with kids too still playing in the streets at ten p.m. It's going to be a long night.

May 15th

Yes, I was right, very little meaningful sleep.

Gave up eventually at 06.38 a.m.

Very cloudy and windy outside, still chilly.

Lou went up to the rooftop terrace but got attacked by a very large seagull, dive bombing at him whilst hissing. He had to make a quick exit and scurry down the stairs at the first opportunity, whilst making a very strange squealing sound himself. It turns out she had a nest to protect with two newly hatched baby chicks.

After a traditional breakfast in the Riad, which consisted of *msemen* (flaky layered bread) *baghrir* (a type of pancake), jam, honey and lots of tea of course we headed off to explore the souk.

Herbalists, spice sellers, metal workers, jewellers,

tanners, fruit, fish and vegetables, all in a labyrinth of alleyways and easy to get lost.

We identified a sign above the alleyway at the entrance to our riad 'Pharmacy' which would be illuminated at night, just in case we couldn't find our way back home.

The biggest hazard in the souk was to avoid the mopeds that hurtle around and weave in and out at some speed, coupled with the challenge of mule carts, wagons and trolley carts carrying the luggage of tourists coming/going.

After visiting the souk we went to the beach for few hours, but it was very windy.

Fish platter for dinner — cold evening.

May 16th

Hoorah, the sun is shining.

We had breakfast in the communal area. Staying in a Riad is a unique experience, but is not for everyone; breakfast is served from one large table, shared by all guests, and by the nature of their construction it is a very intimate space that can be difficult to adjust to. We loved it.

Our riad had six rooms all with unique and traditional decor, it was well kept and clean, and the view from the terrace, reached by climbing a very narrow couple of flights of stairs, gave an amazing view of the Medina, the city ramparts and the ocean.

We went to the beach for the day; truly living up to its reputation, it was very windy again, it's surprising where sand can end up if you get my gist.

Later we found a rooftop terrace bar and restaurant for dinner called Taros, a lively rooftop café with great views, half decent food and they served alcohol.

May 17th

Off to Marrakech today, travelling eastwards inland for 166 km.

The coach took us three and a half hours.

The funniest sight so far on the way, we saw the goats feeding up in the trees.

A rather unusual scene... yes, cloven-hoofed goats perched high up on the branches of trees munching on the fruit.

They only climb one particular type of tree, the *Argania spinosa*, or the Argan tree, a prickly and thorny tree which produces yellow flowers and small fruit.

The nut of the fruit is used to produce Argan oil.

Now, here is the scientific part... the goat eats the fruit, but cannot digest the nut, this then passes through their digestive system which softens the nut, the nut is then excreted by the goat and is gathered and ground to produce Argan oil.

It was truly a bizarre spectacle.

We were later to see the old ladies sitting on very low stools, legs akimbo, hand grinding the nuts to expel the precious oil.

We arrived in Marrakesh at 14:30 and were immediately pestered and followed by a very annoying taxi driver, it seems to be a recurring theme.

Managed to flag one down further up the road, but the taxi driver took us to the wrong address. We then walked around for about fifteen minutes, again pestered by the locals, one teenage lad on a pushbike in particular, offering to show us the way — for a price.

We were excited when we eventually came across Riad Dar Rosa but it appeared there were two, so Mustafa escorted us to the one we had booked which just happened to belong to his sister Fathima!

This riad was just as beautiful as the last, a traditional Moroccan house with stunning architecture, and an interior garden and courtyard. However, the decor was shabby and in need of a facelift or some TLC.

After unpacking and freshening up, Fathima took our dirty washing, as we had been travelling for two weeks now with no laundry facilities; it was washed, dried and folded by the evening.

A visit to Marrakesh would not be complete without a visit to the Medina, with its ancient walls and over twenty huge gates the central courtyard is where people continue to live a traditional way of life. We walked to the Medina, wow, an overload on the senses, and an onslaught of sights. This place was mad.

Haman bathhouses, snake charmers, horse and carriages, sellers, beggars, acrobats, folk dancers, carpet weavers, knickknacks, fakes, monkeys, mopeds, cars, bicycles, eateries, street food vendors, ice cream vendors... ... you really need eyes in the back of your head, but you really shouldn't worry about the hectic atmosphere, just dive right in there and soak it all up.

After getting exhausted just walking around and keeping our wits about us, it was time for dinner. We sat upstairs in a restaurant which had panoramic views across the square.

Lou had his first Tagine of beef, I had Moroccan chicken skewers and salad, ... all washed down with, and you've guessed it, water.

May 18th

Decided to go on the city tour of Marrakech today.

After breakfast we headed off to the bus stop. The bus took us all around the city and we learned that Marrakesh has three main regions.

The Medina, or the old fortified city, still one of the busiest cities in Africa, serves as a major economic centre and tourist destination.

Real estate and hotel development have grown dramatically here in the twenty-first century.

The Menara gardens area is the second, where there are lush gardens with an esplanade at the entrance to Avenue Prince Moulay Rachid, where looking across to the pavilion, once used as a summer residence by a former sultan, you can see splendid views of the Atlas Mountains on a clear day.

Seventy per cent of the Moroccans that live in this area are wealthy and under thirty years of age.

Then there is the commercial area, where you can find the Alzamar Centre, a mall built for the tourists amongst a plethora of five-star hotels. Unfortunately, it is over-run by fast food joints selling pizza, burger, taco, chicken, coffee and ice-cream vendors.

The tour was interesting, very excited to see camels, baby camels, palm trees, olive trees and more camels.

We learnt a lot of very interesting facts, my favourite being:

The Moroccans favourite drink is tea, made of green tea and mint.

It is said that one should have three cups poured from the same pot in a row first thing in the morning.

'The first cup is bitter as is life itself, the second is strong as is love, and the third is sweet — as is death.'

This evening we found 'Sky Lounge' set on the top of The Pearl Marrakech which offered a panoramic restaurant and terrace bar.

It has spectacular views of the ochre city, the medina, the gardens and you could see all the way to the Atlas Mountains too.

We had dinner and wine here, why wouldn't we? Because it cost more than the three nights we had paid to stay in the riad, that's why!

May 19th

The ticket we had for the Red Bus Tour was still valid, so we decided to go back to the Menara Mall and have a look around.

We weren't really interested in shopping, but right next door was the Marrakesh Savoy Hotel... Rude not to pop in for a cocktail enjoyed in the cosy atmosphere of the lobby bar. I had their signature cocktail 'From Marrakech with Love', a delicious but rather potent mix of whiskey, crème de cacao, kahlua and vanilla liquor.

Phoned and spoke to Ju from there, she seemed okay.

On the way home back to riad we went for a walk through the Menara Gardens and around the Medina for one last crazy time.

May 20th

Next stop, this time travelling by train, Marrakesh to Casablanca, 243 km heading north.

Casablanca is the largest city in Morocco, located in the

west, bordering the Atlantic.

It is the chief port and the largest financial, economic and business centre in Africa.

It took us only 2.5hrs, then almost same again to find the hotel, it turned out we had gotten off the tram seven stops too early.

It seemed that we walked for miles, asked several people for directions, including tourist police and eventually found it, Hotel Ambassadeurs, and blimey, what a dump.

The elderly man on reception is ignorant, our room is filthy and dark with mould on the walls and ceilings, the bathroom and toilet looked like it hadn't been cleaned for weeks, there was thick dust on the ledges and the bed sheets... well don't even go there, and I'm sure the hotel was being used as a police knocking shop. At the time we were booking in local bobbies were arriving, sitting on a bench in line, and as one came down from the lift, the next one went up!!

Got out of there as soon as we could to go for a walk.

Literally everything around it was shut too, couldn't even find a place to sit and have an ice-cream/coffee.

'RAMADANADINGDONG'

We ended up in McDonalds, yes but we had no other option, completely against Sarah's rule when travelling.

Walked around for ages and then all of a sudden heard some laughter and music and we had stumbled across, by accident, probably the only bar/restaurant that was open.

Casa-Jose, a delightful Andalusia-influenced tapas bar that sold Moroccan wine (produced in the region) and typical Spanish dishes such as calamari, *patatas bravos* and a multitude of other seafood dishes. Excitedly we went to wash and change, then came straight back for dinner where we enjoyed sardines, calamari, tuna salad, avocado and prawns with wine, delicious.

May 21st

We decided to go for a walk along the beach, and walked and walked and walked... still found nothing open except, you've guessed it, McDonald's, thank Allah.

Sat and had an ice cream and drink and decided to walk back.

On the way we visited the Hassan II mosque. Foreigners were not permitted to enter, it is the world's third largest mosque and was built to commemorate a former king's sixtieth birthday. It is a vast building sitting on a rocky outcrop next to the ocean, said to accommodate 25,000 worshippers inside.

Most of Casablanca is a real dump; we nicknamed it CasaBeirut, a bombsite of a destination.

A city of contradictions, a sprawling European economic centre, imposing Hispano-Moorish and art deco buildings alongside severe social problems, rundown facades and extreme poverty and filth.

Our only saving grace today was that after 15.6 miles of walking we had finally found what we were looking for — Ricks Café.

We scurried back to the pigsty hotel to wash and change.

I showered quickly, didn't want to spend too much time in the filthy room.

I put on a dress and my brand-new sandals, DMs that I hadn't worn yet, only to find that they had been worn by someone. I know this because the buckles had been loosened and the soles were scuffed and dusty. I reckon it must have been the maid because she certainly hadn't cleaned the room; she had probably been prancing around in the room trying on my clothes too, singing with my toothbrush as a microphone, who knows?

Rick's Café — what a jewel — had Casablanca redeemed itself?

Themed on the movie, this is a serious restaurant, fabulous ambience from the very moment you walk in the door. You really do feel like you are on a film set.

During World War Two, Rick, a nightclub owner in Casablanca agrees to help his former lover Lisa and her husband escape the war where Morocco and Rick's Cafe was a crossroads for spies, traitors, Nazis and the French resistance, but soon Lisa's feelings for Rick resurface and she finds herself falling back in love with him.

The release of the film was rushed because of real life events; some say it was due to be filmed here at Rick's Cafe in Casablanca but instead was filmed almost entirely at Warner Bros Studios in California.

Famous for the film's quote's *of all the gin joints in all the towns, in all the world, she walks into mine* and *Play it again, Sam* (referring to the song *As time goes by*) as you sit in Rick's place it certainly reflects the vibe you would expect, Sam (or HasSam probably) definitely does play it again. A wonderful last night in CasaBeirut.

May 22nd

We get out of that dump of a place nice and early, moving on further north up west coast to Tangier today, 293km by train and took just over two hours.

Straightforward enough but arrived early and our contact JiJi said our apartment wasn't ready, so guess what? went to McDonald's to sit and wait for her. She would come and collect us, we were told.

How disappointed we were when she did come. She took us to a completely different apartment to the one we had booked, a dark, dingy fleapit of a place. There was also a scabby Moroccan lady who lived there. Jiji said our original apartment had occupants that were not due to leave until tomorrow, and we would have to stay here for the night and move at midday tomorrow — NO WAY.

We quickly searched the Internet to find a hotel for the night. Jiji started to cry and apologise — she said that the agent had double booked and left it up to her to sort out.

We booked into the Hotel Miramar about half a mile up the road, Jiji took us there in her car and said she would return and pick us up at midday tomorrow.

Very cross, but not her fault, poor woman.

Hotel Miramar was nice, overlooking the marina, but quite noisy as it was on the junction of the main road.

Showered and changed we walked up to the marina, and had dinner in a tiny little traditional Moroccan place. They sold wine but it was expensive; £25 for one bottle of house wine.

I had the best chicken tagine so far — a traditional Moroccan dish of chicken braised with spices, garlic, onions, carrots and potato — very pleasantly surprised.

May 23rd

It's Ju's birthday.

Had breakfast in the hotel, buffet style, only £4 each. Thought it was easier than to go out and try and find something open e.g., McDonald's!

It was lovely actually; cereal, yoghurt, pastries, boiled eggs, cheese, ham and toast.

Jiji picked us up as she said she would to take us to the apartment.

Wow, what a difference; now this is what we booked originally. The size and location were superb.

A really big apartment, two bedrooms, bathroom, kitchen, dining, sitting room and a huge balcony overlooking the beach/sea and very long esplanade.

Settled in, we went straight to the supermarket to buy some provisions to self-cater as there was still nothing really open.

We Googled where we could buy wine, and found a small Spanish supermarket! Walked there, three miles but worth the effort — we brought eight bottles of wine and eight cans of beer (as much as we could carry) after being ushered to a side room and behind a hidden curtain by the owner to choose the wine we wanted.

We felt like naughty schoolkids.

The walk back was exhausting — three miles, but we were pleased with our purchases and could now relax.

Spoke to Ju to wish her happy birthday. I know it won't be for her, it will never be the same again.

May 24th

Up early again today — noisy with the traffic again along the main road.

Breakfast on the balcony; boiled eggs, croissants and jam.

Funny what sights you see, a train of camels walking up the beach today.

Red bus tour, this time Tangier. I think I love doing these, you see so much, and learn so much about the place you are visiting, then you can return later to see your favourites in more detail during the rest of your trip.

Did you know that the Chinese brought the fruit, satsuma, over to Morocco in the early 1800s because of the fertile land and the climate? They started to grow them here but instead of calling them satsuma's they called them Tangerines (Tangier LOL)

Some also say Poseidon lived here, and after the death of his beloved mother Tanja, the city of Tingi was renamed Tangier in her memory.

Local taxis are Mediterranean blue in colour to represent the reflection of the ocean and the Mediterranean seas that meet in the Straits (of Gibraltar).

Later on, we sat on the huge balcony watching the world go by. Lots of single boys/young men were out with apparently nothing to do, just walking around aimlessly, not talking or interacting with each other, kicking stones along promenade, old footballs on the beach. Haven't really seen any women, not for virtually the whole time in Morocco — do women have to stay at home during Ramadan? I am not really sure.

Lou cooked dinner, pasta with a bolognaise sauce.

Interestingly we haven't had any wi-fi or Internet access at all today, not even 4G on data roaming despite being logged in with a strong signal no access to any social media either. Could this also be something to do with it being Ramadan?

May 25th

Still no Internet?

It was lovely sunny day though, so we had breakfast and

decided to go to the beach. It felt really weird, again lots of young boys/adolescents and men — but not a single woman — just walking around in silence, standing, sitting, laying on the grass and beach with seemingly nothing to do.

Three younger kids were each taking a turn riding a bike back and forth in front of us. It's as if they have never seen a woman before.

I tried to FaceTime my family as it is the Lilley annual party at Hylands Park in Chelmsford today, something we do as a family every year. We have such a big family on both my mum and dad's side, and it is a fantastic way of all getting together for a massive picnic. Relatives come from far and wide to meet up for this fabulous event filled with food, fun and laughter.

We have one each May for the Lilley (Dad) side of the family, and one in August for the Humphreys (Mum) side of the family. Unfortunately, the connection was very poor, and after trying everyone I could think of I managed to get through to my great nephew Dylan. The line was terrible so I didn't really get to see them all properly, but as every year there was a nice big crowd of them.

Dale managed to call though; he and Ed are in Miami for a friend's wedding.

They had just been kayaking; it was so lovely to speak to him.

Chapter Two
Spain

May 26th

Up early — breakfast on the balcony.

Packed up, showered and tidied up — out of the apartment by eleven.

We got a taxi to the port where we boarded a ferry to cross to Algeciras, ninety-five kilometres; it only took just over an hour, we then hopped straight on a bus to LaLinea.

A Spanish city in the province of Cadiz, Andalucía, it lies on the eastern isthmus of the bay of Gibraltar/Spanish border, and only five minutes to walk across the border to Gibraltar.

As we arrived at the bus station, it was so exciting to see 'the Rock' and even more exciting to find that that our accommodation was literally five minutes up the road.

Hostal Campana was in a great location but very basic, we had our own room but the shower and toilet were on opposite side of the corridor.

Wasting no time, we went straight out to explore, eat and drink.

We found a wonderful little square full of tapas bars, I ordered pork ribs but the food was ropey and not as expected, I basically got about six bones. Each had about half a centimetre of meat and (mostly) fat around the edges. Thankfully it came with a jacket potato (but microwaved —

not the same as oven crispy, and no butter)

Still the place was lively, and an Irish bar was open, so we went for a nightcap. A great band came on stage, good sounds with the happiest double bass player ever. Ended up staying, dancing, laughing... latest night out so far. Bed at one a.m.

May 27th

Up and out, ready to spend the day in Gibraltar.

This British colony of Gibraltar is only five kilometres long and 1.2 kilometres wide. A heavily fortified British air and naval base that guards the Straits of Gibraltar, a British overseas territory, a symbol of British strength that is commonly referred to as 'the Rock', which according to Homer, was created when Hercules broke the mountain that had connected Africa and Europe.

It is home to more than 500 flowering plants, olive and pine trees, many mammals including rabbits, foxes and the famous Barbary macaques which have roamed the Rock for hundreds of years.

Crazily enough, to cross the border you have to walk across the tarmac of the airport runway, of course checking there are no aircraft imminently taking off or landing.

We went straight for a 'full English breakfast' including my first cup of tea. Nectar!

It was beautiful in the plaza, there was a full brass band playing, so we stopped for a while and took a short video to send to Mum and Dad.

Then we headed for the Rock.

We had to queue for a while to get our ticket for the cable-car, but made it.

I was standing right next to an open window in the cable-car looking down as we ascended up to the top of the rock, suddenly, on reaching the summit, a monkey jumped onto the car right in front of my face. I jumped out of my skin!

The rock was amazing, standing 426 metres high; it was truly breathtaking to stand on top of the viewing platform where you can see for miles.

It's impossible to miss the monkeys, they are everywhere, and fascinating to watch (from a distance) when they appear to be posing for pictures but are probably ready to pounce and pinch your wallet, sunglasses, or food if you get too close.

After exploring we were hungry again, so we decided to do what everyone else probably does and stop off for a fish and chip supper on the way home.

May 28th

Had the most terrible sleep, three men in the room next door were very loud most of the night playing music, talking and making a pungent smell of weed so we decided to leave Hostel La Campana one night early and try out a little houseboat we had seen the day before.

Went online and booked it… a perfect little haven, a delightful houseboat with a rooftop terrace, overlooking the Rock, and marina, right next to the beach.

Very clean and modern inside with shower, toilet, and pull-out double bed.

We put our table and chairs out on the boardwalk, cooked, ate lunch, later dinner, drank wine and watched the beautiful sun, setting behind the rock.

Very peaceful — no noise.

May 29th

Packed up the houseboat only to realise that Lou had left the tarpaulin cover out from the table and chairs. During the night it must have blown away! We searched and searched to no avail, so he nicked the one from the next door boat — hope he wasn't seen on the CCTV!

Heading up the east coast by bus today, our next destination was Malaga.

It's known as the cosmopolitan capital of the Costa del Sol (Coast of the Sun).

One hundred and thirty-three kilometres and almost 2two hours later, we arrived.

Carolina, or Caro for short, picked us up from the bus station.

I first met my dear friend Caro in 2002 when she came to England from Spain to work in the Emergency Department at Princess Alexandra Hospital in Harlow.

We immediately became friends and have remained friends since she returned to Spain in 2010.

My first memories of Caro are that she always wore vivid colours with a mismatch of patterns and odd socks, she always maintained a free spirit, she day-dreamt — a lot, she had a care-free attitude, she made creative art, loved music, writing, singing, dancing, sculpting and painting. She valued freedom, creativity and change.

She taught me the meaning of *Chiringuito*, (inspired by the laid-back beach bars) it translates to a small enterprise, usually a bar selling drinks and tapas where friends meet. We later named our party bar at the end of our garden chiringuito.

We always talked and joked a lot about 'Sundays'… Caro hadn't changed one bit, and is the same today as when we first met almost twenty years ago!

Caro had bunked off work to come and pick us up; she took us to her apartment where we would be staying a few days. She was always a very generous and happy-go-lucky kind of person.

We went for a walk down to the beach, it wasn't far from the apartment, ten to fifteen minutes max, you could see it from the window and the balcony. Had a bite to eat, fish goujons and got some provisions from the supermarket.

On the way back we got lost, took a wrong turn up a very steep hill and managed to walk around in circles for nearly two hours.

Finally found our way back, then Caro came home with Candela, her daughter.

What a delightful little girl she is.

She took us to a local joint she knew, ordered mixed tapas including calamari and squid, which were delicious.

Poor Candela fell asleep at the table as by now it was late, around 22:30, so we went home to the apartment.

May 30th

Woke up to the smell of fresh coffee that Caro had made before heading off to work. They had already left for work and school.

Decided to have a day on the beach.

There was a light breeze, but hot, the sea was a bit chilly though — still early season.

Later we went to chiringuito along the beachfront for tapas again, very tasty.

Keen to learn more English, I taught Candela to say the

phrase 'all right geezer' in a cockney tone of voice. She is quite a flirt with the men (like her mum) and it was hilarious watching and listening to her shouting it out to almost every man that came by.

We walked the short distance home to Caro apartment, laughing, skipping, dancing and singing.

Mostly Queen songs, they were Candela's favourite group and she had learnt to sing them in English; *We are the Champions* and *I want to break free* were ringing out in the streets of Malaga that night.

I think I really like this way of life…

Malaga has a typical Mediterranean climate and beautiful sandy beaches, as well as many sites to see, art museums, shopping and delicious cuisine.

It is also the birthplace of the famous Spanish artist Pablo Picasso, born in 1881, he was a painter, printmaker, ceramicist and theatre designer.

He was the most dominant and influential artist of the first half of the twentieth century and had a net worth of 500 million dollars when he died in 1973.

He could supposedly draw before he could talk, and by the age of thirteen he was said to have out-mastered his father who was his art teacher. His father then handed over his palette and brushes to his son, and vowed he would never paint again.

May 31st

Lou had managed to get tickets for a train to Madrid! We were going to the Champions League Final, Liverpool vs. Spurs, so excited.

We woke up again to the smell of fresh coffee brewing;

Caro and Candela had already left for work and school.

We sorted out our sleeping bags and a few wash bits etc for our trip as we had not been able to find any available vacant hotels or hostels to stay when in Madrid.

Our bus was scheduled for 22:30.

Candela was spending the weekend with her dad, so Caro drove us into town.

We had a few hours spare so Caro took us sightseeing. We headed to Picasso Plaza, part of the city's Roman era, and operating since at least the fifteenth century.

In the centre of the square is a nineteenth century monument in honour of General José Torrijos and forty-eight of his companions who were shot and killed by the order of Ferdinand VII.

It is also home to Picasso's bronze statue installed in 2008; it depicts Picasso sitting on a marble bench sketching with a pencil, and like all the other tourists I sat next to him for a holiday snap.

The house in which Picasso was born is also located in the plaza and is now a museum.

As we turned the corner we were greeted by hundreds of ladies and gents dressed in traditional Spanish costume.

There was a huge ornate carriage and two mighty bulls with the procession. It turns out that there was a religious ceremony going on called Semana Santa, a tradition across the whole of Spain which celebrates Via Crucis (the way of Christ).

To mark the event, all of the fraternities of Malaga take their journey of penitence through the city whilst carrying large floats and images of Christ and the Virgin Mary.

We watched for a while, and took more photos of the

beautiful ladies in their flamenco finery.

We stopped off at a lovely traditional Tapas bar in town for dinner before heading to the bus station... here we go, allez, allez, allez!

Our bus to Madrid left on time at 22:30, jam-packed full of football supporters, mostly Liverpool but some Spurs. Everyone was in good spirits though (or full of spirits, he, he).

It was stopped three times on the way but we were virtually unable to move as now the alcohol consumption had finished and most had shut up with the football chants; there were half comatose bodies lying in the aisle of the bus, and we were on the back row.

June 1st

Arrived at 05:30 very tired as we had virtually no sleep and made our way to the fan zone for Liverpool supporters — Salvador Dali Plaza.

Like many public squares in Madrid, it is surrounded by many restaurants and cafés.

It contains the Dolmen de Dalí sculpture and on the granite floor, are bronze slabs with relief sculptures of fossils, archaeological elements, references to telecommunications and texts with literary phrases.

On arrival the Plaza was virtually empty. Not the case in a few hours, I expected.

Had a coffee, and seeing as we had quite a few hours to kill, decided to get the Metro and take a look at the Wanda Metropolitano Stadium where the game would be played. It's a modern stadium which officially opened in 2017 and is home to Athletico Madrid.

On the way back decided to visit Madrid 2nd Football Stadium — Bernabéu.

A colossal stadium with a seating capacity of over 80,000, and home to Real Madrid.

We spent the rest of the day in Salvador Dali Square fan zone. It was absolute crazy, dancing, singing, flares, chanting, drinking... what an experience... we brought some booze in the local supermarket, El Cortes Ingles, as did most others, the staff couldn't get the shelves filled quick enough.

We bought a T-shirt, nicked a sun-visor and joined the party.

The UEFA had made a rule that the fan zone, both Liverpool and Spurs, should be closed before kick-off.

Shame as it would have been much more fun, and probably safer to have big screens and stay confined to their respective squares.

Instead, everyone dispersed and attempted to cram into packed bars to watch the game.

Anyway, we managed to watch the game, got drunk, and Liverpool won 2–0. Excellent day.

Made our way back to the train station around midnight we think (neither of us remembers) it was locked, so just got into our sleeping bags for a few hours' shut eye.

Never slept rough in my life, but woke up at 04.30 and found that we were surrounded by tens of others doing the exact same thing!

June 2nd

Tired, weary but in a good mood we caught the coach back to Malaga at eleven a.m., and finally arrived there at five p.m.

Caro and Candela picked us up from the bus station and

we headed straight to the beach. We felt knackered but surely a dip in the sea could sort that out.

We had a lovely tapas dinner at a beachside Chiringuito — sardines, Russian salad, fish platter, and king prawns.

Candela was rather impressive, taught us how to eat BBQ sardines correctly, lots of seasoning, freshly-squeezed lemon and then start at the head, nibble to the tail then vice versa back up the other side. She is a dream of a little girl, way ahead of her years.

I phoned and spoke to Ju, she was a bit down, hopefully I cheered her up. I miss her.

June 3rd

Lou and I got the local bus into town.

We visited the Port, rode around on the tuktuk train, walked through the park, saw the wild parrots (colonised here from Argentina), and visited the bullring, before making a pit-stop for a drink in the rooftop bar at Marriot AC hotel over-looking the park and the port — beautiful.

Caro and Candela met us for dinner; guess what — tapas again but delicious, I could eat it every day.

We booked tickets for a van Gogh live exhibition tomorrow night.

Spoke to John and to Jeff, all seems okay at home.

June 4th

I did some washing, cleaning and general housework for Caro, then it was beach day for Lou and me. It was a beautiful sunny day, we had a lovely salad for lunch.

Later we caught the bus into town to meet Caro, Candela and Caro's mum and went to the van Gogh live exhibition.

He was a Dutch post-impressionist painter, born in the Netherlands, who in just over a decade created over 2,100 works, most of which date from the last two years of his life.

He was plagued with mental health issues, and had several admissions to asylums; he cut off the whole of his left ear during one of his breakdowns.

Tragically he died after without knowing the acclaim his art would receive at the age of thirty-seven.

He committed suicide, shooting himself in a field behind a chateau in France.

Paella for dinner, bus back to apartment after nightcap at Rinco Victoria.

June 5th

Early start, we're off to visit the Nerja Caves today.

The caves are a well-known tourist attraction, a series of caverns and chambers that were discovered in 1959 by a group of locals searching for bats that stretch for around five kilometres.

Two bus changes later we arrived, taking just a couple of hours. Nerja is a charming old fishing village with a fabulous stretch of beach called the Burriana with rows and rows of chringuitos serving the best seafood, paella and tapas around.

Not for the faint-hearted though, this town is very steep and hilly.

After a trip to the caves, which were fascinating, we stopped off at Chiringuito called 'AYO' as recommended by Caro, famous for its rustic cooking over a blazing hot log fire of the biggest paella you have ever seen. It's open from sunrise until sunset, serving constantly, freshly made and freshly eaten. (As many plates as you can eat included). Delicious.

June 6th

Tapas festival on promenade tonight!

Had a haircut in local salon, went to beach for a few hours before heading home to wash and change, made some 'slime' with Candela.

The tapas festival was fun, you brought a ticket for two euro, which got you tapas and a drink… Live band, lots of fun, and great value for money.

June 7th

Sad to leave Malaga, it has been so lovely to spend time with Caro and Candela but we're moving on to Granada.

Our stay with Caro and Candela reminded me of my friend Tracy. She came to our house one afternoon for tea and four days later she was still with us.

Tracy has been my friend since the start of my nurse training. She was in the set below me but we socialised together in a large group.

Tracy is one of life's most special women-she is glowing, kind and loving. She radiates beauty. I love everything about her, the good, the bad and the ugly. She is the type of friend that would stick by you through anything and her loyalty is unbeatable.

I know that if I called on her at any time with my eyes full of tears; she would be the first to my door.

She makes me laugh, she is crazy and she has a great sense of humour.

If you find a Tracy in your life, you are very lucky.

The bus left at 14:00, we travelled 126 kilometres, and arrived at 15:45.

We found our accommodation after a short walk through the cobbled streets, Hotel Jeronimos, and checked in.

I wanted to get tickets to go to the Alhambra Palace but, gutted, they were sold out as they only let in seven thousand visitors a day. There was nothing available until 23rd June.

I was very upset. It didn't even occur to me to get the tickets in advance, although I have been there before I really wanted Lou to see it.

Dale took me, Ju and Mum there as a surprise for Mum's eightieth birthday in 2011.

However, we did manage to get a ticket for a guided tour around the grounds of the palace for tomorrow.

June 8th

Dale's birthday, I wish he was here with us, or that we were there with him on his special day.

Got up after a terrible sleepless night. It turns out that directly under our room window there was an all-night tapas bar... We asked reception if they could move us to the other side of the hotel but were told that they were fully booked and there were no vacant rooms.

We decided to go on a tuktuk guided tour of Granada, taking in the cathedral, bullring, and the palace albeit at a distance.

Of course we stopped several times for refreshments and were given tapas on each occasion. These included ham on toast, soft cheese and herb stuffed pepper with tortilla, meatballs in ragu sauce, paella, pasta in green pesto and cream sauce, and pork chop with fresh tomato slices!!

With our bellies suitably full we headed off to the walking

tour with a lovely guide called Cynthia.

She was Spanish but fluent in English and made for a very interesting two hours, educating us about the place.

Alhambra translates to 'the Red One' originally constructed as a fortress in 889 AD before being renovated and converted into a royal palace of Muslim rule in the thirteenth century. It is now a UNESCO World Heritage Site.

Most of the buildings are quadrangular in plan with all the rooms opening on to a central court, connected by smaller rooms and passages.

The palace is full of symbolism, and you see the Muslim hand emblem on most of the archway entrances. The most important of these is at the arch of Puerto de la Justicia.

It is symbolic of the Muslim faith and resembles their five values:

Give to the poor.

Fast for Ramadan.

Visit Mecca.

Pray five times a day.

Be faithful forever.

Most of the tiles, if not all in the palace are green or blue. This is deliberate and represent:

Blue — for the sky.

Green — for the land.

There is one room in the complex that was never lived in as the emperor died before its completion; it was designed by Leonardo da Vinci.

It is one large square on the outside to represent the emperor, and completely round on the inside, representing the world.

The ideology behind this was that the emperor 'ruled the world'.

Alhambra Palace — put it on your 'book-it' list everyone.

On the way home from the tour, I noticed a sign in the street right above our hotel, for a Terrazzo of Monastrie I said to Lou I wondered if it was our hotel as we were right next to the monastery, and blow me down, checked it out and on the fifth floor of our hotel, was the most amazing three-tiered rooftop terrace!

Cocktail o'clock it was then!

Spoke to our son, Dale, on the phone, where does the time go? Love him so much and miss our chats, fizz, fun and dancing.

Happy birthday darling.

9th June

Disturbed sleep again as the tapas bar downstairs did not shut until 07:30, FFS.

Went out for a walk as we had seen a flyer for a classic car show and parade. My brother Gary has always been into cars, and owned a fair few classic cars over the years, forever tinkering with the car engine, or customising the bodywork with his mate at the end of the street called Russ.

He used to go to Santa Pod, a race track in Podington, Bedfordshire, which is a drag racing venue built on a disused WWII air base, once used by the 92nd Bomb Group.

Lou, Dale and I went with Gary and Mandy once, Dale wore his 'mechanic's boiler suit', Gary always used to buy him one every time he went and we used to hand sew the various advertising material badges onto the sleeves, like you do in the Guides or the Scouts.

It was a great weekend watching the 'funny cars' being raced using rocket propellers along the track, eating hotdogs and sleeping in the back of Lou's old Ford Transit van.

Gary still has a love for cars, his pride and joy which takes pride of place to this day in his garage is his 'Little Red Corvette'. My dad drove me to my wedding in it over thirty years ago.

We watched classic car show and parade, it was great fun, most of the car owners were dressed up for the occasion in costume relating to the style/era of their prized possession. They cruised up and down the main street showing off their immaculate customized vehicles.

On the way back we stopped off at the cathedral, where there was a service in progress. We sat through the service but obviously it was given in Spanish, so we couldn't understand it.

Later I spoke to Ju who sounded a little better today and I told her we were going to try and find the tapas bar we had visited nine years ago, but couldn't remember what it was called.

Ju WhatsApp-ed me in no time, it was called 'La Gran Taberna' and we had passed by it several times throughout the day. It was just around the corner, so we went and found it.

I ordered a Vino Blanco, Lou a beer; a ham/cheese/herb and garlic omelette tapas arrived!

Second round — sausage/onion and crisps tapas arrived.

Third round — grilled pork chop tapas arrived.

No dinner required.

Perfect end to Granada!

10th June

Leaving today, travelling by bus further up Spain's east coast to Roquetas de mar, on the Costa de Almeria, famous for its fish, super beaches and amazing tapas where we have booked a cute little apartment called Apartment La-Mineria.

ALSA is the name of the leading operator of Spanish coaches, established in 1923 it provides a modern framework for transport all over the country by road.

Their buses are ace, you get allocated seating, in a luxury recliner chair, and in our experience so far, they are always on time.

When we arrived the apartment was lovely, on the fourth floor right next to the beach. It had a kitchen and dining room, a bedroom and nice-sized bathroom, and two balconies. We didn't have much of a plan whilst here, just to relax, chill and have a week of sightseeing, it is quite exhausting.

So we went to the local supermarket for some self-catering provisions, Lou cooked and we sat on the balcony to watch the beautiful sunset.

We called and spoke to Mum and Dad, Pam, and sent Dale a WhatsApp.

11th June

We woke up early today; the sun was shining so we went to the beach for the day. I had a swim in the sea, although it is still a little chilly.

Lou later went for a walk and came back with the most delicious ham, tomato and mayonnaise rolls, I don't know why but food like this always tastes much better when the sun is shining and you are abroad.

Lazed around and listened to some favourite tracks on the i-Pod and really did nothing else all day, bliss.

12th June

It's Wednesday today, it's so easy to lose track sometimes.

We needed some exercise so went for a nice long walk along the promenade to find the bullring. They fascinate me, the architecture of the structure mainly, I often wonder how they built these impressive structures without all the tools of today.

On the Spanish TV at the moment, they are showing the annual finals and we have seen some excerpts when flicking channels, although we can't watch it for long, just the beginning part with the showmanship/costumery.

In medieval Spain it was considered a noble sport and almost exclusively dominated by the rich who could afford it. Did you know that the most successful matadors can earn up to $75,000 just for appearing?

Nowadays bullfighting is largely on the decline with some regions in Spain banning the sport. Well, they call it a sport but the animals are pushed to extreme exhaustion, it is never a fair fight, more like a ritualistic slaughter.

We walked for over three miles, although the bullring was closed for maintenance the museum was open, so we went in. On display were some fabulous exhibits of elaborate matador costumes and capes which can fetch up to and way beyond $50,000.

13th June

We did not do much today, it was overcast and a little

breezy, although we did go for our daily walk along the promenade, only 3.6 miles today.

I thought I would be clever and cook dinner having been inspired by the tapas we had in Granada.

Pork chop with a crème fraiche and green pesto sauce with rice. Sounds delicious, eh? Edible, but I put far too much pesto in it; Lou as usual was polite and ate it, saying it was okay.

Later I phoned and spoke to Ju; she is keeping busy doing some painting for Dale. I also spoke to Michelle; everything seems fine at home, so that's good.

14th June

So flipping windy overnight, felt like gale force with all the tiles in the suspended bathroom ceiling clattering.

We decided to go on the tuktuk tour around Roquetas town today but there was not much to see. It felt like we were just driving round and round the back streets looking at the lovely villas, some were very nice indeed.

We ended up at the port and took a look at the castle, called the Castillo de Santa Ana, it is a fortification built in the sixteenth century and was used for the refugee inhabitants who lived near the port.

It was largely destroyed following an earthquake in 1804, but was restored and now houses photography, art exhibitions, concerts and speeches.

We decided to stop off for some refreshments, wine, beer and the now obligatory tapas.

Pork tenderloin and sweet red cabbage, fillet of beef with balsamic drizzle, whole chargrilled squid, and a local flat white fish with potato chips and red pesto.

Lou phoned and chatted to Pam.

15th June

We were awake early again, so after breakfast on the balcony we went to the beach, there was a warm breeze today, not windy like it has been.

Later we went back to the apartment for a swim in the pool; it was the first day it was open today.

Spain has very strict rules and regulations that all communal and public swimming pools have to follow; they all open on the same date (around mid-June), they all have to have as many lifebuoys as there are sets of steps, they all have to have a lifeguard on duty whilst the pool is open, they all have to comply with daily pool cleaning, disinfection and proper use of chlorine, and they all have to provide shower and changing room facilities.

Lou went shopping and said he was cooking dinner.

He made delicious paella; we flicked the TV on and saw that tonight's live bullfighting was being broadcast from the bullring in Roquetas, the same one we visited a few days ago.

16th June

It's Father's Day today.

We had a celebration fry-up for breakfast which was yummy. It was a little cloudy today so we went for a nice long walk again.

I managed to speak to Dad, he has had a nice day, we also spoke to Dale and he told us that he is going to meet us for a short break when we get to Barcelona, he will bring his friend Rosemary. So exciting, we cannot wait to see him.

Later we chilled out on the balcony; we watched Soccer Aid and ate hotdogs for supper.

17th June

Up nice and early today as we are moving on. The next leg of our travels takes us off to Cartagena and La-Manga east coast of Spain heading north.

Our bus to the main terminal was at 07:15. The bus arrived spot on time, at first, we were the only passengers but it quickly filled up along the way with locals going to work.

At the main bus station, we boarded our ALSA bus for our onward journey to La Manga, and as previous experiences, the four-hour journey was very efficient, with comfortable, allocated seating, free Wi-Fi and a USB port.

Two hundred and forty-three kilometres travelling again up the east coast of Spain towards La Manga, was a lovely coastline drive.

La Manga (translates as 'The Sleeve') is a strip of land and described as a paradise between two seas, the Mar Menor and the Mediterranean in Murcia.

It is only twenty-one kilometres long and 300 metres wide.

All along the strip on both sides there are numerous white sandy beaches, rocky outcrops and impressive marinas, as well as a great selection of bars, cafes and restaurants.

We finally arrived at our villa after a very long, very steep uphill walk. The instructions to get into the villa were very confusing and it took us ages to gain entry.

It's really a lovely place, three bedrooms, two bathrooms and a very large balcony overlooking the sea, the pool is huge too and no one around it.

After settling in we went to the supermarket, as we usually do now, to get some provisions. This meant another long walk and it was exhausting in the heat, carrying the shopping.

18th June

Today it's the start of Royal Ascot.

One of the highlights of the year at home.

Ascot is an iconic British racecourse for thoroughbred horse racing which has been operating since 1711.

A friend of mine, Marie, always organises a girls-only day trip to this glorious annual event. Style and elegance come into focus as my girlfriends and I dress to impress in an eye-catching array of extravagant, classic, chic and elegant outfits.

Last year Dale treated me, and for the first time in my life I had a hat privately commissioned for the occasion.

Awon Golding is the most splendid milliner who just happens to have her studio next door to Dale, an award-winning milliner who specialises in fun hats and headpieces and has a loyal following of global icons such as Lady Gaga, Kylie Minogue and Meghan, Duchess of Sussex.

My hat was unique, panama style with the most vivid and bright colours of pink and green hand-cut goose feathers, it felt and looked fantastic.

The refined splendour of Royal Ascot is always a fabulous day, meeting up at nine a.m., admiring everyone's fabulous outfits and hats (mostly supplied from Marie's own business, Hatopia) the coach trip there to Ascot in Berkshire whilst eating Barbie-dolls homemade egg mayonnaise or salmon sandwiches and drinking champagne, seeing the royal procession, guessing the colour of the Queen's outfit, visiting the parade ring, placing our bets, eating and drinking copious amounts of alcohol, winning/or losing, it doesn't really matter, dancing and singing around the bandstand with the celebrity presenters, my favourites are Ed Chamberlain, Oli Bell, Francesca Cumani and Matt Chapman.

We had breakfast on the balcony, croissants and coffee whilst looking at the photos already posted on FB of the girls, Katie my niece has taken my prestigious place this year! All the girls really look splendid, all forty-one of them, well done Marie, a colossal effort executed once again.

Lou and I went down to the beach and we had a swim in the sea, it's still a little nippy, but getting warmer.

We watched Ascot data-roaming on my phone, but it is pouring with rain.

I did manage to FaceTime my niece, Katie, and also chatted with friends, Ruth, Trala, and Barbie-doll et al, they're all a bit tipsy LOL.

We had spaghetti Bolognese for tea whilst sitting on the balcony watching the birds, ubiquitous yellow-legged gulls, and hunting swifts… hundreds of them.

It's a popular destination for ornithologists who come here to see blackbirds, starlings, chiffchaffs, monk parakeets, doves, pigeons, sparrows, linnets, whinchats, warblers, greenfinches, kestrels, avocets, shelducks, egrets, and flamingos!!

Dale text — all of his paintings had sold at the private view in a gallery in Athens — genius.

19th June

We didn't really do too much again today, it's really weird but when you move on from destination to destination, it is quite knackering and you really do need a couple of days to recover.

We did walk over to the Mediterranean side of La Manga and spent most of the day on the beach.

Whilst there we watched Royal Ascot again. Frankie Detorri had four winners, later we ate the rest of the bolognaise for tea on a jacket potato which was delicious, and watched a film on DVD about the IRA which we had already seen, but cannot remember where, maybe on a plane somewhere.

20th June

Just opposite our villa we could see a small island, and each day had watched people wading over at low tide to walk upon it. It was where some of the aforementioned birds lived. Nicknamed the 'Island of seagulls', we decided to take a walk over ourselves but I just couldn't do it.

The water was calf-high so you couldn't see the bottom, the sandy bed was too soft and claylike squiggling through my toes and the water was full of jellyfish.

Now, some of my friends know about my unfortunate incident with a jellyfish a few years ago, it is a very funny story.

We were in Malta on holiday spending the day on the beach; we had taken a lovely picnic of egg, ham and cheeses with mixed salad and a carton of our favourite cheap plonk Don Simon.

Lou was lazing around in the sea on his Lilo, so I decided to join him.

If any of you has ever been to the beach at Bugibba, you will know that the entrance into the sea is via steps from the rocky shoreline.

There were quite a few locals and holidaymakers on the gangway to the steps so I decided to try and clamber over the rocks.

Feeling it was quite treacherous I thought it may be wiser to sit on the rocks and edge my way to the sea using my bottom and hands to steady myself.

What a mistake! As I lowered myself to the rocks my foot slipped and my body plonked down with a splash and a thud… immediately my derriere was struck by an immense pain, like a red-hot dagger plunging into my butt cheek just adjacent to my bum hole slightly north of my fanny. I let out a feeble scream, not wanting to draw attention to myself, and frantically started to wave at Lou to get his attention so he could come and help me.

Lou looked across for a split second, smiled and waved, then carried on in with his blissful float on the Mediterranean.

The pain was excruciating, I didn't know what to do, I immediately started to feel sick, clammy and tachycardic. I was worried that I had been poisoned and that I may collapse into a full-blown anaphylactic shock. I hurried to the lifeguard post where two very young, and very fit men were on duty.

Poor things, I thought, as I ran in crying for help, cocking my leg up to show them a now ever-increasing in size, swollen, red-hot raw patch in between my fanny and my bum hole which resembled the map of Malta in its shape.

The two young men quickly attended to my needs by dousing me with neat alcohol, then applying cold compress pads around my privates.

They told me not to worry, it was a jellyfish sting, and although it had 'injected me with toxins locally' it wouldn't poison me systemically.

I stayed in the first aid hut for around fifteen minutes with the guys gently pouring and dabbing alcohol using cold pads before limping back to the beach clad with several cold compress pads hanging out of my bikini bottoms around my crutch.

Relaying my ordeal to Lou, who thought I had been in the sea enjoying myself, I felt really sorry for myself and the two handsome lifeguards who had probably now been traumatised for life.

The day had been ruined, I went back to the apartment, was sick and had diarrhoea, laid down on the bed with my arse under the fan, and fell asleep — for six hours!

I've been very wary of jellyfish ever since, and have a permanent 'branding' of the harrowing experience on my nether region. Funnily enough it still looks a bit like the outline of the map of Malta.

It reminds me, whilst writing this journal, of the only other time I can remember being truly embarrassed, and it was not very long ago.

We have a Lay-Z-spa in the garden, it was a hot sunny day, and I decided to have a dip in the spa. My dad, Eddie, was popping round in about an hour, so I had time to relax, or so I thought.

After about twenty minutes (the spa has an auto cut-off after thirty minutes) there was a rat-a-tat-tat on the door. Thinking to myself 'he's early', I jumped out of the spa, hair and body dripping wet, shouted out 'hang on I'm coming' wrapped myself in a towel and opened the front door.

It wasn't Eddie at all, but the postman! I apologised babbling that I thought he was my dad, that I had just got out of the spa, and sorry that I was dripping wet.

I closed the front door, glanced in the mirror only to see that I had the most massive bogey (you know the type, white and slimy, the kind you get when you have been under the water) smeared right across my upper lip…

So, nothing else for it, if the sea was full of jellyfish today, we would go back to the pool, we were the only ones there and it felt like our own private villa. We mucked about having a diving competition, and discovered the 'boomerang' app from Instagram. It was so funny making silly clips of each other.

Later we had a roast chicken, salad and bite-sized roast potatoes.

That night we saw the International Space Station go over and I used my new binoculars (another lovely retirement gift, from Sally, Jude, Jo, Andy and Sue from the Minor Injury Unit) for the first time.

21st June

We still felt tired so we decided to have a pool day today, with a picnic and watch the races from Royal Ascot.

John and Keeley (my twin brother and sister-in-law) were going today.

Like us, they are keen on horse racing; John has part-shares in a thoroughbred racehorse too.

Unlike me he really studies the form; he mainly bets on favourites and does double/triple accumulators. I tend to pick the number five, my favourite and lucky number, or a horse that has 'diamond' in its name, as this was my nickname at school 'Diamond Lil', failing that then I tend to go for any gemstone, ruby, opal, emerald, sapphire etc.

I've seen their picture on Instagram this morning, they look a million dollars.

There is not really much to do or see here in La Manga

(unless you're a Tweeter) so it is very peaceful and relaxing.

I spoke to Mum and Dad today, they are both all right and have been watching the racing, too.

22nd June

We went to the small bay beach today, it was quite a walk, but we like the exercise, we listened to some music on the i-Pod.

It's quite weird when listening to some music, you 'find' things that you haven't heard for ages, and forgotten how good it sounds even after many years. We were working our way through the alphabet, playing an album from each artist, before moving on to the next, today's list was:

A- ABBA (of course!)
B- Barry Manilow
C- Coldplay
D- Depeche Mode
E- Elton John
F- Frankie Goes To Hollywood
G- Gary Newman
H- Heatwave

The sun is blazing hot; I paddled in the sea whilst keeping my beady eyes open for any pesky jellyfish.

We spoke to Dale, who is still in Athens on an Art residency. They went out clubbing last night, and by the sounds of it, they all got completely wasted.

Ed's dad is there with them visiting, Ed lost his phone.

Dale's friend Rosemary is going over to meet him in a few days as Ed has to leave to come home for Glastonbury.

My Facebook was mad this evening, apparently everyone in Harlow and its surrounding areas were asking what the 'loud explosion' was that it seemed everyone had heard.

It turned out that there had been a sonic boom from an RAF fighter jet which had been scrambled to intercept and escort a Ryan Air plane with a suspect package on board into Stansted Airport, where they arrested a twenty-eight-year-old woman on alleged terrorist activity.

We decided to got out for dinner, to 'Cocktail Café van Gogh', #2 of places to go in La Manga, a nice place to relax, drink some decent cocktails and eat some delicious food — we had mixed grill for two and it was lovely. Not so lovely walking back up the ginormous hill to our villa though, with a very full belly.

23rd June

Our last day in La Manga was spent around the pool, but today it was crowded. All Spanish, I expect they had all come for the weekend.

We had our usual picnic of ham, egg, cheese salad with some Don Simon.

It's strange that when you get a group of Spanish people together at the same time, they all appear to speak at once. It sounded like a swarm of insects, getting louder and louder, reaching a crescendo and then… silence.

They all disappeared, probably for their siesta.

Time to move on early doors tomorrow, bus to Cartagena then travelling further north. We're off to Benidorm, affectionately known as Benners!

24th June

Well, we were up early today, travelling up the east coast by ALSA bus, just under two hours, and 174 kilometres. Flipping hot.

Benidorm is a seaside resort on the Costa-Blanca, formerly a small fishing village in the sixties, now a popular tourist destination and home to expats.

We found the hotel easy enough, Estudios Benidorm in the Old Town.

The apartment was quite small but adequate with modern décor and good air con.

It was also within easy walking distance to both beaches — Levante and Poniente.

On arrival, as usual, we tried to find a supermarket to get some provisions, but they were all closed (supermarkets do not open in Benners on a Monday).

Having got the taste for tapas we decided to Google 'best tapas bar in Benidorm Old town'.

The tapas bar, 'Zodiac', was literally metres away from our hotel, so off we trotted. A lovely place in Rufaza Square full of local people, enjoying local food — a hidden gem.

It didn't disappoint, if you ordered a bottle of wine for seven euro you got six tapas too, so two bottles wine (one red, one white) equalled twelve tapas, yes twelve!

A mighty feast of sardines, prawns, salmon, paella, mussels, jamón, manchego, calamari, pork, beef escallops, patatas bravas and croquettes, all for just fourteen euros.

A superb evening, home to bed, very full and happy.

25th June

Well, we had a bit of a lie-in today; we woke up just before nine a.m., so headed off to the supermarket to get our supplies before setting off to the beach.

The Spanish certainly have it sussed when going to the beach. They all get there early, stay until lunchtime, all seem to disappear at the same time for hours, and then all turn up again late afternoon.

The most impressive part of old town Benners was that they have a designated platform for disabled persons, with very hard-working girls and boys who take individuals into the sea on great big buoyant sunbeds, the individuals have fun floating, splashing, swimming about, then the lifeguards wheel them back in, shower them down and help to dry and dress them... superb, well done, Benners.

Apparently there has been massive press in the UK today about the 'invasion of Portuguese man-o-war jellyfish' in Benners today, luckily we didn't see any!

I spoke to Ju this evening; she is going back to work tomorrow.

26th June

Decided to go and explore today, so went for a walk to find the bullring, and as usual, seemed to take the long way around. We found it easily enough but it is closed permanently and looks rather dilapidated, although the press reports are that the local council are planning to rejuvenate it.

We walked right along the promenade into Benners' new town.

Brits abroad spring to mind, most of the men were fat, pasty white but with sunburnt areas where their vests have been, tattooed everywhere, had pierced nipples, beer guts on full view, or were wearing a football shirt! The women had short hair which was badly dyed pink or purple, were virtually all wearing baggy tie-dyed multicoloured sleeveless dresses, had four plus earrings in each lobe, and were also tattooed. I wondered why women in their latter years also think it is okay to go without a bra when abroad?

We walked down the main area for nightlife called 'the strip' famous for Sinatra's, Talk of the Town, West End Show Bar, The Red Lion and many more.

We walked 6.5 miles in total.

I spoke to Ju to find out how her first day back at work went. She managed three hours which was great, she feels really low, but has taken her first massive hurdle, she did it!

27th June

Instead of the beach today we went to the rooftop terrace of the hotel. No swimming pool but plenty of sun-loungers and a cold shower to help you cool off.

We didn't do too much else during the day as it was scorching.

In the evening we went back to Zodiac. This time, wine — yes — and tapas, including crab, prawns, paella, mussels, meatballs, and anchovies.

28th June

It's exactly twelve weeks today since, Jeff, our brother-in-law, died, it's very sad still; it seems like yesterday but at the same time seems forever ago.

We decided to go for another walk to the indoor market as I wanted to buy a new bikini and we had missed the big outdoor one which is held on Wednesdays and Sundays only.

It's called Mercaloix indoor market. Honestly, maximum effort for minimal reward, walked 1.2 miles in the blistering heat, and the nicest thing there was a fresh butcher's stall, and a meat and potato pie stall.

What a load of rubbish, tut, tut and more tut.

Lots of bling for a waste of money, cheap and nasty shoes/bags/purses/dresses, with most of the stalls selling the same stuff.

Not a worthwhile shopping trip, and I came home with an empty bag.

On the way back to the hotel, I tried to withdraw some cash at the ATM. The first machine tried to charge me two euros, so I cancelled the transaction only to find the second and third machine I tried both declined?

We got back to the hotel and I checked my on line banking to find that 402 euro had been debited from my account — so either someone got lucky (maybe first machine did dispense the cash after we had walked away and pocketed my cash) or Visa made a mistake and need to credit my funds.

Annoyingly I had to spend the next hour on the phone trying to sort it out.

Out for dinner tonight as it is our last night in Benners.

We found a lovely rooftop terrace bar 'Planta21' so we went there first for a nice G and T and a large *Cerveza*. It was beautiful, overlooking the majority of Levante Beach, with wonderful views.

We sat in the Old Town for dinner al fresco. Lou had paella, and I had lamb chops with salad. We watched the world go by; there were lots of VERY drunk people.

Barcelona tomorrow.

29th June

Our bus to Barcelona left pretty much on time. We found our seats, settled down and prepared for a very, very, very long journey.

We had several pit-stops on the way travelling further north up the east coast for 500 kilometres.

The journey was not the best. We were sitting behind a single mum and four children, one of them just a small baby doing what babies do!

We finally arrived at seven p.m. and found our hotel, the BruStar Gotic, what a pigsty! Not a hotel at all, just a pokey room in a residential apartment block, and it was not cheap compared to previous stays. Oh well, one night only. We were excited as tomorrow we will meet up with Dale and Rosemary.

30th June

We were up at seven, and out of that place as quickly as possible. We hardly slept a wink; the mattress on the metal frame bed was one of those really old spring mattresses. Well, it was just like sleeping with Sooty and Sweep in the bed with us. Oh, the noises with every single toss and turn.

We set off on foot using the phone for satellite navigation and found the Arts Hotel easy enough.

Now you're talking! However, we did get off to a bad start.

Dale and Rosemary were already there in reception but their room was not ready.

It was so wonderful to see Dale; it's been almost eight weeks now.

Reception said our room was ready but when we were shown to it, it was not what Dale had paid (an arm and a leg), for a room with a sea/harbour view on the twelfth or above floor. We had been allocated a room overlooking the main road/roundabout on the second floor.

He was very unhappy with customer services, and it took the whole day, as well as many conversations with the manager of the day to be moved.

The hotel was superb, much better than anything we had stayed in so far.

Very clean, smelt heavenly, very large room, two double beds, an office area, massive shower, bath and complimentary luxury toiletries.

Lou and I had literally gone from rags to riches.

There were two pools, one adult only, the other an infinity pool.

Breakfast was included, buffet style, you name it, they had it (apart from one guest who demanded ice cream!)

The hotel had many sculptures and works of art and beautiful fresh flower arrangements everywhere. I think we are going to like it here.

Dale and Rosemary went for a nap, whilst Lou and I sat round the pool laughing at some of the guests' antics.

One obviously wealthy young female guest wearing a Versace 'fits where it touches' swimming suit, kimono-style wrap and oversized floppy hat spent literally an hour posing on the edge of the pool whilst her 'assistant' desperately tried to get the photo of the day.

Another guest on the sunbed next to me ordered some lunch. 'Erm, can I get the chicken Caesar salad, said in a Yankee accent, 'but could I get that without the chicken, no parmesan cheese please, no croutons please, and oh, can I get the sauce on the side?' So basically, he had iceberg lettuce!

Later we all walked down to the port. We found a typically Spanish tapas restaurant and sat down for another feast — pig's cheeks, mussels, patatas bravas aioli, jamón, and eggs.

1st July

We hopped on the sightseeing tour bus to go and see Camp Nou, home to Barcelona FC. WOW what a place. It's colossal, and seats 100,000 fans. We booked a basic entry ticket and one audio guide which was perfectly adequate. The tour pathway was easy to follow with corresponding numbers at each point of interest to press on audio guide. Walking through the museum was awesome, the silverware particularly amazing.

We saw the immaculate pitch, the private chapel, the press room, we sat in the manager's chair, and we walked down the tunnel.

Very impressive, we thoroughly enjoyed the visit which lasted around three hours, so it was great value for money too.

We then hopped back on the tour bus to our next destination — Sagrada Familia — perfect.

The Sagrada Familia is a mighty spectacle, a truly exceptional temple designed by the genius Spanish architect Antoni Gaudi, and is one of his most famous works. Today more than 135 years after laying the cornerstone its construction is still incomplete and work continues on this amazing basilica, not expected to finish until 2026. Unfortunately, tickets to enter for the day were sold out, so we couldn't go in, shame. It gives us a great excuse to come back, though.

So, nothing else for it but to stop for a Scooby snack and refreshments, chicken skewers, calamari and potato and vegetable croquettes.

On the way back to the Arts Hotel we saw many more spectacular sights in Barcelona. I would like to do the Gaudí tour of the city, one day.

He was an architect born in 1852 and was known as the greatest exponent of Catalan Modernism; his works are definitely recognisable and most are located in Barcelona.

He was knocked down by a tram in Barcelona in 1926, and died from his injuries three days later.

We met Dale and Rosemary after a freshen up and sat in the hotel bar drinking champagne of course. We then went to a harbour fish restaurant called 'Sabores Mediterráneos' for a fish supper. Dale chose the best dinner, a super huge mixed seafood platter, gorgeous.

Now, we really should have headed back, but it was too tempting to pop in to the casino… we set ourselves a limit of fifty euros each.

Rosemary and I were too quick to flutter away our euros so we sat in the courtyard drinking gin, chatting and laughing whilst Dale and Lou carried on gambling.

Time flew by; before we knew it the time was now four a.m!

2nd July

Michelle's birthday.

Keeley's sister Jane became a nanny, her daughter Rebecca gave birth to Dexter.

Off to the Picasso Museum today, 'In the name of the father' exhibition — wow — it houses 4,251 works by the artist and is the most complete art collection in the world.

Barcelona shaped Picasso's youth and adolescence, it is so fitting that the permanent exhibition is housed in a medieval mansion and it is fabulous.

Next, we walked to Las Rambles, a tree lined boulevard which stretches for 1.2 kilometres and cuts through the heart of the city, vibrant and lively, fresh markets, craft markets, plazas, street performers and painters, there is even a mural painted by Joan Miró on Las Ramblas.

The boulevard is also famous for becoming a 'red light' district at night and is crammed full of prostitutes,

Rosemary and I spent an hour on the beach later followed by a swim in the hotel's infinity pool.

More fizz before heading out to dinner, this time 'Rossini Italiano', I know Italian in Spain? Lasagne, carbonarra, garlic prawns and garlic bread swiftly followed by one (actually four) for the road in the hotel bar.

3rd July

We met Dale and Rosemary in the hotel for our final breakfast before parting ways.

Orange juice, tea, coffee, yoghurt and cereal, ham, eggs, toast, marmalade — yummy.

Dale and Rosemary headed to the airport to fly back home whilst Lou and I headed for the bus station to go to Lloret de Mar.

We have had such a great time in Barcelona, now I feel like Cinderella again.

Just over an hour later, still travelling north up the east coast, and 75km later we arrived.

Blimey, do you think we could find the apartment? We must have wasted at least two hours trying to find the place.

So, we stopped for a G and T and phoned the agent Victoria. We were literally next door to it! Victoria escorted us; it was just across the road, five minutes maximum.

The apartment was lovely, and as usual when self-catering we went straight to the supermarket for supplies.

Lou cooked us an amazing dinner of steak, asparagus and sauté potatoes and it was delicious.

4th July

We had a bit of a lie-in today, and woke up at nine thirty. Victoria popped to the apartment to replace a broken patio chair and supply some cooking utensils.

We had croissants and boiled eggs for breakfast before heading to the beach. The sea is crystal clear today so we had a swim in the sea and watched the comings and goings of sightseeing boats, jet-skis, banana boats and generally people having fun. It was a lovely, lively little cove.

Phoned Ju today, she's doing so well.

5th July

Awake early today, so ventured out for a nice long walk.

Lloret's beach is lovely, we walked right around the cove and along the promenade to Castell de Sant Joan de Lloret de Mar. It dates back to the eleventh century.

The castle was damaged by an earthquake in the fifteenth century, but was rebuilt.

The war that the English fought against Spain and France which ended in the Battle of Trafalgar had a disastrous effect on the tower when it was bombarded by the British Navy, which destroyed the fortified site. The castle remains in disuse to this day.

A great little find, on the coastal path.

Not a whole lot to see in terms of structure as only a small portion of the castle remains, but with great views from the top.

Very hot today, so sweaty Betty after 6.4 miles.

In the evening we just chilled out on the balcony, listened to some music, and drank a few G and Ts.

7th July

My brother Gary's sixtieth birthday today.

Another unfortunate incident with an ATM, it deducted 303:50 euros from our account balance but did not dispense cash-argghh.

I had researched Lloret and found that there was an amazing cemetery here, listed as the fourth best attraction in Lloret, to visit, so we set off to find it.

Wow, what a place. Built in 1896 the Modernist Cemetery is full of Catalan funeral art, with the most magnificent monuments, tombstones and pantheons, which really wouldn't be out of place in a museum.

Religious or not you couldn't fail to be impressed by this place and it is a must-see if you ever find yourself in Lloret.

We then headed to the 'Church of St Romà' a Catholic church built in 1509, known for its blended architecture, from Gothic to modern, and its sixteenth century art.

It is one of the most emblematic monuments in town. It has a fabulous mosaic dome, and like many buildings already mentioned, inspired by Gaudi.

During the Spanish Civil War the church was looted and destroyed but is now completely renovated.

Inside the church is not so grand but it features some fascinating art and an altar.

The plaza on which the church sits is lively with plenty of tapas bars, it would be rude not to!

8th July

It's cloudy today, but warm.

We went for our usual walk, around town and to the small market.

I wanted to buy a small over-the-shoulder bag to carry my phone and glasses in, but mostly souvenirs and clothes, so I came away empty handed.

We did stop off for a sneaky G and T and we were served some complimentary tapas of calamari, yummy.

9th July

Even cloudier today, and looks like it may storm.

Every Tuesday there is a big market in Lloret, so off we went, but disappointingly, all the stalls, as we've experienced so far in most Spanish markets, seem to sell the same old tat!

I had a haircut; it's much easier for me to go to the barbers, rather than a ladies' salon. The men seem to cut it much better, like a boy, but no Nike ticks shaved in to the back for me LOL.

Seeing as we didn't do much yesterday, and the dinner I tried to cook last night was pretty rank, we decided to go out. We had seen a really nice little restaurant close to our apartment that was advertising T-bone steak.

Then the rain came, accompanied by the loudest thunder and blinding lightning, the rain was torrential, nothing else for it but to sit on the balcony and wait for the storm to pass.

I Face-Timed our niece Katie, she was round Mum and Dad's, with Dylan and Riley.

The Internet is a wonderful invention, isn't it? There we were, hundreds of miles away, but able to see and speak to family in real time. Incredible.

Well, the sun did come out again, so we went to the restaurant, we both chose the 'special' T-bone steak, salad and fries, all for 7.5 euros each.

Lou seemed to get really drunk, so on the way home we stopped off at the Nag's Head for a nightcap.

It turned out that the bar owner came from Edmonton. We struck up a conversation whilst watching a Celtic football game, and amazingly he was the brother-in-law of a girl I worked with at the local hospital.

It really is a small world.

10th July

Not surprising but Lou is hung over today.

Moving day though, so have to get cracking.

We tidied up, packed, left the apartment and headed to the bus station.

We have enjoyed our stay in Lloret, who knew it would be so nice?

Next stop would be Girona, just for one day, before travelling to Nice on the overnight bus.

The journey was only forty kilometres so only took forty-five minutes.

We planned to leave our luggage at the station and then explore but the baggage hall was full. For plan B we quickly googled and found a site called 'nannybag'.

Basically, you book online, then they send you the address of a participating business/shop, you take your bag there, drop it off for safekeeping for however long you need, then collect it when you are ready!

On our way to drop off bags I got stung on the right thigh, who knows what by? But I suddenly had the most intense burning pain and immediately my thigh began to swell. I made Lou suck it (as I had seen my dad do following wasp/bee sting) then I went into a bar and asked for some ice.

Girona is a gorgeous little city in the north-east of Catalonia known for its medieval architecture, its Jewish quarter, its medieval walls and its cathedral where lots of scenes for *Game of Thrones* season six, were filmed.

The old town stands on a very steep hill, and to reach the cathedral you have to climb eighty-six steps. The cathedral dominates the skyline and when you reach the top (hard work in the blistering heat) you are greeted with the most wonderful, panoramic view.

Girona is also famous for the Eiffel Bridge, built just before the Eiffel Tower by Gustave Eiffel. It spans the beautiful Onyar River which runs through the heart of the city and is constructed with vibrant red iron bars criss-crossing harmoniously.

It was really lovely walking along the river looking at the colourful houses or 'Cases de l'Onyar', nineteenth century houses that standout due to their distinct shades of deep orange, yellow and rich browns.

We decided to have traditional Spanish fare for our last supper, so we found a typical Spanish chiringuito and shared a wonderful paella.

My leg was still so painful, and burning hot to touch as well as being rock hard, dimpled and swollen.

Well, it was time to catch the bus to the airport where our next bus was scheduled to leave for Nice. We arrived three hours early, so just had to sit and wait. Luckily, we had two cartons of Don Simon in our backpacks.

The bus came on time, we settled down for some sleep.

Chapter Three
South of France

11th July

Five hundred and sixty-six kilometres and seven hours later we arrived in Nice, France.

It was very early in the morning (05:30) and we had no clue where to go so we decided to head for the port.

On the way we found a little coffee shop that was open, it had a handful of locals in, so we stopped off for a cappuccino, freshen up and brushed our teeth.

Our apartment would not be ready until two p.m., so we walked around the port and along the promenade.

Would you believe it? There were already lots of people on the beach and in the sea, at 06:45!

Our sister-in-law Keeley and her BFF Tracy were already in Nice, they have a girly trip once a year, and it just happened to be at the same time we were visiting.

We found their hotel, set in a pedestrian street in the old town — Hotel Cresp — and sat outside the small bakery next door ready to surprise them… and waited… and waited!

Finally, after what seemed like an age, they emerged from the hotel front door to our loud cries of, 'Bonjour, surprise, surprise.'

They had a cycle tour booked for the morning, so we were grateful to be able to use their room to leave our backpacks, shower and change, before venturing off to see some sights.

We headed off to Castle Hill. Ideally situated on the shore and nestled between the port and the old town, it is home to almost twenty hectares of wooded grounds, shaded paths and numerous viewing points allowing for exceptional views across the Bay of Angels.

The castle which once straddled the hill is just ruins now; it once stood within fortified walls alongside churches, convents, markets, hospitals and noble towers, and was home to the town's administrative and legal authorities.

A communal cemetery sits just outside the city wall and it contains some remarkable monuments in terms of architecture and stature.

After a few hours Lou and I walked back to the Promenade des Anglais and sat on the beach with an ice cream.

Keeley and Tracy met us and we enjoyed some wine on the terrace at their hotel before heading off to find our apartment.

It wasn't too far from theirs, about ten minutes' walk, a charming little studio, perfect for our short stay.

We met up with Keeley and Tracy later; we had a reservation for dinner at 'Fine Guele' which had been recommended by the concierge at their hotel.

There is a very locally well-known chef here with apparently impeccable credentials.

We sat outside, the finest ingredients were assembled with flare, the menu was not too extensive that you couldn't choose. I had devilled eggs to start, followed by pan-roasted duck and seasonal vegetables. They also served Billiecart Salmon, my favourite champagne — Result!

12th July

So excited today, I have been waiting to visit this next place for I don't remember how long... Monte Carlo! Lou had been here years ago whilst travelling with a mate; he always said he would bring me here one day, and true to his word!

We departed from Nice Ville to Monaco Monte Carlo on a train.

We headed straight to the port to see the spectacular yachts, and oh my, the wealth of some folk, surely, they could spare some, or share it? that wouldn't be too much to ask, would it?

Next stop the most famous gambling and entertainment complex in the world — Casino de Monte-Carlo, the opulently decorated marble and bronze casino which has all the glitz and glamour that has made it famous, just as you would imagine it, and exactly as you would see it in the films.

An elegant Beaux-Arts building built in 1863 in the Napoleon III style, it is breathtaking and I couldn't believe that I was actually here. Interestingly the citizens of Monaco are forbidden to enter the gaming rooms of the casino.

We couldn't get in, either! Despite following the dress code, long trousers, collared shirt and no flip-flops, Lou was not allowed in as his big toe was showing through the end of his sandals, LOL.

We were allowed in to the slot rooms where I quickly lost ten euros. It was fun and definitely another recommendation for your 'book-it' list.

Parked up outside were some equally impressive automobiles — Aston Martin, Porsche, Maserati and Rolls-Royce to name but a few.

Next, we headed off to the principality of Monaco and to

the palace where we got on a tuktuk for a mini tour.

Did you know that:

Monaco is the second smallest country in the world after the Vatican City in Rome.

The first Grand Prix was held here on April 14th 1929.

Monte-Carlo means Mount Charles in Italian.

After an exhausting day sightseeing, we sat on the harbour in Monaco drinking a lovely ice-cold aperol spritz before heading back on the train to Nice.

We showered and changed, then Lou and I headed to a local restaurant called 'Popples' they had a live band playing, dinner was lovely, so was the company and the entertainment.

13th July

Up by the alarm today, as we were meeting Keeley and Tracy for croissants and coffee, before they leave to fly home.

It's been great spending time with them, albeit just a few days.

We went to the beach, but it was so hot, thirty-seven degrees in the shade, so frequent dips in the sea were required. The undercurrent and waves were really quite strong on the coastline, so when you tried to get out of the sea the current kept drawing you back in... It was fun to watch locals and holidaymakers falling at the last hurdle, being swept back under, then emerging with some degree of disorientation.

We had a lovely quiche for lunch, from the bakery we had got the croissants from earlier.

Tomorrow is Bastille Day, so tonight big celebrations are planned along the promenade.

The fireworks were something else. We were dazzled by the pyrotechnics which were choreographed to music belting out from the many speakers erected along the promenade. We took our own wine and nibbles and found our spot to watch the action, all tightly and expertly controlled from barges just off the shoreline.

The display was stunning with vibrancy, colour, flashes, glows and bangs.

Thousands of people were out with their families and friends to commemorate the day.

14th July

Bastille Day is a national holiday in France, which commemorates a turning point in the French Revolution and dates back to 1789.

We decided, as it was our last day in the South of France, to go to Cannes.

We walked to the train station and jumped on, half an hour later we arrived.

Cannes is a resort town on the French Riviera probably best known for its annual film festival, as well as its association with the rich and famous.

The oldest residential area, Quartier des Anglais, houses some of the grandest of villas, built to reflect the wealth and standing of their owners.

The tuktuk tour took us around the town, and takes you back in time, along the promenade, through anecdotes about cinema, the legendary Palais des Festival, the Forville Provencal market, the medieval old town of Le Suquet with its panoramic viewpoint across the bay, Le Castre Museum, Palm

Beach, to the port and around most of the famous Cannes hotels, including the Majestic, Carlton and Martinez.

If only walls could talk, most of the rooms have been celebrity hangouts of film legends, with slinky suites, star-spotting bars, the best spas in town, sophisticated dining and discreet partying.

The port is jam packed with luxury yachts, carefully being tended to by private chartered crews. Oh, to be rich.

We stopped off there for an aperol spritz before catching the train back to Nice.

Spoke to Dale this evening. He had an online delivery from the supermarket and had cooked dinner at our house for Pam, Jess and William.

Chapter 4
Italy

15th July

It's our niece's husband Ashley's birthday today.

It's also our dear friends Lolly and Ian's wedding anniversary.

We are moving on too, next stop Genoa, Italy.

One hundred and eighty-four kilometres travelling the coastal road and crossing the border.

The weather today is shocking, dark black skies and pouring with rain for entire journey. The bus was over an hour late, and we eventually left at ten thirty, a journey that should have taken around two and a half hours took almost five.

Anyhow, we managed to find Hotel Britannia, and things started to brighten up.

Genoa is a port city in the north-west of Italy. It is known for its role in maritime trade over many centuries, and is the birthplace of Christopher Columbus.

After settling in we went for a walk around the port, but first impressions were that it looked pretty gloomy. The streets were steep, hilly, like a maze and mostly very narrow. We stumbled across the cathedral which was very impressive, we will go and take a closer look in the next few days.

Of course the first thing we fancied to eat was a traditional Italian pizza, and there was no shortage of choice.

I always find it most fascinating that the fewer ingredients and the thinner the base, the more delicious they taste.

Walking back to the hotel we took a turn up a very tiny, dark and menacing lane, there were African-origin men (mostly) lining the entire length who appeared to be dealing 'goods' from boxes/bags/suitcases. We were glad when we safely got to the end.

16th July

What a difference a day makes, the sun is shining and it is a glorious day.

Guess what? My favourite — the open top bus city sight-seeing tour.

This city is attractive, historic and very educational with wonderful buildings and architecture.

Interesting facts:

As mentioned, it was home to Christopher Columbus, the most famous Italian explorer who went to sea at a young age and is said to have found new lands called 'the Americas'; incidentally by accident whilst he was searching for a new way to get to China and India, hoping to profit from the lucrative spice trade.

We stopped and hopped off at this tiny dwelling where he spent his youth. Although heavily reconstructed in the eighteenth century, the house is now a 'museum' furnished in a style which is in keeping with Christopher Columbus's era.

Marco Polo, an Italian merchant and explorer who served as foreign emissary to Kublai Khan of China was also imprisoned here after joining the army when Venice was at war with Genoa in 1298–99.

The Cathedral di San Lorenzo is very distinctive and impressive and is the most important church in Genoa. Its façade is majestically black and white stripes; it sits imposingly in the heart of the city, and was built as a dedication to San Lorenzo Martire and it guards the ashes of the patron saint San Giovanni Battista which were brought here at the end of the First Crusade.

The Cathedral was bombed by the British in 1941 during WW2 but survived the attack and inside the Cathedral you can still see the bomb.

Jeans were invented here, in 1873, by Jacob Davis and Levi Strauss! Originally designed for miners as the denim fabric, with the addition of copper rivets at the places most fabric trousers ripped — the pockets and the flies were sturdy and could withstand hard work.

The open-top sightseeing tour was a triumph, we thoroughly enjoyed the day.

Carbonara for dinner for me, lasagne for Lou.

We spoke to Dale this evening; I miss him, love him and cannot wait to see him again.

17th July

Our sightseeing bus ticket was still valid, so after a super buffet breakfast we headed off.

Lou wanted to go and see the football stadium but it was rubbish, no Camp Nou, that's for sure.

However, we had heard of a spectacular cemetery here in Genoa, but it wasn't part of the bus route, so we got off and walked (around five kilometres) to find it.

This place is a hidden little gem… WOW.

It's called 'Monumental Cemetery of Staglieno' and is an extensive cemetery famous for its sculptures.

A nineteenth century burial ground crammed full of ornate tombs covering more than one square kilometre and is the second largest cemetery in Europe with over two million graves.

It was like visiting an outdoor museum of the finest neoclassical, realism, symbolism, art nouveau, art deco and gothic works and sculptors.

It also contains the graves of British Commonwealth servicemen and women from the first and second world wars.

The Staglieno has been subject matter for album covers (Joy Division), books and films *On her majesty's secret service* — Bond.

If you ever go to Genoa it's another one for your 'book-it' list!

Opposite our hotel was the Savoy which had a rooftop terrace.

It was the perfect place to have pre-dinner cocktails before dinner.

We're moving on again tomorrow.

We have had a lovely time here, it is so beautiful.

I spoke to Ju on the phone, she is doing very well, then I rang Mum and Dad.

Dad had seen the specialist today regarding his disabling spinal canal stenosis and been placed on the waiting list for surgery.

18th July

A nice hearty breakfast to start off, cereal and yoghurt, eggs and bacon, fresh orange and coffee, and Lou had a slice of Genoa cake!

Travelling south down the west coast of Italy to Florence today.

We caught the bus locally for the 232 kilometres three-hour journey.

Our seats were not allocated this time, and the bus was full, and the only availability was the middle two on the back row, so it was really not very comfortable at all.

The bus terminal was seven miles from Florence, but there was a direct tram link in, so we jumped aboard, and then had a 1.8 kilometre walk to apartment.

It was a cute ground floor apartment, with a tiny terrace which reminded me of the opening sequence of *Coronation Street* — all it needed was a cat sitting on the fence!

As usual we went straight to the local supermarket for provisions and we brought some fresh mussels, chips and bread for tonight's dinner, it was yummy.

Laundry done, dinner eaten, and bed… feeling exhausted.

19th July

We woke up really early and had boiled eggs with soldiers for breakfast, followed by some toast and jam before heading out to explore.

I wanted to get the sightseeing bus so we went to the local tourist information centre. The lovely lady there advised us against it, stating that the streets in Florence with most of the tourist attractions were far too narrow and the big bus is unable to access the tiny, cobbled streets.

We opted for a personal guide in a golf-type buggy but they were all booked until three p.m.

So, not to waste any valuable time, we headed on foot to the Michael Angelo Plaza. It was a lovely walk, along the River Arno, with a pit stop on the way for a wine and a beer.

Crikey, the walk up the hill was very steep and quite a challenge in the heat, but wowee! What a view.

The Piazzale is dedicated to the Renaissance sculptor Michael Angelo, with the huge monument, a bronze replica of David, transported up the hill on 'poggi ramps' by nine pairs of oxen in 1873.

Once at the top the view captures the heart of Florence from Forte Belvedere to Santa Croce, across the lungarno and the bridges of the Arno, the Duomo, the Palace, the Bell Tower and the rest of the city and the hills.

It is just stunning.

On the way back down, we stopped for an aperol spritzer and a beer, with a complimentary tomato bruschetta — grazie.

The golf buggy was fun, just Lou and I with a local guide.

We were taken on a tour around the old town and loaded with many interesting facts:

- The river Arno goes all the way to Pisa.
- Over eight million books and manuscripts are held in Florence National Gallery.
- The River Arno flooded Florence in 1965 losing thousands of famous art works and artefacts.
- Santa Croce Church is the burial place of Michael Angelo and Botticelli.
- Its cathedral is the third largest in the world after St Paul's in London, and St Peter's in Rome.

20th July

Today is our thirty-fourth Wedding Anniversary, blimey how did that happen? Time flies.

We have decided to have a nice day out today, so we went straight to the train station and caught the 09:56 train to Pisa.

We had already booked our ticket online to go up the Leaning Tower of Pisa at 14:30, so, on arrival we had a walk around, stopped off for a cocktail and lunch (pizza) before heading to the tower.

What a sight, the tower was leaning much more than it appears on the TV and in photos.

A free-standing bell tower with a four-degree lean as a result of unstable foundations, veering upwards in a permanent defiance of gravity, the tower is the third oldest structure in the city, built between 1173–1372, it is 183 feet high and has 296 steps.

No wonder it is a 'Wonder of the World'

The climb up was tricky, and exhausting. I am not sure that visitors will have the opportunity in the future, the stairs are very worn and, in some places, slippery. It will probably resemble a helter-skelter in years to come.

Around the tower, within a most beautiful landscaped square, is home to Pisa's other main sights, the cathedral and baptistery.

The Pisa cathedral is candy striped and has a graceful tiered façade; it is a medieval Roman Catholic cathedral and is one of the grandest architectural masterpieces of Tuscany.

It contains sixty-eight marble columns from Sardinia; the number represented the number of churches in Pisa at the time of its construction.

There were lots of tourists of course; all trying to capture the best pose — 'holding up the tower', 'pushing the tower over'.

I decided to stop and help a lone female traveller and take some shots for her, crouching down with camera pointing up to make sure I got the whole tower in the frame. As I stood up my own phone fell from my shorts' pocket, the screen smashed completely.

Gutted.

We had a lovely day in Pisa, though. Another tick off the 'book-it' list.

21st July

So excited as today we are off to the Uffizi Gallery, and the Accademia Gallery.

The Uffizi Gallery is one of the most famous art galleries in the world and a place that I had always wanted to visit. Now here I am.

A monumental building built in 1560 originally constructed as administrative and legal offices.

My goodness, it contains masterpieces from the greatest Renaissance artists such as Botticelli, Michael Angelo, Leonardo, Raphael, Rubens, and Rembrandt.

The icon of the gallery is 'The Birth of Venus' by Botticelli.

Look it up, the painting was found by the National Gallery after lying unidentified in its vaults for more than 150 years. It depicts the goddess Venus arriving on shore after her birth, emerging from the sea fully grown. It is worth more than ten million pounds.

After spending around three hours at the gallery we headed off to Galleria dell'Accadamia. Thank goodness we had a pre-booked ticket as the queue was right around the block with tourists excitedly waiting to see 'David', arguably the Western world's most famous sculpture.

The gallery was established in the 1700s and in 1873 the original statue of Michael Angelo's statue was transferred here.

I must admit, I had total immersion into this statue.

C.501 it is carved from one single piece of marble, it took Michael Angelo three years to make, it is 17ft tall, and he was the tender age of just twenty-three.

The magnificent nude man, at the height of physical vigour, intense expression of strength, courage, power and invincibility is absolutely colossal, powerful, moving, impressive, stunning, and certainly made me feel very emotional.

Did you know that some say David's willy is so small for a reason? It's because it had retracted in fear due to David's imminent battle with Goliath! Every day is a school day!

Absolutely splendid!

Feeling exhausted we headed back to our apartment. We have walked quite a distance today; my watch tells me it is nine miles in total.

We roasted a chicken for dinner, and had some nice fresh salad.

Then we planned the next part of our journey, next stop Rome.

We found a nice Airbnb and booked our bus to take us there.

Today was the conclusion of the golf British Open — won

by Shane Lowrie.

22nd July

Still feeling exhausted from all the excitement yesterday we lazed around for a bit before getting ready for today's adventures.

Off we went for a walk to find the Florentina football stadium; Lou likes to have a look, but this one was not at all impressive, and closed!

On our way back we stopped off at Piazza Santa Croce to see the basilica (we had passed it on the golf buggy tour a few days ago).

Among the many highlights of the church as you walk through its hallowed walled you will find a bell tower, a fascinating crypt, and sixteen chapels!

Santa Croce also hosts three cloisters; a covered walk with an open colonnade, designed for silent contemplation, prayer and meditation.

It is the burial place of Michael Angelo and Galileo, Dante also has a memorial here but his sarcophagus is empty (as he was exiled from Florence).

It even has a Henry Moore sculpture in the gardens *Warrior with Shield.*

Henry Moore had an infatuation with Florence and he gifted this work to the city before he died.

If you ever go to Florence this is a definite must-see.

Next, we went to the rooftop terrace bar next door to the Savoy (strangely the Savoy didn't have one?) Strawberry Fields Bellini anyone?

I also had my phone screen fixed, the young chap did a

great job and it looks like new.

We went home to our apartment and packed up ready for tomorrow's move, too tired to go out or to cook we got a takeaway… No, not pizza… Chinese and it was delicious.

I've really liked it in Florence, I think it equals my all-time favourite two European cities to visit, Valencia and Rome, a charismatic city you would be sorry to miss. I would like to come back again, one day.

23rd July

We left the apartment in Florence, caught the tram to the bus station, then the bus to Rome that we had already booked.

Allocated seats this time on the front row of the bus, lovely, we settled down for the three-hour journey, 273 kilometres heading south down the west coast of Italy.

Well, we arrived on time at about two thirty, then everything went pear shaped.

We walked across to the train station as we needed to get to Roma Termini, there was no one to help, so after toing and frowing, Lou checked the main departures board, shouted at me to run as the train we needed was about to leave at platform six.

We quickly jumped on the train; it departed, in completely the wrong direction — fifty-two miles in the wrong direction to be precise!

Finally, the train had its first stop, we got off and jumped straight back on the next train on opposite platform and headed back to where we came from!

Feeling het up we hailed a taxi to get to our location, and got totally ripped off, paid twenty-eight euro for less than a two-mile journey… oh, well.

Our apartment was gorgeous, a fifth-floor penthouse, big and spacious with a gigantic balcony.

The host had left us free wine and biscuits.

As usual we went shopping for provisions, and settled in.

24th July

We woke up early today and had already decided not to do too much.

It really is exhausting after moving day, as is sightseeing.

Anyhow, we did go for a 'little' walk, and nine miles later we had visited the Colosseum, Palatial Hills, Trevi Fountain, Pantheon and Vittoriana — the museum and largest national monument in Italy!

The Pantheon never ceases to amaze me, built in 113–125 AD, you turn a corner and there it is, this gigantic wonderful building in the middle of Rome.

But, of course, it was there before everything else around it, right?

Built by Hadrian as a Roman temple, it is now a church, it's free to get in, and once inside all you can do is marvel at its marvellousness!

A cylindrical building with a central dome, opening to the sky, known as an oculus.

How they built it is beyond any comprehension, go see for yourself!

It is very hot here at the moment, locals say that it is a heatwave and some temperatures are reaching record highs.

We sat on the lovely balcony, Lou cooked chicken and roast potatoes, we listened to some football commentary on the radio, and rested.

There is no wi-fi in the apartment at the moment, so I contacted the host who said they would come and replace tomorrow.

I spoke to Ju via WhatsApp, she seems okay. I miss her.

25th July

The anniversary of Lou's dad Bill who died two years ago.

We had breakfast, poached eggs on toast and fresh orange juice before heading to the Metro not far from our penthouse.

Saint Peter's Basilica and Square is just glorious, although we have been here twice before it is still as breathtaking and a testament to the religious, artistic and cultural significance of Rome.

Located within the Vatican City, it is the largest church in the world, and is regarded as one of the holiest Catholic shrines.

Two hundred and eighty-four Doric columns and eighty-eight pilasters embrace it, 140 statues sit on top of the colonnades (all created by Bernini) the entire interior is lavishly decorated with marble, architectural sculpture, reliefs, and gilding. There are several chapels, a nave and a great altar, there is also an extensive vault leading to the crypts below (although there is no public access to this now, we saw it on our previous visit).

The genius Michael Angelo was responsible for the design of its grandest feature, its dome; he also painted the ceiling in the Sistine Chapel.

Free to enter it is immense, incredible, stunning, monumental, magnificent and a visit to Rome would not be complete without a visit here.

We've heard that the Pope gives a public audience sermon on the last Sunday of every month, that's three days away and before we leave so were going to try to come back.

Back to the penthouse but wi-fi still not replaced, pizza for dinner.

26th July

It's Friday.

We already decided to go to Piazza Barbarini today, so we got up early and had breakfast, scrambled egg on toast with a smiley tomato ketchup face on!

I always used to do this to Dale's scrambled eggs, so we sent him a photo of it.

The piazza is especially renowned for its centrepiece, the Fontana del Tritone, designed by Bernini.

Four dolphins hold up Triton, the god of the sea, as he jets water out of a seashell. It's beautiful (but not a touch on the Trevi fountain which is just around the corner).

The piazza is also home to 'Bernini Hotel' an iconic hotel which was very popular in the sixties, frequented by movie stars and singer superstars who supped, sipped and simpered here.

It's a great spot for lunch and a glass of Chianti — be rude not to.

Then we walked up to the Crypt Ossario, again we came here last time we visited Rome but it is just so fascinating.

Here lies a crypt that began with a practical purpose; there was no longer room in the small cemetery of the nearby monastery, so the bones of exhumed monks had to be placed elsewhere. The Capuchin monks left the monastery and took up residence here where they would transport and sort the remains of the deceased monks.

The bones were 'arranged' in a certain order along the walls depending on status.

It is a corridor containing the remains of around 3,700 dead, with six rooms; Crypt of Resurrection, The Mass Chapel, Crypt of Skulls, Crypt of Pelvises, Crypt of Leg and Thigh bones and the Crypt of Three Skeletons with a placard which reads 'What you are now we used to be; what we are now you will be'…

Had a little walk around town, found a wine cellar that sold Billie-Cart Salmon, so just had to buy a bottle. I will save if for when we meet Dale and Ed in Venice.

Did I mention that they are coming to meet us on 12th August?

27th July

Lou wanted to go and see the Olympic Stadium today, so off we set with his directions. He said it was at the end of the Metro Line and then around half an hour's walk… Well, it was but in the opposite direction to the way we had come.

It was like a Benny Hill moment, head scratching, walking around in a circle, map upside down, then map round the right way, more head scratching, then back down the steps to get back on the Metro, back in the direction we had come from.

Anyhow, we eventually found it and there just happened to be a diving competition in progress.

We walked around the huge stadium and surrounding complex, and there was plenty to see. The 'Stadio Olimpico' itself is the largest sports facility in Rome, once the centrepiece for the 1960 Olympics, and host of the opening/closing ceremonies it is now home to Lazio and Roma, shame there is not a game scheduled.

The diving competition was still in the knockout stage; we sat and watched for a while, and had a drink before heading back to the penthouse.

The sky has turned very black and menacing, I think we are in for a very big storm, maybe 'the clash of the titans'!

28th July

It's my eldest brother Jeff and sister-in-law Marion's fortieth wedding anniversary today. Wow.

Sure enough, my goodness, last night, what a storm. A battle between Romulus and Remus, David and Goliath and the Clash of the Titans all rolled into one.

I have never seen anything like it; vicious, savage, mad, tempestuous, angry, turbulent, brash, strong, proud, lavishing, blinding, deafening and perpetual.

The whole sky was a kaleidoscope of razor-sharp flashes of lightning, opening holes in the cloud which then collapsed causing rapturous thunder with dagger-like fire spears of rain lashing down against the window frame.

Lou had slept through the whole thing!

We were on the Metro just after eight, heading straight for the Vatican City.

Entry to the Vatican Museum and Sistine Chapel is free on the last Sunday of the month.

The weather was still terrible, although the storm had passed and it was warm, it was still raining. Never mind, we had our cagoules.

The queue was substantial, but once the doors opened, we moved forward quickly, and upon entry we swiftly made our way to marvel at the Michelangelo Fresco in the Sistine Chapel.

It took four years to paint, the complex design includes several sets of figures, both clothed and nude, which allowed Michelangelo to demonstrate his genius, the book of Genesis and the hands from 'the Creation of Adam' being the best known.

Initially he sought to engage assistants to speed along the work as quickly as he could, but was unable to find suitable candidates, and painted virtually the whole ceiling alone.

A supreme masterpiece of pictorial art.

Of course, there are numerous other pieces of art in the museum including works by Francis Bacon, Matisse, Munter, and Salvador Dali... the list goes on, you really could spend an entire day here.

We hot-footed it to St Peter's Square next to see the Pope delivering his sermon. We were very lucky to witness such an event with thousands of worshippers all congregating, hoping to catch a glimpse of the man himself!

It was very moving, although we didn't understand a word. I logged on to Facebook and did a live stream video so that all of our family and friends could see it, too.

Lunch of spaghetti with tomato sauce next.

Later in the day we tried to meet up with my nephew Rory and his girlfriend who were here in Rome for a short stay. Unfortunately, we kept missing each other so we headed back to the penthouse for the rest of the day/evening.

The maid had been and swept/watered the plants on the terrace.

She had also hung our washing out to dry!

29th July

This morning was a chill out few hours. We spent some time sorting out backpacks, packing and tidying up ready to leave Rome tomorrow.

I received a panic call from Jess at home. She had noticed that our car was missing, she wasn't sure how long it had been gone for as she had been in bed all weekend hung over!

I phoned Dale to discover he had been home to collect it and driven with Ed to see his family in Huddersfield — phew — panic over.

Dale said he and Ed were looking forward to meeting us in Venice.

So for our final night in Rome, we ventured out to find a restaurant recommended to us by my brother John.

We found it OK, just off Piazza Navona, it was called 'Cul De Sac', and what a delightful little wine bar.

Looking very traditional, it was cramped, both inside and out, with 'no frills' long pine benches and tables, lucky we managed to get seated outside.

The reasonable prices and an encyclopaedic wine list ensure this place is always popular.

Thank goodness for Valter, our waiter, who helped us out with recommended dishes and accompanying suitable wine. We shared a home-made pate to start then I had meatballs with mash potato, and Lou had what Valter described as a Romany dish, typically for the poor, of slow-cooked stewed oxtail.

It was bloody delicious.

The most famous fountain in the world 'Fontana di Trevi' was calling us back to see it one last time.

I absolutely love this place, the first time Lou brought me here (he always said he would) I cried, tears of extreme emotion and deep love.

You can hear it and feel it before you see it.

It is a sprawling baroque-style fountain which depicts Neptune on his chariot, being led by Tritons, with seahorses representing the moods of the sea.

Legend says throw a coin in the fountain using your right hand over your left shoulder to make a wish; great things will happen, and one day you will return to Rome.

Throw a second coin in and you will have romance, and throwing a third coin in will ensure marriage.

It is truly magical.

Home to bed.

30th July

Up and about early enough. Boiled some eggs and buttered some croissants for our journey ahead.

Again the bus was bang on time, we settled into our allocated front row seats and got to Naples in no time, 226 kilometres in two and a half hours.

It's the birthplace of Sophia Loren.

We met Alessandro, our Airbnb host, was waiting to show us in to the flat. It is lovely BUT right on the junction of Piazza Sanità which is FULL of kids/adolescents who congregate on mopeds... Oh, the noise!

31st July

Our nephew JJ's birthday today, and our friend Leafy's too.

Well, we got up early and decided to go on foot and explore the Bay of Naples.

We passed by the cathedral, a sample of beautiful architecture containing a large number of fine works of art, and the seat of the archbishop.

It is dedicated to Saint Gennaro — the patron saint of Naples — and contains a phial of his blood which is reputed to liquefy on occasions, and when it does, it guarantees good fortune for the year to come.

Down by the bay we stumbled upon a film crew and some actors who were busy shooting a new movie called *Seven Days to Fall in Love*.

There was quite a crowd because the star of the movie was a famous Italian actress called Serena Rossi.

Soon after we walked on to the Castel dell'Ovo which was once a Norman castle and fortress, later inhabited by hermit monks. Then we had a mooch around Borgo Marinaro, a charming little fishing village.

Here we stopped off for a cheeky aperol spritz and a beer, only to be served olives, crisps, pizza slices and mini sausage roll tapas!

On the way back to the flat we stopped and purchased a three-day tourist travel card, our plan was to use it to visit Pompeii and Sorrento whilst we were in Southern Italy.

My watch tells me we have walked 9.4 miles today.

I spoke to Ju, up and down but on the whole, she is doing great.

1st August

Up early, showered and out by nine a.m.

Off to Pompeii, so excited to see it.

When staying in Naples you just have to visit Pompeii, don't you?

It was easy enough to get to on the train from main Garibaldi station, and only took an hour.

Some friends told us not to bother with Pompeii, but to go to Herculaneum instead; I disagree.

This is an ancient Roman city that was buried under four to six metres of ash and lava following the catastrophic devastating eruption of Mount Vesuvius in 79AD.

This preserved site features excavated ruins of streets and houses. Pompeii had been an important inland port, a place of trade, industry and business famed for its fermented fish sauce! Its people were a mixture of wealthy elite, professionals and slaves. The various inscriptions also attest to bakers, bath attendants, grape pickers and prostitutes.

The Lupanar (officially the largest) brothel is the most famous. It demonstrates that the women provided their services in cells usually only big enough for a stone bed, there were no windows or doors (maybe curtained off) but the condition of the brothel was of no concern to their owners or their clients as most of the sex workers were slaves.

Murals from the brothel depicts the women as erotic and exotic, with fair skin, naked except for a 'bra' and in a variety of sexual positions with young, athletic-looking men.

There are also many examples of graffiti.

Wealthy persons did not frequent these establishments because of the availability of mistresses or slave concubines who would fulfil their sexual needs.

There is also a principal square, basilica, theatre, Roman baths, taverns, bakers, oh, and so much more to see.

One of my favourites is a charming little house called 'House of Lovers' named for an inscription that translates 'lovers, like bees, wish life to be as sweet as honey'.

The site was abandoned until the eighteenth century, and since then about three fifths of the total area has been recovered.

It is absolutely fascinating-and vast, we spent most of the day here.

Another tick off the 'book-it' list, and surely somewhere to come back to?

After a late lunch at Delzie pizza restaurant of mixed chopped salad with chicken and mozzarella cheese thin crust pizza (to die for) washed down with wine, we headed home on the train.

We sat on the balcony and watched the 'mental moped mating rituals'.

2nd August

Out early once again, this time we're off to Sorrento.

The train was packed; we had to stand all the way, both tourists and locals out for the day.

Coffee and croissant on arrival followed by a nice little jaunt around town on the tuktuk train.

It's a busy seaside resort, perched on a cliff it seems. We had a few hours walking around the shops, cafés and bars, and we also had a look around the harbour.

On the train back we stopped off at Herculaneum, a residential town which was also destroyed by the eruption of Mount Vesuvius.

Much smaller that the site at Pompeii, and less impressive but with better preserved buildings.

We later visited the San Gaudioso Santa Maria church which was on the piazza Sanita, for a fascinating tour of the underground catacombs. The burial grounds dated back to the third century, still complete with frescos, bones/skulls etc.

A mysterious place... the price of entry ticket is used to support the local community with local work and clean-up projects.

Lou cooked ravioli with tomato passata for dinner.

I spoke to Mum and Dad, then Ju who is enjoying getting on with some painting.

Dale went to the opera at Glyndebourne today with his friend Raqib.

3ʳᵈ August

We both woke up today and felt completely exhausted after the last two days which were full on.

Lou went to get his haircut, whilst I cooked us some brunch, sausages, eggs beans, fried bread and jam.

It was on the agenda to visit the San Paolo Football Stadium, so we set off. As we approached it we noticed that there seemed to be a lot of police around.

Anyhow, we walked around the stadium but it was closed.

As we got to the main gate there seemed to be some hustle and bustle, then a coach arrived, the team coach, the gate opened, and the whole Napoli football team exited. They were travelling to Marseille for a game tomorrow!

When they left the kind security guard wagged his finger at us and let us in to the ground to see the pitch, it made Lou's day.

I had read a review on a nearby pizza joint that had a Michelin star. It was just around the corner to our flat so we went there for tea.

It was called di Cira Olivo and was #1 for pizza in Naples.

It didn't disappoint.

Naples has plenty of important history, architecture, fine churches, art galleries, museums and catacombs yes.

But it is also home to meetings, beatings, cheatings (we saw several street brawls) and kisses, near misses (mopeds) and pisses (openly in the streets). It is dirty, overbearing and crime ridden, beware of your own mortality as mopeds career past you, whilst shady figures loiter around your pockets, but it is a taste of 'real Italy'.

4ᵗʰ August

It's our last day in Naples, right outside the flat in Piazza Sanità there was a funeral taking place. The piazza was full of hundreds of mourners, and then along came the hearse... a great big stretch Maserati!

Lots of police around too, in official uniform with medals, lots of locals out and mourners keen to get the briefest of touches on the coffin as it was being carried into the church.

We figured it was either somebody very important, or a well-respected member of the Mafia?

After watching the procession, we headed off to the Madre gallery of Contempory Art. It was free to enter.

Recently restored and refurbished the museum is dedicated to exhibitions. It also contains an extensive library.

On our visit we were lucky enough to see works by Jeff Koons, an American artist recognised for his sculptures that depict everyday objects, most notably balloon animals in stainless steel and Anish Kapoor, a British Indian who is most commonly recognised for his striking sculpture at the 2012 Queen Elizabeth Olympic Park; the ArcelorMittal Orbit.

Most days whilst in Naples we used the Metro. There was a station close to the flat, and every time we went down the escalator, we saw a homeless man just sitting there.

He didn't beg, or pester anyone; he just sat there with his sad eyes and empty expression.

I decided to stop off at the supermarket where I brought him a carton of juice, a fresh sandwich, some biscuits and some chocolate, an orange, banana and an apple.

I travelled down the escalator for the last time, and there he was, I crouched down and placed my offerings on the ground in front of him.

His face was beautiful, and I am sure that his eyes were welling up; it felt nice that even for just that second, he seemed happy.

Lou and I had meatballs, gravy and mash for dinner before an early night, moving on again to Rimini.

5th August

Virtually no sleep, oh goodness, the mopeds! Constant noise all night.

The bar opposite was also open all night; in fact, it was just closing as we left the flat at 07:10!

A long journey today, travelling northbound up the east coast, 516km, but not direct, we had an hour and a half stop over and changed buses in a small town called Pescara, before our final destination of Rimini. Total journey time just over seven hours.

Well, the bus stopped seven kilometres out of town, so we walked to the local train station, followed by another bus ride, and finally arrived at our Hotel 'Rosy', unfortunately there was nothing rosy about it at all!

A tiny room, shower head that was literally over the toilet (which you had to sit sideways on) and a balcony about two foot wide and four foot long, with a 'lovely' view of a brick wall. The ceiling fan didn't work, neither did the air con.

I complained straight away. The miserable man on reception said we had to pay five euro a day to have air con switched on! No way, and after some heated discussion he finally agreed to switch the air con on for free.

Feeling tired and completely stressed, we went out for dinner and had a lovely pizza with mixed salad to share.

Back to shitty hotel; spoke to Dale and Ju before bed.

6th August

Up for breakfast which was quite nice, buffet style, continental, but did get told off for taking coffee out onto the terrace.

We headed off to the beach, but walked and walked for ages... all the beaches were 'private' you had to pay seven euro each plus another seven euro for a parasol = twenty-one euro a day just to go on the beach!

Rows and rows and rows of them.

We eventually found a tiny strip, which wasn't private, so we settled down to relax.

The sea is very shallow here, it's the Adriatic Sea, and so there is no tide. We had a nice day.

We decided to go back to the same restaurant for dinner

tonight. To be honest, there were hardly any others to choose from, but this time the food was shocking,

We ordered mussels and chips, waited ages for service, and when it arrived almost half of the mussels had not opened. Lou got the right hump and started sulking, so I went and complained; the head of service tried to say that it was quite normal for that to happen with mussels! Err, no, we've had mussels many times before, eventually got a discount on the bill and left.

7th August

Cloudy and breezy today, then around lunchtime began to get very windy.

Didn't really do much, just planned and booked next move to Bologna.

Went out for dinner, I had chicken fillet, potato and salad. Lou had lasagne.

Going to San Marino for the day tomorrow.

8th August

Up early and ready for our day trip. Breakfast first, again lovely continental buffet style before heading for the train to the bus station, and bus to San Marino.

It is the world's oldest sovereign state, surrounded by Italy. Of the Earth's 196 completely independent countries it is the fifth smallest, a landlocked micronation.

It is beautiful, very picturesque old buildings, tiny narrow windy cobbled streets, souvenir shops, and the most stunning views of nearby towns and surrounding countryside.

There are three castles here, which feature on the national flag, between two of the castle towers there is a path which follows the city wall along the cliff face, it really reminds me of a Disney film or two 'Let it go, let it go'.

There is also a Basilica and a large Piazza where you can just sit and watch people coming and going, whilst enjoying a nice glass of wine and a thin and crispy authentic Italian pizza.

There seemed to be a commotion going on outside the palace. There were lots of tourists taking photos of a very handsome man. Of course I jumped in there and asked for a selfie having no idea who he was. Later we asked in the restaurant and the waiter snatched my phone and was excitedly running around showing everyone the picture of me with this handsome man. I still don't know who he is, singer, actor, prince, who knows?

There are no cars, and it really has a medieval feel and is quite charming.

We had our passports stamped at the post office/tourist information centre, an excellent souvenir of a visa tax stamp and official ink stamp over the top.

After another tiring day we headed back. Lou called Bunny and they had a nice long chat.

If you ever dreamt of visiting Rimini, then stop... don't bother, it sprawls across the Adriatic Sea, and is one of the most famous seaside resorts in Europe with fifteen kilometres of sandy beaches, and that's about it.

San Marino, on the other hand, is a gem not to be missed.

9th August

We set off from Rimini to Bologna today, an hour and a half bus ride.

We found our apartment easy. A gorgeous studio with its own garden, right next to the train station (although you wouldn't know it).

As usual we went to the nearest supermarket for some provisions, this time it was —

Lidl!

10th August

A nice leisurely start to the day before heading off to explore.

Bologna is the oldest university town in Europe dating back to the eleventh century, a colonial city famous for it hundreds of arches built originally to shade the horses.

Not so much to see compared to other Italian cities, a lovely Basilica which was just as glorious as the rest we have seen in Italy, The Fountain of Neptune (naughty, originally considered too sexy with nymphs squeezing water jets out of their breasts and Neptune appearing to have an erect penis) and the *DueTorri* towers (both leaning) built as a competition between two families to show their wealth, and to demonstrate which family was most powerful.

They were both constructed in 1109, and sit at an intersection of five roads which lead to the five gates of the city walls.

We climbed to the top of Asinelli tower — 498 steps — again not for the faint hearted but we were rewarded with the spectacular views across Bologna's red rooftops.

Then we went for (a very long) walk to see the football stadium, the 'Stadio Renato Dall'Ara' home to Bologna FC. Not very impressive although it has hosted the FIFA World Cup twice.

Had an ice cream to cool down before catching the bus back.

My watch tells me eight miles today.

11th August

Decided to do nothing much at all today, just meandered around, caught up with some bookings, did some washing and packed up bags ready for moving on tomorrow.

Lou popped to the supermarket for some dinner; he got some nice steak and some salad.

We're off to Venice and will be meeting Dale and Ed.

I can't wait to see them both.

So excited.

12th August

Up and out of the apartment early, first on the train to Bologna Central, and then to bus stop for FlixBus to Venice — yippee!

One hundred and fifty-four kilometres and just over two hours we arrived with ease following an uncomplicated journey, but then it all went wrong again!

Our satnav took us completely off track. We walked, crossed bridges, walked more, crossed back over bridges for what seemed like forever. Following about another hour on the river boat we finally ended up at our destination for one night 'Sunny Hostel'.

It was situated on the island of Giudecca, along a large promenade overlooking the canal and the main Island of Venice.

Venice has more than one hundred islands, no roads, just canals. The main canal thoroughfare is called the Grand Canal.

To make the islands of the Venetian lagoon habitable early settlers drained the lagoon, dug the canals and used the earth to make a shore and banks. On top of the banks, wooden platforms, and then stone was placed, then the buildings were constructed on top.

Crikey, it was so hot in the room, no air con and a split-level with bed upstairs, and we all know that heat rises.

Anyhow, we went to the shop and brought some wine, cheeses and biscuits. Luckily the hostel had a roof terrace, so we sat admiring the view for a few hours before heading to a local restaurant for lasagne and spaghetti bolognaise.

13th August

We crossed from La Giudecca to Venice main island by river taxi, so excited to see Dale and Ed today.

Again, the satnav took us the wrong way and like yesterday we walked over who-knows-how-many bridges and canals.

The books say everyone gets lost in Venice. How could you not in a city with over one hundred islands, 150 canals, 400 bridges, and six districts?

We made it eventually, the delightful 'Residenza Corte Antica', a recently renovated bed and breakfast right in the heart of Venice.

We checked in and put the Billiecart fizz on ice ready for when Dale and Ed arrived, and set off to explore.

Venice is a hauntingly beautiful place, it dates back to the fifth century and is crammed full of Renaissance and gothic palaces, piazzas, bridges and the most splendid basilica.

Dale and Ed didn't arrive until late afternoon, so we drank our fizz whilst freshening up before heading out for dinner.

We sat to dine in restaurant 'la Calcina' on the beautiful

panoramic terrace on canal Giudecca. I had sea bass and sauté potatoes, Lou and Dale had pizza and Ed chose pasta and pesto. We laughed, ate, drank wine and chatted, catching up with all the gossip, it was fabulous.

When we got back to the B and B, Dale told Lou that he had booked us in to a luxury 5-star hotel for our last two nights in Venice as a treat for his birthday.

14th August

We all met for breakfast, there was so much to choose from, so we had a hearty breakfast before heading off for the day's sightseeing.

First stop the Jewish quarter, or ghetto, an area in which Jews were compelled to live by the government. The gates were opened in the morning at the ringing of a bell in St Mark's Campanile, and locked in the evening, and strict penalties were imposed on any Jewish resident caught outside of the area after curfew.

Now things are very different, and everyone is welcome, there are five synagogues (only two are used), a school, an OAP home, a restaurant and a bakery.

Next, we walked to San Marco, stopping on the way for refreshments. Ed found a Magnum ice-cream shop, you could make your own, his was white chocolate and covered in smarties, marshmallow and honeycomb.

We also walked over Ponte-de-Rialto, the oldest and best-known bridge in Venice.

The bridge has a massive arch which is twenty-four foot high, allowing for the passage of galley ships, and has three walkways — two along the outer balustrades — and a central row full of shops selling jewellery, linens and Murano glass. It is very impressive.

San Marco square is very busy today, we will come back.

We decided to have a nice lunch — pasta — with wine of course, and then it was time for a ride on the gondola.

The most iconic image that you see in every magazine or TV show/films about Venice, so when you finally get to visit of course it's on our 'book-it' list.

The symbol of history, tradition and undeniable romance, formerly used by the upper classes, a flat-bottomed wooden boat, hand-built in the workshops called *Squeri*, the crafts and careers often passed down from father to son for generations.

Yes, they are probably overpriced and overrated, but who cares? Such fun.

Ed and Lou felt tired so they headed back to the B and B whilst Dale and I carried on being tourists. First a cheeky G and T and Negroni.

Next stop for us was the Collezione Peggy Guggenheim — if you are interested in art then you must visit this collection.

Peggy Guggenheim was an American heiress who lived in Venice for thirty years. This is her private collection located here in her former home; she is also buried in the gardens, in a grave with her dogs.

It is an eclectic mix of pieces from her favourite modern artists, including Francis Bacon, Jackson Pollock, Pablo Picasso and Salvador Dalí.

We then went to Gallerie del'Accademia to see the George Baselitz exhibition, the gallery's first ever exhibition of a living artist. A German painter, known for his figurative, expressive paintings. I had never heard of him before, but Dale educated me and I did find his inverted figure paintings depicting the artist and his wife, twice life sized and upside down, quite engrossing.

A busy day today, after a quick shower and change we headed out to a restaurant for dinner, Lou had found it on TripAdvisor highly recommended for fish dishes. When we got there, it was fully booked and there were no tables available for an hour and a half.

We booked a table and went back to the Ponte di Rialto to see it at night and have a few drinks. It looked even more beautiful — all lit up, and the Grand Canal really is grand.

Dinner was worth the wait, but there was a mix-up with the bill. The total was 219 euro, but they charged my card 2,219 euro!

I immediately realised because I received a text from Lloyds Bank! The manager came out, checked his machine, and saw that it had been processed for 2,219.

I think it was a genuine mistake, but the manager was unable to reverse or cancel the transaction.

After discussion, as tomorrow is a bank holiday here in Venice, the only solution was for the manager to reimburse me in cash. He did, after we promised we would return it if I could sort the error out with my bank — he trusted us.

15th August

Breakfast was lovely again, but sadly Dale and Ed are leaving today. We checked out of our B and B and they came with us to book us into the Hilton Hotel.

Hilton Molino Stucky situated back over La Giudecca,

once a flour mill, this huge building is now a luxury hotel.

Our room overlooking the canal was perfect, very large and the bed was so comfortable. We also had a bath which we hadn't had for four months!

There was the most splendid rooftop terrace and infinity pool too.

Dale upgraded us on check-in to full access of the executive lounge which served breakfast until ten, then snacks and drinks until nine, with a 'happy hour' five until seven where you could mix and drink your own cocktails, beer or wine at your hearts' content (or until you fell over!).

Our last two nights in Venice — perfect.

Dale and Ed made off in style. They looked like something out of a Bond movie, zooming off in a speedboat taxi to the airport... it's been super; these last few days... miss them already.

I phoned Lloyds, and guess what? The transaction had taken place, and the money withdrawn from my account. The lady said there had been a 'scam' by many restaurant and shop owners doing exactly the same thing, especially if the transaction has taken place later on in the evening, and by the time the account holder realises it is too late! Lucky the bank had texted me at the time — phew, at least I had the cash, but what if it was counterfeit? I took it to the hotel concierge and they checked each note individually, thankfully it was real.

The rest of the day Lou and I sat around the infinity pool, later we went into the executive lounge, ate the food on the buffet, and dra9nk the cocktails/wine until we couldn't physically eat or drink anything else.

We went to bed around 11:30, only to be woken by the rematch of Romulus and Remus, David and Goliath and the Clash of the Titans.

The storm was even more spectacular than the last, No kidding, the rain lashing down looked like fire spears, the sky an eruption of violent disturbance of the electrical condition of the atmosphere — charged like giant capacitors in the sky.

This time I tried harder to wake Lou up to witness this force of nature, this exhilarating spectacle, but I think he's in a red wine coma.

16th August

It's Lou's birthday — he is fifty-gr-eight.

Surprisingly he is feeling okay, so after breakfast we jumped in a water taxi to revisit Piazza San Marco, home to the iconic St Mark's Basilica, the Doge Palace and the Bridge of Sighs.

We queued to enter the basilica, it didn't take long. This stunning building dates back to the eleventh century.

The main façade is ornamental and gothic, it has five domes, and almost the entire inside roof is covered in gold mosaic as a status of its wealth and power.

The altarpiece is the famous Pala d'Oro, a masterpiece of Byzantine craftsmanship; it contains 1,300 pearls, 300 sapphires, 300 emeralds and 400 garnets.

After a few hours in the piazza I think Lou was having a bit of a relapse, so we headed back on a water taxi to the hotel.

The barman made Lou a special shot for his birthday, and after snacks and happy hour in the executive lounge again we sat on a bench along the canal — this time drinking happy birthday fizz.

Spoke to Mum and Dad, Pam, Duchess and Lolly, and Dale of course.

17th August

Sadly, it's time to check out of this magical, romantic and just-like-you-see-in-the- movies place called Venice.

We took a water bus to the ferry port, only to find that there were two, and we were at the wrong one.

Blimey, the lady at ANEK ferries office helped us out, but we would be cutting it really fine as the port we needed was three bus changes, and one and a half hours away, on public transport!

I think she phoned a family member, calling him a taxi driver, to take us the forty-five-minute drive for forty euros. Still, thankful we got there in time for our longest journey yet... A twenty-six-hour ferry crossing from Venice to Igoumenitsa in Greece.

Chapter 5
Greece

18th August

1,196km, north to south of the Adriatic Sea, and an exhausting ferry crossing later we arrived in Greece.

To my delight in the early dawn this morning I had the opportunity to witness a shoal of dolphins following and appearing to play in the wake of the ferry. They do this rather like a surfer catching a wave, they 'ride' the wake for a bit of forward momentum which enables them to travel greater distances with less effort.

The ferry had nice clean toilets on board, and showers, so we could freshen up and change our clothes.

The crossing was okay too, I haven't got very good sea legs, like my dad, but the Adriatic was literally like a millpond.

Igoumenitsa is a coastal city in north-western Greece and is the capital of the regional unit of Thesprotia and Epirus, it's a nice little port but there seems little else here.

The Hotel Oscar was not the best either, in dire need of a makeover, but very near to the port, the staff are friendly and welcoming and we are only here for two nights to re-charge our batteries.

We had dinner this evening at the hotel restaurant.

We spoke to Dale and Ju, they have booked India, and will spend the next few weeks organising our itinerary — YIPPEE.

19th August

Out to explore, trying to find the ferry, bus, train... anything to get us out of here as there is literally nothing but the ferry port.

We booked to go Corfu, Kavos, yes Kavos tomorrow.

TripAdvisor recommended a nice seafood restaurant nearby, so went there for dinner but it was closed down. We did find another just by the port so we had a pizza, our first Greek salad and wine for dinner.

20th August

Checked out and headed for the port to get our ferry to Corfu.

It only took an hour, 62 kilometres.

We tried to find 'Sandy beach resort' but after walking up a very long hill luckily a taxi driver pulled over and transported us for five euro each.

Kavos is a small village on the island of Corfu in the municipal district of Lefkimmi. It gained popularity in the post-war era as a resort devoted to tourism. It was once popular with young holidaymakers and the (in)famous 18–30s (now defunct).

'Sandy Bay' was cute, the staff again were very welcoming and friendly. Our room wasn't ready so they gave us a free drink at the bar, followed by another!

The proprietor came and took 150 euro from me for payment, but I was sure that I had already paid in advance on booking, I checked my account, and I had, so he quickly refunded my cash. You really have to have your wits about you, as it is easy to get done over!

Anyhow, after checking in we walked about a mile into Kavos town. Goodness me, the main strip was literally like a ghost town, all the 'party animals' were asleep I guess?

We got some provisions at the supermarket but decided to have dinner in the restaurant at Sunny Bay. I had beef stifado, one of my all-time favourite Greek dishes, Lou had kebab and we shared a Greek salad.

We spoke to Dale; he is off to Germany tomorrow for a wedding.

21st August

Not the best night's sleep, not that it was noisy or anything, but the bed was really creaky and it got light really early.

We went to the small beach — private to Sunny Bay — and chilled for most of the day.

Lou cooked pasta with hot dog and ragu sauce and we researched flights to India from Istanbul.

Booked to fly to New Delhi on 27th October.

22nd August

We got up late-ish today, although not such a good sleep again.

Lou sat on the balcony to plan the next leg of our trip, so I went to the private beach for an hour.

We walked into town and had a look at Kavos beach, surprisingly it was really small, but fully equipped with tourist facilities, as you would expect.

The beach is sandy, the waters are clear; there are snack bars, beach bars, umbrellas, sunbeds, and water sports.

But… where are all the people? It's deserted.

Corfu is the second largest island in the Ionian group, and many consider it to be the most beautiful. The tourists must all be staying in Corfu town because they certainly are not here.

I had my hair cut on the way home; the hairdresser was from the UK and had stayed in Kavos following a holiday nine years ago.

She was telling me that the place had really gone downhill since the ban of 18-30s holidays, she also said that over the past few years the rate of male suicide in the resort was shockingly high, last season there had been twelve!

We have booked up for a boat trip to visit Paxos and Anti-Paxos at the weekend, and booked in for the 'Greek Night' at the hotel tomorrow. Should be fun.

23rd August

We went to the beach for the day today before heading back to wash and change for the Greek night.

A traditional Greek night with live entertainment including Greek music, traditional dancing, belly-dancing and Zorba dancing (performed by men, holding onto each other's shoulders, waving a napkin, traditionally danced in Greek tavernas).

The menu for the night was tzatziki, tyrokafteri and taramasalata all served with pitta bread, followed by pork and chicken souvlaki, homemade Greek sausage, fries, pitta and salad, and a desert of fresh fruit salad.

It was really great fun until some drunken little Irish prick (who the dancers had dressed up in their traditional costume for the entertainment of the packed crowd) decided to jump in the pool.

The lead Greek dancing man was terribly upset, he told us

that the costume had been custom made for him and cost two thousand euro.

IDIOT.

24th August

We decided to walk into town early afternoon. England were playing rugby at five p.m., followed by Liverpool vs. Arsenal later. Lou has not seen much sport since we've been away, most of the places we have visited it has not been accessible, so I don't mind. In fact, I quite like watching most sport myself.

My favourite is horse racing but I also particularly enjoy the rugby and the golf.

We had a few drinks in a bar before speaking to family at home.

It's the Humphrey's turn today, party in the park at Greenwich. Like the Lilley party which took place in May, all the Humphreys (Mum's side) congregate at the top of the hill in Greenwich near to the Pavilion Cafe.

If you have never been to Greenwich, then you must. A royal park overlooking the River Thames, home to one of the most iconic views, with the most amazing mix of seventeenth century landscape, stunning gardens and a rich history that dates back to Roman times.

The 183 acres has something for everyone, you can stand on the Prime Meridian, a reference point for the rest of the world with a longitude of 0 degrees, from which every place on earth is measured in terms of its angle east or west from this line.

There is also the Royal Observatory, National Maritime

Museum, monuments, memorials, statues, wildlife (including a deer park), sports and leisure facilities, children's playgrounds, and of course fabulous ancient trees that make for fantastic climbing.

If you are feeling up to it the walk down the hill into Greenwich town is exhilarating, here you will find a charming and historic area of London home to a number of tourist attractions such as the *Cutty Sark* clipper ship, the Queen's House and Greenwich market.

Greenwich market is fondly regarded as one of London's best with its cobbled stone floor, a statuesque portico and the lanes leading into the market are so very quaint. The market is crammed full of boutiques, antiques, books, pop paraphernalia, souvenirs, retro clothing, arts and crafts and restaurants, bars, delicious artisan delicacies and street foods.

There are also florists, butchers, tearooms, a cinema, several public houses and a pie and mash shop!

Again, after calling several family members mobile phones with no answer (all too busy enjoying themselves) I managed to get Dylan on WhatsApp, the line was not great, but I did get to say hi and tell them all that we were missing them.

We watched England thrash Wales, then went to dinner at 'Big Max Diner' I had lamb kleftiko, a rustic traditional dish of slow-cooked lamb marinated in garlic, oil, and lemon juice with tomatoes, potatoes, and feta cheese — bloody delicious.

I have made this at home before, and I will try it again, but it never tastes quite the same when you DIY, does it?

25th August

We're off on our boat trip today, so up early and out by 9:30.

We sailed from Corfu to the magical islands of Paxos and Antipaxos, first stopping off at Antipaxos which has the most stunning silk-like beach and the most marvellous crystal-clear aquamarine waters, like a blue lagoon — paradise.

Here we had some fun, jumping off the sides of the boat into the sea and snorkelling to look at the fancy, vivid coloured fish.

It doesn't have any permanent residents and is only inhabited during the summer months by patrons operating a few tavernas along its beaches.

Then we headed to Paxos; Greek mythology says that Poseidon, the god of the sea, struck Corfu with his trident to create a separate island (Paxos) where he could quietly enjoy his romance with his wife Amphitrite, a sea goddess.

The island is only seven by three miles, and has been called one the twenty most beautiful islands in the world. The west coast is rocky with few beaches, but it has huge sea caves and turquoise waters.

Gaios is the capital of the island and is where we stopped for a few hours.

It's very captivating, a typical fishing village with a very pretty harbour, pastel-coloured buildings, Venetian architecture, a maze of side streets and a pedestrians square on the seafront.

We sat and watched the world go by with a carafe of vino.

The trip was very well organised, the boat was clean and had a shower, there was traditional Greek music played, the schedule was bang on time, and we both thoroughly enjoyed it.

26th August

It was a lazy day for us today, just sat around the pool.

Packed and got ready to leave tomorrow, we have a very long journey ahead.

We walked in to Kavos town for one last evening and went back to 'Big Max Diner'.

They were pleased to see us.

Tonight, I chose beef stamna, again a traditional Greek dish, this time of slow-cooked beef with cinnamon, paprika, nutmeg, passata, rosemary, and garlic with carrots, potatoes and grated cheese.

Almost as good as lamb kleftiko, I'm going to try this recipe when home.

Well, we have survived Kavos, and strangely enough I have really enjoyed it here, although it's definitely no longer like a party town.

27th August

Up at 07:45

Taxi to Lefkimmi

Ferry to Igoumenitsa — twenty-three kilometres

Bus to Athens — four hundred and seventy kilometres

Bus from Athens to Piraeus — eleven kilometres

Overnight ferry from Piraeus to Heraklion (Crete) — three hundred and thirty kilometres

Bus from Heraklion to Agios Nikolaos — sixty-three kilometres

All in all, twenty-eight hours travelling.

OMG

Knackered.

28th August

Arrived in Crete, the birthplace of Zeus, the ruler of the Gods, People and Hospitality.

Known for its varied terrain which ranges from fine sandy beaches to the White Mountains.

Completely knackered with nowhere booked, we found a bar which had wi-fi so we sat with a lovely frothy coffee for nearly two hours... there was a small studio apartment not far called Angeliki apartment so we booked and headed off to find it.

Olga, the owner, let us leave our bags there whilst she was preparing the room, so we went to get some provisions (as usual).

Lou cooked dinner and we sat on the balcony to eat before retiring to bed.

29th August

Woke up, Lou asked me what I thought the time was? 09:14 was my guess, pretty accurate as it was 09:13!!

After such a long journey yesterday, we decided to just relax. We had eggs, bacon and tomatoes with toast before heading to the beach.

Angeliki's apartments were shabby on the inside, but on the outside very pretty with blossoms. It sat on some white-washed stairs halfway up a small hill right next to the seafront.

It was very breezy on the beach, but I went for a swim in the sea. My watch told me I had only swam fifty-one metres, but it took me around twenty-five minutes, so I figured against the breeze and the tide it was for like 750 metres, I was okay with that.

30th August

Agios Nikolaos or Agnik for short is a small coastal town in the north-east of Crete, set upon three hills. It is an arty, leisurely, sleepy yet bustling town.

The place has three faces to the sea.

The lake and port, Kitroplatia beach and the marina.

The lake, Voulismeni, is a folklore inspiring deep body of water which is connected to the sea by a narrow inlet of water.

It has distinctive vertical walls reminiscent of a volcanic crater; many believe it was created by a sunken volcano, that it is bottomless and the mouth to an underground river leading to Santorini.

Some also believe, that when the Germans left Crete at the end of WW2, they sank their guns and armoured vehicles in the lake, but these have disappeared and have never been found.

The lake is pretty, with lots of cafés, bars and restaurants are set around it and there are ducks, fishing boats and hills with a little park above it.

We had a walk around the town, I wanted to get some decent face cream, the stuff I had brought from home had run out long ago, and I had been using whatever I could find in the supermarkets.

I always try to look after my skin, cleansing, removing my make up religiously, toning, and using a good quality moisturiser. Funnily enough I haven't worn a speck of make-up yet on this trip, apart from the odd bit of mascara and that's it.

At work once I was helping an elderly patient to have a wash. She had the most amazing skin and when I asked her what her secret was she replied that she had moisturised every day for the last seventy plus years, with the simplest of products — Vaseline!

We had a walk around the bay and the port, I had a little paddle in the sea but I am sure that my ankles were being nipped by the little fishes.

31st August

We decided to have a day out of the sun today, so went sightseeing (ish) although not as much here to see compared to other destinations.

We saw the Abduction of Europa statue, which represents unity, peace and solidarity, and then, the Horn statue of Amalthea, which represents an eternal symbol of abundance. I could go on for the rest of this book trying to explain, but Greek mythology, it's fascinating...

We looked around the little boutiques and souvenir shops, stopped off at Voulismeni Lake for a drink and a bite to eat, burger and chips which resembled something more like a pattie of meat from a can, possibly dog food?

1st September

Olga had left us a little gift in the fridge last night as a thank you for staying in Angeliki apartments, a bottle of wine and a small bottle of traditional raki.

Unbeknown to me I accidently put the bottle of raki out, instead of the water, of which Lou had woken in the early hours and taken a large thirsty swig of!

For those of you who don't know, raki is a clear brandy made from grapes and raisins, then flavoured with pungent anise, very potent (80–100 proof) usually diluted with water and served as an aperitif — so funny.

Today we went on the tuktuk tour of Agnik; we saw the mosque and the church, but not much else.

Beef stifado for dinner and some lovely cocktails.

Moving on tomorrow, not going very far, just along the coast to Malia.

2nd September

We left Agnik today, short bus ride of 29 km and just over half an hour later we arrived at Yiannis Manos Hotel.

We found the apartment easily enough, thank goodness for data roaming and sat nav; it's helped us out so much on this trip.

The apartment is nice enough, it has two pools, a lovely bar and we have a balcony overlooking the front main strip.

Supermarket trip completed we relaxed by the pool before cooking meatballs and mashed potato for tea.

3rd September

Dale has a small show of his new etchings at Edel Assanti Gallery at the weekend.

My family are all organising to go and see. Oh, I so wished that I could go.

I am feeling a little homesick, I miss home and family sometimes, I miss Dale all of the time.

We sat around the pool today, had a swim, Lou researched somewhere to go out for dinner and found #1 on TripAdvisor of where to eat in Malia.

Guess what it was called?

'The Red Lion Gastro pub and Restaurant' LOL

I had ribs and wings and it was flipping delicious.

4th September

Breakfast on the balcony this morning, sausages, eggs, toast and fresh orange juice.

We went for a walk into town but really not much to buy at all. So expensive and mostly tat and rubbish apart from some lovely Greek dishes etc… but can't buy them, can't carry them!

We walked down to the seashore and sat in a lovely spot on the rocks for a drink.

Later I had a swim in the hotel pool before chilling out on the balcony.

Lou cooked 'deconstructed' cheeseburger using up the leftover mince, cheese and tomatoes that we had in the fridge.

I had a lovely long chat with Ju tonight; she seems to be doing ok.

Jeff would be so proud of her, I just know it.

Listened to podcast of Pop Master, and didn't do half bad!

5th September

Lolled around for most of the day, it's weird that the less you do sometimes, the more tired you feel.

Nothing really to report except that I spoke to Michelle via WhatsApp who was round at Mum and Dad's, so we switched to video call so we got to see them all too.

Elsie was there, my great niece; blimey kids grow up so quickly, don't they?

Packed up our bags ready to move on tomorrow, not far again; Hersonissos.

6th September – 15th September

It only took eighteen minutes to travel 12.2 kilometres west along the north coast of Crete from Malia to Hersonissos.

The Sergious Hotel was literally 200 metres from the bus stop.

A great room, with a huge balcony, and all-inclusive (a treat as we're both feeling homesick).

We spent a whole week (plus an unexpected two days) here. For some reason I did not keep my diary up to date.

Anyhow, the hotel was lovely, I had my laundry done, and we had some great lunches, afternoon tea and cakes, dinners, wine, cocktails.

We met a couple called Tom and Lyn who were with their two friends Derek and June for Tom's eightieth birthday.

Amazingly they had been visiting this resort and staying at the same hotel for the last twenty-eight years... extraordinary.

On Tom's actual birthday the hotel had arranged a special evening. Lou and I were invited to join them on the 'top table', and we drank champagne (I had most of it!).

We watched a Greek dance troupe, an acrobatic show, a magic show, and a flamingo dance show.

We went for a ride on a tuktuk, went to our first ever foam party, drank our way through the cocktail list, and drank Raki!

Hersonissos is a cute little town; it has several blue flag beaches and the typical aquamarine sea that Crete is known for, worth a visit (but not every year for twenty-eight years running)

The food is delicious, the freshest most juiciest Greek salads you'll ever taste, of course not forgetting the traditional Cretan cuisine of meze, pitta, giros, stifado, kleftiko... the list goes on.

All the staff in the hotel have been lovely, great memories.

Dale is currently in NYC at a show with his friends. They were all called into a room as there was a band waiting to play… only The Who. WOW.

Pam (Lou's mum) and Jess have booked up to meet us in Turkey in a few weeks' time; they chose the hotel, so we booked the same one, Hotel Julian, in Marmaris.

Our onward ferry to Rhodes was postponed two days on the trot due to adverse weather conditions but we were emailed to say it would finally set sail on Sunday 15th September.

15th September
We left Hersonissos and headed to Heraklion for the day before our ferry which was due at 10:00, now due at 16:05.

Heraklion is Crete's capital, a bustling city which has undergone a significant makeover in recent years mostly due to its increasing prosperity.

The old harbour is still standing, guarded and protected by the old Venetian Koules fortress; we had a look around, ate a late lunch, and headed to the port.

The ferry was late and didn't leave until 17:50.

The journey of 430km took sixteen hours.

It was a terrible journey, stopping off at six different islands en route, each time the intercom 'bing-bonged' with an arrival announcement, followed by a safety announcement so there was absolutely no chance of any sleep.

16th September
We finally arrived in Rhodes at 09:20.

The largest of the Dodecanese Islands, the name of the

island comes from the ancient Greek word 'Rhodon' — Rose.

First stop Faliraki and the Sunny Sun studios.

We were shown to a pokey little room. Lou was not very happy, as there were no cooking utensils, cutlery, and the crockery wrapped in kitchen roll, in a plastic basket on the floor — no wall cabinets.

There are three single beds, all made up like *Little House on the Prairie* with flowery brushed cotton sheets and a horse hair blanket, there is no shower door, the fridge doesn't shut properly, and there is a stupid tiny and too small curtain on the patio door.

The pool is very nice though and we have a big balcony.

Oh well, we went for a walk, then and a swim before dinner and bed after twenty-six hours awake — yawn.

I applied for our Turkey visa online, all good $20 each.

Dale has gone to Istanbul today.

17th September

Slept well, didn't wake up until nine thirty.

Got ready and headed to the beach.

Described in the guides as one big funfair filled with a multi-ethnic crowd tirelessly in pursuit of pleasure (they're definitely not here today, it's deserted).

The beach is impressive though, golden sands stretching for over 4km with small rocks and pebbles and emerald waters of the Aegean Sea.

Lou went for a walk and brought us back a lovely ham and cheese baguette, boiled egg and some cider and ice cream.

Later on, we headed out to a bar, to watch Liverpool versus Napoli… they lost 2–0

18th September

Another lazy day, got up and went to sit around the pool.

Lou pitched himself under the gazebo for hours researching our next move, we're going to head to Rhodes old town, and it feels like we are having withdrawal symptoms from the culture and sightseeing.

Still, it does you good to have a rest now and then, eh?

We had lovely chicken gyros for lunch, and then had a good swim before heading out for a walk.

Mike's Bar was about a kilometre away from Sunny Sun studios, a sports bar where we stopped for a drink, then another, then another! We ended up staying all evening, had dinner, scampi for me, Lou had a chicken and mushroom pie, we watched the Spurs vs. Olympiacos game.

Dale phoned. Whilst in Istanbul, they had hired a private yacht to take them around the sights along the Bosphorus straits!

19th September

It's Katie, our niece's, birthday today.

Went to the beach for a few hours, had a ham and cheese baguette for brunch, listened to some music through the alphabet again.

A — Alexandra O'Neal
B — Bob Dylan
C — Clash
D — Deacon Blue
E — Erasure
F — Frank Sinatra
G — George Benson

H — Heatwave

I — INXS

J — Justin Timberlake

K — Keane

L — Luther Vandross

M — Michael McDonald

Back to the pool for a swim before packing, ready to move on tomorrow.

Faliraki is a town of 'has been, wants to be again, sadly never will be' beach resort.

Rather run down, dilapidated and dated, though friendly and welcoming.

There are nicer places to visit though; I would skip it if I were you!

20th September

Haven't travelled that far today. We caught the bus from Faliraki and headed north, sixteen kilometres and thirty minutes later, we arrived in Rhodes' old town.

This time we have a lovely self-catering apartment called Gemani.

A bit of a walk into the town, but that's good for our fitness as we haven't had much exercise in the last few weeks.

We walked into town. Rhodes old town is the core of this island's capital, a beautiful and remarkably preserved compact walled city dominated by the 'Palace of the Grand Masters', where medieval meets ancient.

Full of fascinating streets, museums, mosque, tavernas, markets and shops.

There is even a great big concrete diving board about 100

metres off shore, some tourists and locals were having fun diving off and then climbing back up.

21st September

Croissants for breakfast, then walked into town and around the palace, originally a seventh century citadel, it is an exceptional example of gothic architecture. After the island fell to Ottoman rule it was used as a command centre and fortress.

The palace was restored in 1937 and when Rhodes was unified with Greece it was turned into a museum.

Through the cobbled streets around the castle and the fortress there are lots of market stalls, shops, cafes and bars. Lovely bits and pieces to buy, but again, we can't carry them in our backpacks — shame.

I tried to cook a roast dinner, of sorts, it was edible but nothing like home.

Very windy tonight.

22nd September

Last day today in Rhodes, so we decided to get the bus back to Mike's Bar in Faliraki to watch the rugby, football and have a 'decent' roast dinner.

England was playing Tonga in the Rugby World Cup, Manchester United was playing West Ham, and Liverpool was playing Chelsea.

Finally, after five months travelling, we had our first real roast dinner and it was mouth-watering — beef and lamb, roast potatoes, mash, carrots, peas, Yorkshire pudding and gravy.

23rd September

Off to Turkey today.

Our ferry was not leaving until 16:30, so Georgia let us stay in the apartment until midday.

Lou accidently cracked the ice-cube dish last night and was worried so he walked into town to buy a new one.

We got on the ferry as planned; it was supposed to be a 'Flying Dolphin' but was really slow due to high seas.

Eighteen kilometres and three hours later we arrived, it was dark and we had no idea how to get to our destination.

We passed through customs okay and found a cashpoint machine, again, like Morocco, Turkey has a closed currency, Turkish lira, so that was our priority.

It asked me how much I wanted in pounds, so naturally I typed in £200, only to be dispensed the cash in actual pounds!

Now to find the bus station, we knew the rough location from data roaming, but while walking we saw dolmus with the destination of Olu Deniz, jumped on and the driver knew exactly where we needed to go.

Perdikia Hill Resort and Spa Hotel it was called, and blimey, a very good description, flipping heck, what a hill.

Chapter 6
Turkey

24th September

Oh, there it goes again; I had forgotten what it sounded like, the call for prayer at four in the morning!

The hotel is lovely, but very much catered for the Turkish tourist.

There are some very weird foods served in the buffet restaurant, but an outdoor barbeque and pizza oven that serve different dishes every evening.

It really is astonishing how much food some people pile onto their plates, as if it is going to run out, or that they haven't been fed for weeks.

Piggish really, some couples' tables had up to ten plates of food, like a banquet. Of course they did not eat it all, seems such a waste.

It has three pools, one of which is adult only, not that there are hordes of children here.

It also has a small outdoor amphitheatre where they lay on evening entertainment.

We sat by the adult pool today, and then disaster happened.

I got stung!

What is it with me and pesky stings?

I have no idea what it was, only that I felt a sudden, sharp, red-hot burning sensation on my left leg medial to my knee joint.

I got up quick, saw something very large and black fly off, and got into the pool to try squeeze out and cool down the sting.

Once again, I felt immediately nauseous, and ran to the loo with an upset stomach.

Within minutes my leg was rapidly swelling, very painful and burning hot, and after about four hours the entire leg from my foot and ankle up to my groin was solid like a tree trunk.

Obviously, a result of the inflammatory response, my body's natural reaction in an attempt of self-protection. But, by golly, the venom from that critter felt toxic, of course I was not having a full-blown anaphylactic reaction, my airways were clear, with no difficulty in breathing or swallowing, I had no facial swelling, and I didn't feel dizzy, but I felt nauseous and had diarrhoea and could barely move my leg.

25th September

Hardly slept, my leg is still like a tree trunk and I am feeling unwell with a fever and body aches. I might need some help, but for the time being I shall just have to rest, elevate, ice and take some antihistamine and anti-inflammatories.

26th September

What a nuisance, this mishap is really putting the dampers on this 'leg' (excuse the pun) of our journey.

Still resembling one of the ancient trunks we climb up on our annual picnic in the park I have decided to self-medicate. I think I need something stronger systemically. The risk of DVT (deep vein thrombosis) did cross my mind.

Lou and I got on the bus and went into the town; I popped in to the local chemist to buy some steroids.

I had to have them once before, also following a sting to my right arm.

We had been sitting by the river one evening having a beer with friends. I was stung by a wasp that time, over just a few hours my forearm had become three times the size, solid, red and burning hot.

The pharmacist came out to ask what the problem was. I showed her my leg and she was horrified, telling me I should go to hospital.

I reassured her, and told her that I was a nurse, that something similar had happened to me before.

After some discussion which included me promising her that if I felt unwell with a temperature, or any signs of sepsis that I would go to the hospital, I had a short course (five days of 40mgs a day) of Prednisolone.

27/28/29th September

We didn't really do much else, my mishap took care of that, but the steroids were working. The tree trunk leg started to gradually go down, taking on the appearance of a memory foam mattress. When I pressed my fingers into the flesh, they left a great indentation. This is called 'pitting oedema'.

We did go into Olu Deniz — overlooking the village are the Babadag Mountains where it is famous for paragliders who give their tandem flight passengers a panoramic bird's eye view of the stunning blue lagoon whilst experiencing 360-degree turns, wingovers and gliding on the thermal flows during their decent.

I defo would have had a go had I been physically able.

We also watched some football, ate some lovely food, had a haircut, sat around the pool and relaxed.

30th September

Moved on today, travelled 125 kilometres up the west coast of Turkey to Marmaris.

The journey took three hours but we stopped halfway for a drink and loo break.

We had a nice little Airbnb for two nights, Zerkan was the host, he was very nice and met us on arrival to show us to the flat. He was from Istanbul.

We went to the supermarket for supplies, did our washing, had a walk around the town and harbour, then cooked dinner and watched a film on TV.

Pam and Jess will be here in two days.

1st October

Breakfast was lovely, ham and cheese with some fresh baguette, orange juice and coffee.

As we haven't had much exercise recently, we went for a long walk. My leg was now well on its way to getting better, although there was still some residual swelling.

Marmaris is known as the turquoise coast; it has a pebbly beach with a long seafront promenade, and is one of Turkey's most popular holiday destinations.

Marmaris marina was worth a visit, we marvelled at the boats and yachts, some of them were very luxurious, obviously home for the rich on their holidays. Many of the smaller ones were available for private charter too. Now that would be just great if there was a group of you, wouldn't it?

We walked along the promenade, and went to the bazaar,

we mooched and looked around the shops and I brought two new bikinis.

Opposite the flat we were staying in there was a small salon so I decided to treat myself and have a manicure.

2nd October

We checked out of Zerkan's flat and headed on foot to our next stop — Julian Club Hotel — where we will be meeting Lou's mum, Pam, and our niece, Jess, tomorrow who are coming out for the week.

The hotel is all inclusive, so we were given our wrist bands and checked into our room which was okay, overlooking one of the pools; we had a swim and sat around the pool.

The hotel is quite big, but full of chavs, fatties, Brits and kids!

Dinner was delicious; so much to choose from, the waitress was lovely and very attentive so I gave her a tip 'keep 'em sweet'!

I spoke to Ju this evening. The itinerary for the India trip, is coming along nicely, Ju sounds excited, but says she is nervous too.

3rd October

Woke up too late for breakfast, never mind.

Had a walk to the local market, lots of lovely fruit and vegetables, herbs and spices.

We brought some wine and beer for later, as the bar would be shut when Pam and Jess arrive.

The hotel has an animation team called YOLO who appear to work from ten a.m. until midnight, but surprisingly they are really good.

Pam and Jess finally arrived, Pam has a huge room with a massive balcony where we sat, chatted and had a drink before retiring to bed.

It's really nice to see them.

Pam had brought me an early birthday present sent from my friend Ruth. It is one of those all-in-one snorkel masks; you know the ones that are all attached and give you a panoramic viewing field.

Ruth is such a kind person, and so thoughtful. I've known her for twenty years now, we worked together as nurses.

The Hebrew meaning of the name Ruth is 'compassionate friend', and she certainly is that to everyone she meets.

In the Bible, Ruth reminds us to be humble and keep working as God blesses you, remain faithful and work hard, always show kindness, love, respect, grace, honesty, integrity, generosity, virtue and selflessness. Geraldine and Paul chose the perfect name for her!

4th October

My dad Eddie and our sister-in-law Kim have birthdays today.

We met Pam and Jess in the buffet restaurant for breakfast, again lots of choice, lovely fresh food, cereals, fruits, cheese, meats, egg station and so much more.

I borrowed a wheelchair from the medical centre and we walked into town.

We mooched around the bazaar and Pam brought some sandals.

Later we had dinner in the hotel and then played bingo!

5th – 10th October

The Julian Club Hotel in Marmaris is a firm favourite with UK holidaymakers that's for sure, but we spent a lovely week with Pam and Jess.

Mostly in the hotel but we went to a few nice bars… Jaspers, Shadows and Seven Brothers.

We watched some rugby and football.

Jess met a nice Turkish chap, we called him Mehmet.

We joined in the ping-pong drinking game and played a music quiz; we got drunk lots and ate far too much food. All delicious.

We met a lovely waitress called Pelin, and a barman called Gok; they both looked after us very well.

We had a great time in the Hammam too. Pam, Jess and I went.

The Hammam experience is all about leaving yourself in the hands of your *tellak or natir* (male and female attendants).

We started off with a face pack, steam room and sauna, followed by a traditional body scrub with a hand-woven cloth known as a *kese* whilst pouring warm water over you with a small bucket, then a foam wash whilst lying on a warm marble slab called the 'gobektasi'.

Finally, a full body oil massage, designed to revive the mind, body and soul and soften the skin. This beauty custom from centuries ago transports you to a world far away from your everyday stresses. It certainly did that.

11th October

Pam and Jess left yesterday, Lou and I had to stay one more night as we mucked up our dates for our bus to the next destination.

Last night we moved just around the corner, the hotel was

really quite empty but they are closing for the season today!

Next stop Bodrum, so we caught the bus as planned, still travelling 110km north up the west coast of Turkey.

The journey took three and a half hours; we then jumped in a taxi to get to Bodrum Bay Resort Hotel.

The hotel is set on top of a big hill with panoramic views of Bodrum bay on one side and Gumbet on the other — it seems lovely although our room is not as expected — dark and pokey.

12th October

I am not one to complain, but I cannot stay in this room. The bed is broken and made for the most horrendous night, squeaking every little inch you moved.

Also, there was some Russian guy in the room above and I am not kidding, he was on the phone from three to five thirty a.m.

I went to reception to complain about the broken bed, they apologised and said that they would replace it. The maid knew the bed was broken and she tried to help, but her English was poor, and my Turkish non-existent!

We spent the day at the pool and on the beach, but when we went back to the room, the bed was the same!

So... I went back to reception and was twice informed that it had been replaced... it hadn't.

I asked to speak to the duty manager; he promised me it would be taken care of in the next fifteen minutes, so I believed him, how stupid of me.

We went back to the room after dinner and you've guessed it — same bed.

Lou tried to calm me down and said not to worry, he

would remove the bed, prop it up against the wall and we could put the mattress on the floor for tonight.

BIG mistake, we found a huge cockroach, and next door partied on their balcony until four a.m.

I took photos as evidence; you just wait until I see the manager in the morning.

13th October

Absolutely fuming I marched myself off to reception and asked to see the duty manager… it was the same one as last night.

I showed him photos of the broken bed, mattress on the floor, the cockroach etc, and I genuinely think he was horrified.

He quickly took me off to show me another room, with an upgrade, a junior suite — much better, large balcony, clean and bright and it had a bath!

He sent a porter to collect our luggage from the old room, Lou was still there and the cleaner had arrived, someone phoned her and she started to cry, I am not sure if it was the manager telling her off, or worse, sacking her?

We went for a walk into town, later to the hotel gym and for a swim.

I am feeling better now.

14–19th October

Bodrum Bay Hotel sort of redeemed itself.

We spent the next five days here, did lots of walking and swimming, and also went to the gym every day.

The views from the hotel are superb, as mentioned you can see both Bodrum Bay and Gumbet Bay, you can also see the castle, a historical fortification built in 1402.

It has four towers known as the English, French, German and Italian towers — the names of the nations' responsible for their construction.

The Mausoleum of Halicarnassus is well worth a visit too, it is one of the seven wonders of the ancient world.

King Mausolus reigned around 376 BC and built this colossal tomb before his death.

It was destroyed in an earthquake around 1494 and nearly all the materials were then used to build Bodrum Castle.

Now all that you can see are some columns, the stairway to the chambers, some remnants of some statues and some wall plaques — a selection of the original statues that were here are now in the British Museum.

Other sights to see here are Bodrum amphitheatre which dates back to the fourth century and is one of the oldest stone theatres in the world.

In its heyday it was said to have seated 10,000 people. Now, following restoration it seats around 3,000 and is still used for artistic and cultural activities.

And of course, the famous windmills… they were made of stone and lined with wooden planks, and were used in the eighteenth century right up until 1970s as a means to grind flour for the local residents.

The windmills are now derelict, but still rest among the olive trees on the surrounding hills. Only two are still in recognisable condition but their location is fantastic for views across both bays… sunset and dawn are great times to visit.

Once again, I don't know about you but it absolutely fascinates and amazes me how on earth these structures were ever even built — no machines, cranes, engines, electricity etc...

19th October

A long journey today, we travelled further north up the west coast from Bodrum to Çanakkale, 586 kilometres which took nine and a half hours on the bus.

The bus station was miles from the town, but there was a free shuttle bus which dropped us off almost at the front door of our hotel — Set Ozer Hotel — what a little gem — very clean and modern, tastefully decorated, a lovely outside terrace, stunning floor and wall tiles, and location perfect.

We settled in but it was late, so we went for a short walk along the promenade and saw the replica of a Trojan horse, the actual one which was built for the movie *Troy*, that excited me, then we had dinner before going to bed.

20th October

We decided to visit Gallipoli today, just a short ferry ride of twenty minutes.

We hired a taxi driver who would take us round all the memorials.

Although well-endowed with the most fabulous coastline, the Dardanelles straits and scenery, Gallipoli is chiefly known for its grim military history.

In April 1915 Winston Churchill, during WW1, devised a plan to deploy allied troops there, mainly Australian, New Zealand and British, with the expectation of eradicating Turkey from the war.

It was a dismal failure which led to mass casualties and deaths.

The battlefields, trenches and cemeteries here are moving

and numbing.

You really do feel the special spirit of this place, as you visit the Anzac cemetery, the British, French, Turkish, Australian and New Zealand cemetery, as well as the many historic monuments of architectural importance

The Lone Pine memorial was my favourite.

The soldiers killed, almost 200,000 I believe, were mostly between eighteen and twenty years of age. The day of the landings, April 25th, is now celebrated as Anzac Day. This is attended by Turks and visitors from throughout the world.

'Those heroes that shed their blood and lost their lives… You are now lying in the soil of a friendly country, therefore rest in peace. There is no difference between the Jonnies and the Mehmets to us where they lie side by side, here in this country of ours.

'You, the mothers, who sent their sons from far away countries, wipe away your tears.

'Your sons are now lying in the bosoms and are in peace.

'After having lost their lives on this land they have become our sons as well.'

(Mustafa Kemal Atatürk — 1934)

Do not miss this, if you are in this part of Turkey — a definite for the 'book-it' list.

21st October

Up for breakfast of cereal, boiled eggs, toast and jam before heading out for the day, we are off to visit Troy.

Now an archaeological site, Troy is cradled in mythology

and has been the stage for many myths, tragedies, wars and victories for many centuries.

Alexander the Great, Roman emperors, Hadrian and Augustus allegedly visited this ancient city of apparent blessed power.

And then there is of course the ten-year Trojan War. Now there are just ruins, and it is home to a replica Trojan horse (to scale which you can climb up inside) again worth a visit.

Everyone knows the story of the Trojan Horse right? but just in case you are not familiar with it, here it is in a nutshell.

According to legend, the Trojan king's son, Paris, eloped with Helen, the wife of the Spartan King, Menelaus.

Believing that she had been abducted the Achaeans set off to Troy with a huge army, but after many years, the Achaeans realised they could not capture Troy.

They came up with the plan to pretend to give up and retreat back home, but would leave a gigantic wooden horse as a gift.

The Trojans accepted the gift believing it to be an offering to the god Poseidon and took it into their city walls.

Warriors hidden inside the horse sneaked out at night, opened the city gates and let their fellow warriors in to finally capture Troy!

Again, another place worth a visit.

Later we sat by the port in Çanakkale for dinner, lovely, we saw some fighter jets fly over. Scary.

22nd October

Up early for breakfast, same as yesterday, lovely.

It was really weird, but we had to get on the bus, which then got on the ferry to travel 315 kilometres to Istanbul.

Although the total journey time was six hours it was a really nice drive along the coastline of the Sea of Marmara.

As previously experienced the bus station was miles out of town, and when we arrived, we were ushered on to a crappy old minibus.

The driver was ancient; he kept trying to ask us where we were going and then just grumbled back — all in Turkish.

He set off, then after about twenty minutes he just stopped and gestured us to get off.

We knew we were nowhere near the destination, data roaming told us so, we were still over three miles away, but he practically pushed us off the steps of the bus!

A ten-minute taxi trip away we arrived at Hotel Palde.

The hotel and room seemed okay, so we washed and changed and went out straight away for dinner.

We ended up on the Galata Bridge where there are many fish restaurants. Big mistake — and I wish I had read TripAdvisor.

Every restaurant had touts that accosted us, bombarding you with rubbish spiel, virtually pinning you to the front of their premises sticking their menu in your face.

They are expensive tourist traps, our bank balance and stomachs regret eating there. Cold food, half frozen and soggy pizza, leather-like lamb cutlets, ripped off with service charge, then sitting outside charge and another charge which I didn't even know what for. Avoid the temptation if you're ever in Istanbul.

Historically known as Constantinople, Istanbul is the most populated city in the country and the economic, cultural and historic hub. It straddles the Bosphorus straits, the Marmara and the Black seas.

Its population is estimated to be up to nineteen million, making it one of the largest cities in Europe and the world.

Like Rome, it is built on seven hills.

23rd October

Out early, we had lots to see, do, smell and taste today.

Zerkan, the host we had met in Marmaris had given us a list of 'must-sees' in Istanbul.

First, we walked over the Galata Bridge, which spans the Golden Horn in Istanbul, and connects the north and south, overlooking the Bosphorus Straits which divide European Istanbul from its Asian half.

There were lots of fishermen with rods dangling trying to catch their supper.

We then walked to the Galata Tower, a restored fifth century tower and former prison, and a fire lookout tower. We didn't go in but it looked wonderful in the autumn sunshine. It is nicknamed 'the Tower of Jesus'.

Then we went to The Sehzade (Prince's) Mosque, on the third hill of Istanbul (out of the seven total) built to commemorate Prince Sehzade Mehmed who died aged only twenty-one.

Süleymaniye Mosque was next, built in 1550 by Suleyman the Magnificent. Oh wow, what a building, a masterpiece of Byzantine architecture, four minarets, a massive central dome with thirty-three openings, giving it the best light and acoustics and one of the largest mosques ever built in the Ottoman Empire.

Besides its place of worship, it also contains madrasa

(religious institutions), a hospital, school, large kitchen, baths, shops and stables.

I was actually allowed in, I had to remove my shoes and wear a headscarf, and to my delight there was a couple getting married!

Grand Bazaar next — a labyrinth of a medieval shopping mall. A covered market that has twenty-two entrances and over 4,500 shops crammed packed with everything, you name it, and they had it!

It's a fun place to walk around, and very easy to get lost, BUT not cheap like other bazaars in Turkey and the vendors were not keen to barter.

We walked for miles today — 11.7 to be precise.

Another terrible meal tonight — disappointing.

Cold rice, burnt kebab, mouldy tomatoes, undercooked chicken wings, brown salad leaves... We sent it back, they served us with the same food just with the skin peeled off the mouldy tomatoes and the brown salad leaves removed!

We refused to pay the bill.

We then went to local bar to watch Liverpool, Lou got drunk, and Liverpool won 4–1

Had all clothes cleaned at local laundrette.

24th October

Lou is hanging today, awake and then back to sleep several times for most of the morning until he finally got up at two p.m.

We went for a really long walk, across the Galata Bridge into the main town.

I wanted to go to Sephora, they sold my favourite lip gloss there and I was running very low, actually scraping the barrel!

They had an extensive shopping area but Lou was feeling too delicate, so we just brought the lip gloss and then went for an ice cream in the park.

There was a delightful little antique market on the way, and if only I could have, I would have brought a beautiful antique teapot, sugar and milk set, exactly like the ones they use at 'The Wolseley'.

It reminded me of home and my favourite London restaurant. Apart from the fascinating history behind the iconic building in Piccadilly, the Wolseley is renowned for its spectacular interior, classic food and seamless service.

It started life as a Wolseley Motors Limited prestigious car show room, then it became a branch of Barclays Bank, (the bar used to be the manager's office).

In 2003 it became a restaurant, it was restored and renovated but many aspects of its original design remain, such as the Japanese lacquer and eastern influences, the domed ceiling and monochrome geometric marble flooring.

We have been there many times and it is one of the first places we will go when we get home!

On the way home we stopped off at the Spice Bazaar, so colourful and aromatic with rows and rows of spices, heaped into giant domes.

Aside from the spices you could also buy dried fruits such as apricots, figs, dates, strawberries, kiwis as well as Turkish delight, tea, honey, baklava, olive oil, soaps, coffee... another assault on the senses.

Lou then went for a haircut. It was so funny when the hot wax came out and was dripped straight into each ear canal... his face! Then the barber slapped the same hot wax onto both his cheeks.

I spoke to Ju tonight, she is all packed and looking forward to India, I can't wait to see her and Dale.

I also spoke to Dad, he has received his letter for the operation on his lower spine and they are happy to go ahead, he is on the elective admission list and now just has to wait.

25th October

Up early enough for breakfast today, but what a weird choice.

Salad, chips, chicken, kebabs, olives, cheese... so I plumped for some cereal and fresh orange juice!

It was a busy day today, we visited the Topkapi Palace, built in the fifteenth century. It is a sprawling palace, and now a UNESCO World Heritage Site, it was the imperial residence of the Ottoman sultans for almost 400 years.

The gardens, buildings and the church are very imposing, unfortunately large areas are not accessible to the public and there are currently a lot of renovation works going on so we did not see any sultan splendour.

We did see a 'circumcision room' though, a room dedicated to the circumcision of young princes, which is a primary right in Islam.

The room is quite elaborate embellished with a mixed collection of rare tiles which once adorned the ceremonial building of Sultan Suleiman. They were moved here out of nostalgia and reverence for the golden age of his reign.

Ed sent me a WhatsApp to say thanks for his birthday card and sweetie jar that I sent him via Moonpig for his birthday.

A boat trip this afternoon, which included lunch and a pleasant ride along the European coastline, around the Golden Horn and up the Bosphorus to the Black Sea.

We got off the boat for a short break, had a glass of wine and watched the fishermen before heading back down the straits, this time following the Asian coastline, around the Maiden's Tower and back to port.

This iconic landmark has a rich history, located on a tiny inlet which dates back to the fourth century.

It has served many different purposes throughout the centuries including a tax collection centre, a defence tower, a lighthouse, a radio station and a quarantine hospital. It is now a visitor's attraction and museum, it also houses a restaurant.

Tonight, we looked up where to eat on TripAdvisor following our dismal food for the last two nights!

'Bistro Chef' (#2in the TripAdvisor rating) was much nicer, certainly not fine dining, but edible, we shared Et Izgaralar and salatalar (meat grill and salad).

Home to bed feeling exhausted after a few busy days.

26th October

Terrible sleep again, next door came home around half past midnight, and by two thirty a.m. the TV was still on and blaring. I think he must have fallen asleep with it on, but after several attempts at banging on the wall I had to phone reception.

A few minutes later I heard banging, keys and then silence. The night porter must have let himself into the room and turned off the TV.

At breakfast the duty manager came over and apologised, she asked us if we wanted to change rooms but we only had one night left and last night's culprit was due to check out anyway.

The pub down the street was showing the Rugby World Cup, England vs. New Zealand so we went to watch the game. England were victorious 19–7.

We had two more things on our list, so straight off to The Basilica Cistern. (Nicknamed 'The Sunken Palace').

This enormous underground cistern was built to provide a water filtration system for the great palace of Constantinople and was capable of holding nearly three million cubic feet or 100,000 tons of water.

The ceiling is supported by 336 marble columns arranged in twelve rows of twenty-eight of mainly Ionic and Corinthian style.

It was odd, to enter you had to go down a fifty-five-step steep stairway, and then it was almost pitch black. The one pillar that everyone wants to see is held on a plinth of two Medusa heads.

According to one of many myths Medusa is one of three female monsters of the underground world and she has the power to turn anyone that looks at her into stone.

The cistern has been the location for several films — James Bond, *From Russia with Love*, as well as used in video games — *Assassins Creed*, and referenced in books — Dan Brown, *Inferno*.

We have been making a list of films to watch when we get home, and as well as the above these include *Casablanca, Carry on up Pompeii, Troy, Gladiator, Casino Royale, Midnight Express, Seven days to fall in love, Barcelona: A love untold, The Passenger Michelangelo Antonioni, Taken, Mama Mia, Captain Corelli's Mandolin* and *Indiana Jones and the Temple of Doom*.

Maybe we saved the best until last, Sultan Ahmed Mosque aka the Blue Mosque was the final place we had to visit whilst in Istanbul.

This is closed to non-worshippers for half an hour during the five daily prayers, but otherwise open to tourists, and of course we had to take our shoes off and cover our heads, but I was very happy to go take a look.

Inside it was majestic and splendid, the lower level is lined with more than 20,000 handmade ceramic tiles, some very flamboyant representing flowers, fruits and trees, and the upper level is dominated by blue paint and stained-glass windows.

There are chandeliers, lamps, verses from the Qur'an, domed windows, lush carpets and fine sculptured marble.

Outside is just as stunning, domes, minarets, columns, arches, a large courtyard, monuments, a fountain — once again we felt amazement at how this incredible structure was ever built back in the early seventeenth century — wow.

So very excited, were off to India next, I don't think I'll be able to sleep a wink.

Chapter 7
India

27th October

It's Ed's birthday today.

Up early and feeling most magnificent, I can't quite believe we are off to India!

We had a nice breakfast in the Palde Hotel before heading off in a shuttle bus to the airport.

Our plane to Delhi took off at 18:10, here we go!

Flight time was just under seven hours — the only trouble was that we couldn't buy any food, or even a drink on the IndiGo Airlines' flight.

Having no rupees (again India has a closed currency, so you can't get them until you are there) their machine didn't work for contactless or card payment.

After travelling approximately 4,560 miles we arrived in New Delhi.

Customs and immigration then took almost two hours, luckily Dale had booked us a car transfer to the hotel, and we finally arrived at 04:30.

Wow — what a place — Maidens Hotel was ready and waiting for us, three staff, like we were royalty. They checked us in and escorted us to our room.

In our room was a letter from the manager apologising for not being there to greet us on arrival.

'Dear Mr and Mrs Lewis,
 A warm welcome to Maidens Hotel, Delhi.
 We thank you for choosing to stay with us.
 I do hope you have a comfortable and enjoyable stay.
 Please do not hesitate to contact me or one of my senior executives at any time should you need any assistance.
 Kind regards.
 Puneet Kapoor
 General Manager'

28th October
 The Maiden's Hotel is just superb.
 Absolutely gorgeous, an old colonial mansion built by two Englishmen brothers in the late 1800s, which became a heritage hotel in 1903.
 This hotel showcases nineteenth century colonial charm and architecture and was widely considered the best hotel in Delhi at the time of opening. It is an imperial survivor of the British Raj.
 It is a glorious illustration of old-world charm with modern pleasures.
 Breakfast was delicious, we sat in the garden terrace where we watched squirrels play, peacocks roam and small birds chirp sweet songs.
 Puneet Kapoor came to greet us and introduce himself personally!

Lou and I went for a walk to explore and were stopped several times by the same tuktuk man touting for business. We tried to explain that we were not going far today, but would hire him tomorrow when Dale and Julie are here.

We saw the Red Fort, but it is closed today (Monday). It still looks pretty impressive, though.

Loads of monkeys are roaming the streets, there is real poverty here, rubbish everywhere, derelict buildings, homeless, and lots of smog.

And cows, lots of cows just smack bam in the middle of the roads, just stray cows, over five million across India they reckon. They are revered as sacred in Hinduism which accounts for 80% of religion in India.

We stumbled across a funeral, literally around fifty to sixty men piled onto the back of a truck. They got off and passed a wooden stretcher with a blanket covering a body, then carried it to a mound of wood, where they placed it on top, ready to burn.

It's a 'bank holiday' here today, so there are hundreds of locals milling around, as we walked it seemed like everyone was stopping and staring at us, some even approached us for 'selfies'.

Delhi is one of India's largest urban areas; it sits astride the Yamuna River, a tributary of the Ganges about 100 miles south of the Himalayas.

The capital embraces old and new, and the surrounding metropolitan region as well as the adjacent rural area.

It has a population of over eleven million.

I literally cannot wait for Dale and Ju to arrive; they're estimated time of arrival is 02:30 so we have asked reception to wake us up when they get here.

At 03:00 we got the call — yippee — got straight up and ran down the stairs to greet them. I can't quite believe they are standing right in front of us.

29th October

Marion's birthday today.

We woke up at 09:00 and met Dale and Ju in the garden terrace restaurant for breakfast.

The itiniery was set; we negotiated with the tuktuk driver and his friend, and hired them for the next two days' adventures.

First, we were off to Humayun's tomb, the tomb of Emperor Humayun, who ruled over territory in Northern India. It was built in the 1560s, and considered to be grander than any tomb built before in the Islamic world. Constructed in red sandstone with white and black inlaid marble borders, it symbolises the powerful Mughal dynasty.

It inspired several architectural projects including the Taj Mahal.

On our way to the next stop, we saw that there was a horseracing meeting scheduled for later today, so we decided to come back later to saviour the experience.

Safdarjung's Tomb next, a sandstone and marble mausoleum built in 1754 in the Mughal Empire style for the prime minister. It's in the same style as Humayun tomb, not quite as impressive, but still striking. There are four dry fountains that were reported to be reactivated but recent excavation proved unsuccessful.

The surrounding gardens are beautiful.

Back to the Delhi Races. Nearly all men, maybe we saw three or four women! We weren't allowed any phones or cameras but when we got inside everyone was on their mobile phones!

It was great fun and we attracted quite a lot of attention. I am not sure they have ever had Westerners at the racetrack before.

A couple of 'regular punters' congregated around us and gave us some tips stating 'every race is fixed anyway'. Betting was mad, but we took their advice and guess what… we won both the races!

Our drivers waited for us and then took us to see India Gate, a war memorial dedicated to the 70,000 soldiers of the British Indian Army who died in World War One.

The memorial, like the Cenotaph in London, is free of religious iconography.

There were hordes of people there, a band was playing, and then a marching procession followed.

Again, lots of looks and stares, locals requesting 'selfies', especially with Dale.

It was really good fun.

It's been exhausting but finished off with a superb dinner at Maidens; we've crammed a lot in today.

30th October

My birthday! And John, my twin brother's, of course!

We all met for breakfast, and it was once again delicious. Our tuktuk drivers were ready and waiting, and as a birthday surprise they had made us all marigold garlands for my birthday. How wonderful.

First off, we went to Qutub Minar, a soaring tower of victory, over seventy-two metre high, and the highest minaret in India.

The tower was built to celebrate Muslim dominance after the defeat of the last Hindu ruler in Delhi.

A UNESCO World Heritage Site, and again fascinating, how the structure was ever built is beyond comprehension.

Birthday lunch next, our drivers took us to Jamun, a recommended place to eat.

It's a cosy little restaurant with a lovely ambience, blackberry and pink décor (after the colour of the Jamun and its pulp) and delicious bold flavoured food — good shout tuktuk man!

Akshardham Hindu temple next on the list — 'a divine abode of God' an eternal place of devotion, purity and peace.

On the way we were laughing and having some banter between me and Ju in one tuktuk and Dale and Lou in the other.

Suddenly I felt this aura of someone very close to me on my left, then in a fast, jerking movement the pillion passenger on a motorbike loomed in at me and attempted to snatch my bag. Luckily, I had my wits about me (and my bag secured across my torso/shoulder) I stuck my leg out to boot him and they sped off empty handed.

Ju really wanted to see this particular temple, that's why it was on our itinerary.

You were not allowed to take phones, cameras and pretty much any other possession inside with you, security was very tight (rightly so), there is a safety deposit facility, but combining contents of our bags we literally had all our passports, valuable and cash on us.

A shame but Lou and I stayed outside whilst Dale and Ju went in.

After what had just happened Lou thought it was best for us to keep hold of our stuff.

Built in 2005, apparently costing over 100 million pounds, it is free to get in; the complex is colossal and absolutely beautiful.

Ju said that it was one large room dominated with columns and domes, every square inch of the sandstone and marble structure being intricately carved with elaborate reliefs, deities, saints and mythical creatures with a centre piece of a three-metre-high, gold statue.

Outside there were life-sized carved elephants, lush gardens and breathtaking fountains.

A birthday cake was waiting for us on return to Maidens, we were ushered in to the bar, where the candles were lit and the waiters sang happy birthday. I got a card too, so special.

After a quick wash and change it was straight out again, this time to Connaught Place, the main financial, commercial and business centre in Delhi.

Following some nice drinks and snacks (still stuffed from lunch) we sat and watched a famous Indian man singing in the central park (popular for cultural events) before all piling into one tuktuk back to Maidens and into Dale's room for a nightcap, ended up drinking until three a.m.

31st October

If you ever visit Delhi, you must stay at this hotel, it is stunning, everything about it, the building, the gardens, the pool, the rooms, the ambience, the service, the personal touches, all of the staff, and I cannot fault it at all.

I think it is one of the best hotels I have ever stayed in, and I've stayed in quite a few over the years.

Chateau Marmot is on an equal par; very similar is style to Maidens, as in personal touches. It is located on Sunset Boulevard in West Hollywood, and is modelled on a royal retreat in France.

We were going to Los Angeles to see Dale; he had a short term 'artist in residence' which culminated in a joint exhibition at Nino Mier Gallery.

Now, I thought we were staying in a motel nearby, but when we got out of the limousine I nearly wet myself with excitement!

Lou and Dale had booked it as a surprise, I could hardly breathe! I rushed inside where Dale had ordered some fizz.

About ten minutes later I realised I had left my bag in the back of the limo, it had all our cards, passports and over four thousand pounds in cash. Luckily it had been a private pre-booking and the driver came back with it.

'Dear Mr and Mrs Lewis, I am delighted to have you at The Chateau, I hope you have a lovely stay, warmest wishes, Amanda Grandinetti, Managing Director'.

It looks like a gothic fort, access is through a discreet entry and the interior is frozen in time, it has a fabulous courtyard with restaurant, a super pool, massive library/piano room and a cute bar.

The hotel exudes old world charm; it has character, history, romance, and a reputation for being the place to stay for 'those on their way up, or those who are on their way down'.

It is known for long- and short-term residencies of the rich and famous, and is exceptionally good at keeping secrets.

John Belushi died of a drug overdose here in 1982.

Led Zeppelin drove their motorbikes through the lobby in the sixties.

Lindsey Lohan was banned from the hotel after racking up a tab of over $46,000 on cigarettes and candles.

Another on my favourite list is Soho Hotel in the heart of London. It is quite different, but again it has the feeling of personalisation from the moment you step inside its twinkly porch.

This time very modern though, a boutique hotel with ultra-chic decor, vibrant mixtures of colour, sculptures, huge plant pots, neon and contemporary artwork. It has a gym, library and even a cinema.

The bar area is crammed with so much to look at too, my favourite thing is the lovely mural which runs along the entire length of the oak and pewter bar.

The rooms are incredibly spacious, and the bed, well I nearly needed a set of steps to get in!

Sadly we are leaving The Maidens today, but it's time to move on, we still have plenty to do and see in India.

We travelled north in a private car, 244 kilometres and six

hours later, we arrived in Chandigarh, a city in India that serves as the capital of two neighbouring states of Punjab and Haryana. The city is unique as it is not part of either of the two states but is governed directly by the Union government, which administers all such territories in the country.

A friend and work colleague of mine from the hospital, Sheetal, has family living here, so a few days ago she put us in touch.

Her sister Meenu, husband Sumit, their twin girls Bumika and Bhavika and son Aditya had kindly invited us to be their guests for dinner.

Wow, what a fabulous time we had. Meenu had cooked us all a wonderful feast that was truly delicious.

Her family were so lovely, friendly and welcoming, we had lots of laughs, left with very full bellies and laden with gifts!

It was a very special evening.

1st November

Up early today and packed ready for our transfer through the foothills of the Himalayas to Shimla.

With a few hours to kill we decided to visit Nek Chand gardens first.

Now, I had never heard of this place before, but this creation is beyond belief!

Nek Chand was a self-taught Indian artist, who created this eighteen-acre site, yes, eighteen acres!

It started with him clearing a small patch of jungle to make himself a small garden and studio area, he set stones around the little clearing and before long he began sculpturing a few figures from recycled materials he found on the land.

Gradually Nek Chand's creations developed and grew; he worked at night and in total secrecy for fear of being discovered by the authorities.

When finally discovered by the authorities they were torn, as this development was forbidden and should be demolished, however his work was so magnificent after deliberation it was decided to give him a salary to continue his work!

The Rock Garden is now acknowledged as one of the modern wonders of the world.

The sculptures, statues, waterfalls, mosaics, courtyards and buildings now span twenty-five kilometres, and is a UNESCO world heritage site.

Ju placed a small ceramic dove that our niece Michelle had given her high up behind the branch of a 'Baobab' tree within the Rock Garden in Jeff's memory — a lovely moment.

Well, we travelled as planned north from Chandigarh through the Himalayan Mountains, 112 kilometres and two and a half hours later we arrived in Shimla.

Shimla was once the summer capital of British India because of its 'British-like climate'. British soldiers, merchants and civil servants moved here to escape the summer heat.

The presence of bachelors and unattached men meant it was also popular for the wealthy to socialise and ladies looking for marriage, as well as its balls, parties and other festivals.

We had a drink in the hotel before heading out.

It's funny because everywhere in the hotel there are signs;

'WARNING — beware of Monkey, keep balcony door shut if you are not in your room'

We had a walk up to the 'Ridge', through some very narrow streets famous for their small shops selling souvenirs, crafts, jewellery, shawls, scarves, leather, belts and wooden sculptures/carvings.

Tomorrow we are going direct to the train station to try and get tickets so we can travel back through the Himalayas to Kalka on the famous 'Toy Train'; so far, we have not been able to.

Meenu had already tried for us, as had Dale and his friends Awon and Raqib before coming to India, it was a shot in the dark, but our last resort.

2nd November

We had to get up early today if we had any chance of getting a ticket for the Shimla to Kalka 'Toy Train'.

Up and out by seven, we waited for the station to open at eight. A small queue was building, but there were only about a dozen so far.

YIPPEE — success — four tickets on the train — £1 for four of us, that's 25p each.

Step back in time, an incredible feat of engineering, the 'Toy train', built 1903, has over 800 bridges, over 900 bends and 103 tunnels, and is considered to be one of the most beautiful railway journeys in India with breathtaking views of rugged mountains, forests, waterfalls and valleys.

The journey is said to be magical, and to some extent it is, but not so much on our train.

We only managed to get a ticket for economy. We sat on wooden slats which were very uncomfortable, especially for the seven hours and eighteen stops!

Still, we travelled with the locals, mostly Indian lads, and had the delight of relishing the experience, sharing local food which we purchased at the snack stalls at the stations from out of the carriage window on the way.

Wouldn't do it again unless on The Himalayan Queen — a luxury service with cushions, carpets, food, music and no stops, so if you are tempted to do this journey, then I suggest this one, and you must book in advance!

Our driver was waiting for us at Kalka station, he drove us all the way to Amritsar, and after a very long day travelling, almost 300 kilometres in total, we finally arrived at 20:30 and checked in to 'One Hotel GG Regency'.

What a shame, the staff were rude and not very welcoming, the wi-fi is crap and the key cards for our rooms did not work.

Hey ho, we decided to just go out for dinner before bed. There was an Irish bar advertised not far away, but when we got there, it was shut. We walked a little way and found 'Wine and Dine bar'.

We were the only ones in there, but the food was nice.

3rd November

All tired today, so we had a lie-in, and met at midday.

Sri Harmandar Sahib — aka Golden Temple — wow, wow, wow.

- Tobacco, narcotics and intoxicants in any shape or form are not to be carried in to the precinct.

- Shoes, socks, sticks and umbrellas of devotees are to be left outside the holy premises — they will be taken care of by the Sri Harmandir Sahib's employees free of charge.

- Visitors will please wash their hands and feet at the taps at the entrance outside the holy premises.

- Visitors will keep their heads covered all the time they are inside Sri Harmandir Sahib complex.

- Photography is permitted only around the *Parkarma* (water tank)

Full steam ahead, in we went and what a truly amazing place.

Not only a central religious place for Sikhs, but also a symbol of brotherhood and equality where everyone is welcome regardless of religion, class, social status, gender or race.

It has four entrances, symbolising this welcoming, and as well as the temple it has houses, dormitories, a community kitchen, a dining hall and offices.

In the middle is an artificial body of water called the Sarovar, it is believed to have sacred healing powers.

The community kitchen (Guru Ka Langar) is where hundreds of volunteers prepare, cook and serve meals, free to all visitors. It is dished up in the enormous dining hall where pilgrims sit in multiple rows and eat together without being discriminated; they serve over 25,000 people a day.

We joined the queue, were given our stainless-steel, five compartment, *Thali* plates, we sat in line and were served dahl (lentils), sabzi (curried vegetables), rice, chapatti and kheer (sweet rice desert).

Simple, nourishing and delicious.

We then watched in amazement at the clearing and washing of the plates, two rows of at least ten volunteers who have this process off to a fine art.

Throughout the day there are several rituals and recitals that take place. We walked around the Sarovar listening to the melodious hymns, people watching and taking the most beautiful scenes in, to store in our memory banks.

We also had numerous requests for selfies! LOL

Incredible.

Later we got a tuktuk to the Hyatt hotel for a superb dinner al fresco. We were surrounded by water fountains, flowers, soft music and twinkly lights. I had butter chicken — mouth-watering.

On the way back we just had to stop off again at the Golden Temple, it was just as beautiful and emotional as it was during the day.

Lou stayed outside to look after our bags and shoes amongst the sleeping pilgrims.

We found some steps to sit on, Ju and Jeff had watched a programme about the temple and had planned to visit here to sit on the steps together on their next trip to India, ha-ha, she had to put up with Dale and me instead!

We sat on the steps, chatted about Jeff, laughed, cried and then Ju got shat upon by a bird flying overhead — so funny, we really did laugh out loud.

4th November

Another busy day today.

We visited the Jalian Wala Bhag, a place of massacre by the order of Reginald Dyer, General of the British Indian Army at the time of Partition of India and Pakistan.

It took place on 13th April 1919. Many villagers had gathered here to celebrate an Indian festival, and also to protest to seek for independence from British rule.

Dyer and his troops entered the gardens and started to open fire at the crowds.

Thousands were injured or killed, and 1650 rounds were fired.

Then it was off to the Wagah Border Ceremony.

So much fun, this is a ceremony that takes place every single night, it is officially meant to be the lowering of the national flag and formally closing the border between India and Pakistan.

It's more like a massive show off between the Indian and Pakistan military, who can march the fastest, who can dance the best, who can swing their legs the highest, who can get their crowd to cheer the loudest, who can make the most fearful expression, who can beat their chests the most furiously.

Foreigners are allowed to sit in the best seats in the enormous grandstand, (seats twenty-five thousand) so we had a great view of the spectacle. The moustaches, uniforms and the Pakistan soldier spinning at a breakneck speed on his one leg were my favourite.

Off to bed earlyish tonight as we have a red eye start in

the morning.

5th November

Up at four a.m., we take a taxi to Amritsar Airport, flight to Delhi, 450 kilometres, then connecting flight to Jodhpur, 622 kilometres, arriving at destination around 14:30.

Jodhpur is the largest city in Rajasthan, aka the 'Blue City' because most of the houses are painted blue.

The blue pigment indicated that a Brahmin (priest) lived there. It is also said that the blue colour is said to be cooling and have insect repellent properties.

Some also call it the 'Sun City' because the sun shines very bright and hot every day of the year.

Our hotel is amazing, Nirvana, but more like the Best Marigold Hotel! Right in the heart of the old town, an old palace and totally authentic.

Lou and I have the best room, it's delightful, and it has the most fabulous mural hand painted on one entire wall, peacocks, peonies, and princesses.

A beautiful heritage property adorned with art work, carvings and pot plants, full of historic charm, it also still has a small functioning temple within its walls.

We settled in straight away and went out to find the Stepwell.

Toorji Ka Jhaila Stepwell — this is the most elaborate type of water well you will ever lay your eyes on, a well where the water is reached by descending a set of multi-storeyed steps down a vertical shaft with passageways, chambers, steps and elaborate carvings.

They were originally constructed to provide water to the villages, serve as a leisure purpose, a place for social gatherings and religious ceremonies such as praying and providing gifts to the goddess of the well.

This particular Stepwell was built in 1740, I have never heard of them before, it's mesmerising.

Just by the Stepwell there were some lovely cafés and bars, most of them had rooftop terraces, so of course we stopped for a nice wine, beer, G and T and nibbles.

Dale had his hair cut, and a very close shave and while we were waiting outside some beautiful little kids were soon surrounding us 'selfie, selfie please' so we had some fun taking photos.

We then had a mooch around the Sadar Market and the Ghantar Ghar Clock tower, and the surrounding narrow alleys selling vegetables, spices, Indian sweets, textiles, silver and handicrafts.

There was a nice-looking restaurant with good reviews on TripAdvisor, called 'Curry's', we passed it earlier, so we went there for dinner tonight.

I am glad we did, we had a great evening, rooftop terrace, beer, authentic Indian cuisine including butter roti (a buttery Indian flatbread) which is our new favourite and a hubba bubba pipe!

I couldn't do it properly though, I kept laughing too much, and then it made me cough... so funny.

We did have quite a lot of leftovers on the table, so we asked if they could be bagged up to go... we then took them to the family we met earlier... bless them, the children were squealing with delight.

6th November

Up early again today, we met our driver, called Raj, at 08:30 who would be taking us on a Bishnoi village trip.

Bishnois are an Indian tribe who live by the philosophy of protecting everything alive including trees, plants, animals and humans; they live on the border of the Thar Desert near to where we are staying.

Now these trips were originally started by rajas and maharajas to show Indian and foreign guests a glimpse of real Rajasthan culture, the cost of the day is donated to help the poor and needy locals.

First off coffee, followed by a drive to the villages. On the way we saw lots of wild deer and gazelles. We also saw lots of poverty, whole families literally living on the roadside.

We stopped off at a small family-run pottery for a demonstration, Dale had a go on the potter's wheel and was really good at it, and then we had some chai, a tea infused with aromatic Indian herbs, and sugar… it's quite sweet.

Next, we went to a traditional Bishnoi house; we tried turban tying, sari wrapping and opium preparation and tasting!

In India there are two main preparations generally used for smoking opium, madak and chandu. In a nutshell madak is used here, raw opium is mixed with water, and then heated until it boils and forms a scum on the top. This scum is continuously removed until the liquid thickens; this is then strained through cloth.

The opium is smoked or drunk in company of other villagers following the day's work. Westerners have a beer or glass of wine, and Bishnois have opium — simple.

Ju noticed that the lady of the house was wearing a silver tribal taviz amulet, a tube-like pendant which are often filled with prayers and then sealed. The lady took it off and placed it around Ju's wrist, indicating that she could have it... it is lovely, and exactly what she wanted for some of Jeff's ashes.

Raj explained to us that Bishnoi commitment can be seen in their simpleness, in the home, the food they eat (strictly vegetarian) and the way they dress.

Their clothes are 'nature friendly', the men in a white dhoti (and unbelievable how pristine and white it really is), the women in earth colours, mostly red but with oranges and greens. A Bishnoi lady is also frequently seen adorned in gold, this is considered a status symbol, and married women all have elaborate nose rings, earrings and headpieces.

Next off to a carpet, or *durry* weaving cooperative. Here we were given a demonstration of using the loom and shown examples of many different designs.

Dale bought one, and by doing so was helping to support families and hamlets in the Bishnoi community.

We ate lunch with the family, cabbage curry, roti, and Indian raita — it was lovely.

On the way back to the hotel Raj stopped off at a jeweller that he knew. He took me and Ju inside where the jeweller opened up the amulet and very carefully placed Jeff's ashes inside, before sealing back up, using a silver solder. When Raj explained to the jeweller what he was doing, he started to bow his head and offer prayer to Ju; he completely refused to take any payment for his work.

It was very emotional for us all but wonderful at the same time.

Later we hired a tuktuk to take us to the hills so we could have a panoramic view of the 'Blue City', I don't think he understood our instructions, he was going backwards and forwards, round and round in circles, he knocked a driver and passenger off their moped and just carried on driving... Then it was dark, we got out and walked back to Curry's for dinner, it was so nice yesterday we couldn't resist.

7th November

Ju and Jeff's wedding anniversary today.

Up early as we're moving on again, our driver was not picking us up until 13:45 and we still had Mehrangarh Fort to see.

So, after a final visit to the Stepwell and breakfast of toast, jam and coffee, we headed off.

In 1459 Rao Jodha laid the foundation of what was destined to be one of the mightiest forts of all time.

The fort is huge and sits right on the edge of a cliff, it really is incredible, look it up, the scale of the building, it's mesmerising. The intricate carving, the quality and detail of the lattice work is on another level, its magnificent architecture... Once again, how the hell did they ever build it?

The audio tour was a great shout, loads of fascinating facts, my favourite;

We learnt that wives dressed in their wedding attire on the death of their husband, and in an act of devotion and faith they sacrificed themselves at his funeral. This was known as the custom of sati. Through one of the many gates throughout the fort you can see the imprints of the hands left by fifteen of the wives of the maharaja before they died on their husband's funeral pyre.

Today the fort is a unique museum that houses priceless relics and an impressive collection of palanquins, elephant howdahs, cradles, paintings, weapons, armoury, jewellery, turbans and costumes.

And the view from the many open platforms, including the 'Blue City', is breathtaking.

I'm glad we squeezed it in, it was well worth it.

We headed off to Pushkar with our driver as planned, four hours and 185 kilometres later we arrived at Hotel Gulaab Niwaas Palace.

What another cracker of a hotel. It gave us a grand feeling as we arrived, this place is amazing, our rooms are very spacious and overlooking the holy lake.

We have come here to go to the Pushkar camel fair, so an early night before the long day, tomorrow.

8th November

This place is awesome, a bit like a summer fete but an old traditional Indian festival. Thousands of camel, horse and cow traders converge to do business, trading their animals at this fair.

It's mad, the camels are painted, tattooed, shaved, decorated, adorned with jewellery, beads and sashes as well as being raced, danced and entered into beauty contests.

There is a massive showground where today's itinerary

includes hot air balloon flights, a cricket match, a moustache competition, a turban tying demo, a cattle exhibition, a classic dance show, a musical performance and a live concert with fire and light.

We walked around to take it all in, we saw Brahmins giving blessings, many arts and crafts stalls, magicians, dancers, acrobats, snake charmers, children dressed up in traditional costume and big wheel/carousel rides.

Of course, we watched the moustache show and took some amazing photos.

It is mobbed by tribal people from all over Rajasthan, pilgrims from all over India, and photographers, filmmakers and tourists from all over the world.

We also went to the lake, a sacred site for the Hindus, it is surrounded by fifty-two bathing ghats which are a series of steps allowing entry to the lake. A dip in the lake is thought to cleanse you of all your sins. The lake is also surrounded by Hindu temples.

Literally everyone was getting in to the lake — mostly fully clothed, but some naked!

9th November

Ju and I got up early to go to the camel fair again. I think Dale and Lou are burnt out after yesterday so we left them at the hotel to chillax.

We tried to walk, but must have turned the wrong way. A local lad came to our rescue and flagged down a car, the kind driver inside took us in his lovely blacked-out window, limousine-style MPV, for free!

It was much quieter today, we walked around, watched the most amazing little girl tightrope walking, a dancing painted monkey dressed in a tutu and a snake charmer. Ju got offered some drugs — we laughed and ate some fresh Bombay mix.

Being such a holy place alcohol, meat and eggs are completely banned, as are underground vegetables such as potato, garlic and onion. Mushrooms, fungus, yeast and honey are also on the forbidden list.

Pushkar has a magnetism all of its own and if you are anywhere nearby during the Hindu month of Kartika and the extravagant and magnificent camel fair you would be insane to miss it!

10th November

Travelling on again today, 146 kilometres, and three hours later, we arrived in Jaipur.

Alsisar Haveli — a heritage hotel in the 'Pink City' — an oasis in of calm smack bam in the middle of Jaipur.

Lou and I have the best room again, with a four-poster bed and a mattress that's like a marshmallow — it embraces you when you lie on it — so comfy.

The Haveli was built in the late nineteenth century. It was originally a nobleman's townhouse, serving as a holiday home for the Alsisar family, when they came to Jaipur to visit the royal family. Today it is a luxury hotel but still operated by the Alsisar family.

No time to lose, we swiftly arranged for a tuktuk driver to take us sightseeing.

First on the itinerary was the Hawa Mahal, or 'palace of the winds'.

Probably the most recognised monument of Jaipur, built for royal ladies to enjoy people watching, the day-to-day goings on/dramas and processions through the city behind the safety and confinement of this pink sandstone façade without being seen.

Its elaborate and fancy architecture has 953 windows with lace-fine décor, balconies, domes and spires.

I really can imagine how much fun it would have been and I can visualise their faces whilst gossiping together about those less fortunate and wealthy.

Next stop Man Sagar Lake and the Jal Mahal palace — so beautiful — an artificial lake, with a 'floating palace' which once served as a hunting lodge for duck shooting!

Unfortunately, you can only look at the palace from the roadside, entry inside is deemed too risky for fear of collapse seeing as half of the palace walls are below the water level.

The palace is apparently going to be renovated and will eventually become a luxury hotel — gives us an excuse to come back, eh?

We stopped off at a small row of market stalls, Dale and Ju had a fresh coconut drink, then we went back to the hotel for dinner, followed by drinks on the roof terrace. We played cards, too.

11th November

Breakfast was delicious; we sat in the hotel gardens and had eggs to order, toast, jam and coffee before heading out on today's adventure.

Dale and Ju really have thought this leg of our trip out to the max, and we are sure not to miss a thing.

The Amber Fort, and lots else is planned, so we'd better get to it.

On the way to the Amber Fort, we saw a snake charmer at the side of the road. The tuktuk driver stopped and we got out. The snake charmer placed a turban on Dale's head and started to play his whistle — out popped the cobra from the straw basket. Sure, it was just for us tourists, but it was funny.

This mighty fort sits on top of an eleven kilometres hill and is very impressive. It was a very long walk up — tuktuk are not allowed up the hill — years ago you used to sit on a palanquin on the back of an elephant for the ride, but thankfully this custom, deemed as inhumane, is now frowned upon.

Full of Hindu and Muslim architecture it was built in 1592, it has courtyards, gardens, bastions, watch towers, commanding views, pavilions, carvings, murals, beautiful stained-glass windows and the famous Hall of Mirrors which is totally encrusted with small mirrors and glass, it glitters in the daylight, twinkling like stars.

We then went to see the Panna Meena Ka Kund Stepwell.

Quite a bit smaller than the Toorji Ka Jhalra in Jodhpur but still staggeringly impressive.

Again, this stepwell was used to collect water, to bathe in and as a resting place; it was also used for religious ceremonies.

It is square shaped and has seven flights of stairs to descend before reaching the well — no railings of course so it does feel a bit like you are going to topple over and fall in!

The tuktuk driver then took us to an 'elephant sanctuary', but it seems more like a money-making scam.

We did see two elephants, yes, but then they asked for money to look at them, feed, wash, paint and ride on them!

We left after making a donation. Next stop, the monkey palace.

What a place this is, a large Hindu temple complex called Galtaji Temple, aka Monkey temple due to the massive colony of rhesus macaque and langur monkeys that live here.

The tuktuk driver dropped us off at the bottom of the hill and said we must walk up, and my, it was another very long walk up, and then down the other side.

Halfway there Ju was going to give up, so she rested whilst Dale, Lou and I took a short hike up to the small sun temple where we were blessed by a holy man.

When we finally arrived at the temple complex, it took about thirty minutes. There were hundreds of pilgrims bathing away their sins, accompanied by hundreds of the monkeys playing, jumping on the rocks and being fed peanuts and bananas.

Even though the temple is home to the monkeys it is dedicated to Ganesha, the elephant god and not Hanuman, the monkey god.

We hitched a ride back with some locals who offered us a pillion seat on their mopeds for 50p each! Lou walked — stupid!

On the way home we popped in to a nice little cocktail bar — Paladio — a classic Indian colonial-style joint, Ju had found it whilst doing her research — several cocktails later we were quite tipsy.

12th November

Today would have been Jeff's birthday. Strange because it's a full moon tonight, his favourite song was The Waterboys' *Whole of the Moon*, which Ju had played at his funeral.

Breakfast on the patio again, delightful fluffy scrambled eggs on toast.

Off we went to visit Jantar Mantar this morning. An observatory built in 1728 with nineteen architectural astronomy instruments made of stone designed to measure the positions of the stars, altitudes and to calculate eclipses.

I didn't really understand it, and really should have read up about it before our visit.

We then went on a little tour around the 'Pink City', so named as all the walls of the old city are painted this colour.

We stopped off at the Albert Hall Museum, and wow, what a building, full of wonderful exhibits of ancient Indian sculptors, artefacts, carpets, textiles, tribal dress, paintings and musical instruments.

It was originally built as a concert hall and is named in honour of Prince Albert, the husband of Queen Victoria.

We then walked around the Pink City and found our place for a late lunch. The restaurant 'LMB' (Laxmi Misthan Bhandar) had been recommended by Dale's friend Raqib who used to frequent this place with his grandfather.

The waiter helped us with the menu, and we were not disappointed.

Eat with the locals they say — perfect!

Back to the hotel for a swim in the pool, and change before heading out again, this time to Rambagh Palace for drinks and snacks. Formerly a maharaja's palace, royal guesthouse and hunting lodge, now a luxury hotel this place retains its elaborate splendour.

We sat on the garden terrace, drank cocktails, were entertained by some Indian dancers, watched a little boy play a flute to the full moon, (they do this every full moon at Rambagh Palace) we lit a candle for Jeff and Ju had her palm read.

The palmist told her that she had some upset recently, but she was going to turn a corner, be very happy and prosperous, and live a very long life!

13th November

Off again today, we travelled 200 kilometres to Ranthambore, which took four hours.

Famous for its national park and Bengal tigers, a vast wilderness covering 500square kilometres.

Ranthambore is a wildlife sanctuary in North India known for its Bengal tigers, established in 1955 by the government of India and declared one of the Project Tiger reserves in 1973.

We are staying in the Ranthambhore Heritage Haveli, a traditional Rajasthan-style building with wonderful architecture amongst the rural surroundings of the national park. Again, it is beautiful, nice big rooms, a lovely pool and gardens.

We are booked on a safari tomorrow, so the rest of the day we spent in the hotel.

I secretly went to get measured up. There is a tailor within the hotel, he is going to make me a tunic and trouser suit, it's called a *Salwar Kameez*.

Buffet dinner at the hotel, before a few drinks on the terrace and bed.

14th November

A 5:15 a.m. start, the jeep safari waits.

We had our own jeep, rather than going in a massive one with twenty tourists.

Our driver and a guide greeted us and off we went.

The road to get right into the National Park was very dusty and uneven, it was really cold too, but we had blankets for our knees and feet.

We drove around zone ten in the park for around two hours; we saw deer, antelope, peacocks, buffalo, eagles… but sadly no tigers.

Back to the hotel for breakfast which was all ready and laid out for us.

I had a swim before setting off again for our second safari.

This time we went to zone eight. Our guide was much better than the one earlier, really informative and desperate to find an elusive tiger.

Deer, antelope, water buffalo, eagles, owls, monkeys, osprey, peacock and a leopard which is quite rare we were told, but again, no tiger.

Never mind, it's been a fantastic day.

Dinner at the hotel again, buffet style, before drinks and a game of cards.

Lou and Dale had a political debate about Brexit and immigration.

15th November

Off to our last stop in India with Dale and Ju, really excited as we are off to Agra.

Two hundred and seventy-five kilometres, and six hours later, we arrived.

Tajview hotel does what it says on the tin — gives you a fabulous view of the Taj Mahal from your bedroom window!

Once again, the hotel is superb and it has a lovely rooftop terrace (but the smog is really bad today).

Lou and Dale went for a little walk, Dale had his hair cut and a massage in the middle of the street. The barber's friend was holding his mobile phone with the torch on so he could see!

We had the most delicious dinner in the hotel restaurant, AND they sold champagne. Dale was happy, the waiters were really friendly with us, we shared some fun banter with them.

Early to bed as we have a big day ahead tomorrow.

16th November

We were up and out by eight thirty, in an attempt to beat the crowds visiting the Taj Mahal.

Surprisingly the streets leading up to and around it, were some of the filthiest we have seen in all our time so far in India. There were open sewers that the locals had to step over right outside their dwellings to access the street, the kids were like ragamuffins, the tumble-down shack houses were made from corrugated iron, cardboard, wood or plastic sheeting, the smells were disgusting, there was rubbish literally everywhere.

Then, right in the middle of this slum stands the most beautiful building you have ever seen.

This building represents India like the Eiffel Tower in France, Sydney Opera House in Australia and Buckingham Palace in the UK.

Described as the most extravagant white marble tomb ever built for love.

It was constructed by Emperor Shah Jahan in memory of his beloved wife Mumtaz Mahal who died in 1639 whilst giving birth to their fourteenth child.

Taking twenty-two years to build it was completed in 1653, Jahan had planned to build an identical one for himself in black marble but only the foundation had been laid before he was deposed and imprisoned in Agra Fort by his own son, Aurangzeb.

He believed his father would spend all the treasure of the Mughal empire building a second Taj Mahal, there would be no money left for him. He imprisoned Jahan so that he could get his hands on the throne.

Jahan spent the rest of his life there, looking out along the river Taj, directly at his creation. After his death his body was floated up to the Taj Mahal and entombed next to his beloved Mumtaz.

We walked around this universally admired masterpiece and it truly does live up to its reputation as being one of the most beautiful buildings ever created.

Inside is equally as impressive, an eight-sided chamber ornamented with pietra dura (an inlay of semi-precious stones) and marble.

The building is the pinnacle of Mughal architecture, symmetrical with a dome and four minarets. These lean outwards very slightly; in addition to providing aesthetic balance, they would fall away from the main crypt in the event of a disaster like an earthquake — very clever.

The Taj Mahal is said to constantly change colour throughout the day, purple, grey and pink at sunrise, dazzling white at midday and an orange-bronze when the sun sets.

We then found 'Jeff's bench' and Ju scattered some of his ashes on the grass. We all cried...

To lighten our mood, we found a rooftop terrace bar, overlooking the Taj Mahal we sat for a drink and lots of laughter.

We also watched some locals on their rooftops training homing pigeons. The flock reacted to their owner depending on his whistle and waving of a cloth.

Homing pigeons' compass mechanism relies on the sun, using its position and angle to determine their path of flight. It is said that they can find their way home even if they have been transported to a destination with no visual clues, and their navigational skills have been put to use over many decades from the ancient Olympics to world wars.

Fascinating, mesmerising, absorbing and captivating.

Well, we couldn't sit there all day watching the pigeons, so next stop Agra Fort.

As non-Indians we had to pay four times as much as the locals for entry, as we have in most of the tourist attractions in India.

A red sandstone and marble fortress built as a military structure, Shah Jahan later transformed it into a palace, and ironically it eventually became his prison.

It is colossal, an incredible construction full of labyrinths, passageways, pavilions, bathing ghats, courtyards, mosques, a stepwell, bastions, palaces, marble jalis, stone lacework and delicate carvings.

The Khas Mahal is my favourite, it was the palace of Mumtaz Mahal, made of marble, decorated with the most beautiful lattice work, and once upon a time encrusted with gold, gems and precious stones — over the years these have been picked out and stolen by the tourists — I wish I could have reached one — some of the high pillars still have them — I defo would have nicked one! LOL

A place to observe and absorb.

Well, it's our last evening in Agra. Ju and I went back to the slum street we had walked down earlier on our way to the Taj, I had seen lots of severe poverty and felt a tremendous and intense sadness at the sight of India's class and caste divide, but nowhere quite as shocking as here.

The feeling that the youth cannot escape the reality of their own lives, unable to tackle the burden of health equalities, mortality, and inequalities in standard of living muddle around in my head. I want to help, but I feel sad at the significant realisation that my efforts would be in vain.

Anyhow, I had ten football shirts in my rucksack that I had been carrying around since Istanbul. This was definitely the place to distribute them at last.

Obviously not all the boys we found down the street were 'lucky' enough, but seeing the faces of those who got a shirt was priceless, and gave me a warm feeling of joy and pleasure.

17th November

Up for breakfast at the Tajview hotel before heading back to where it all started, Delhi.

Ju had a henna tattoo done before the car picked us up.

Two hundred and thirty-seven kilometres, and four hours later, we arrived at Radisson Blue Plaza. Another splendid room, and Dale has upgraded us to a premium package, so we had complimentary wine, drinks and snacks.

We washed and changed before making the most of the lounge bar until Dale and Ju had to leave for their flight home.

It's very sad to say goodbye, I shall miss them, Lou and I are so grateful for all the booking and planning, we definitely couldn't have designed such an amazing and orchestrated itinerary.

18th November

It's our first day waking up with no Dale and Ju, the last three weeks have been breathtaking, my goodness, truly an adventure we never thought possible.

I went down for breakfast this morning alone. Lou was still asleep, I had bacon!

Most of today was spent at the hotel; we have made the most of our upgrade. Thanks Dale.

19th — 22nd November

Travelling 1,885 kilometres heading south — flight from Delhi to Goa.

We are going to have a rest for the next few days, as the last three weeks have been full on.

Goa is one of India's gems, a state in the west colonised by the Portuguese in 1510.

With its natural harbour on the Arabian Sea and wide riverways it was ideal for the seafaring Portuguese who were intent on controlling the spice route from the east.

It has a very distinct character from the rest of India. Skirts replace saris, and its magnificent palm-tree-fringed beaches offer travellers the hedonism of sun, sea and sand.

We stayed at 'Casa de Goa', relaxed on the beach, listened to the waves, watched the fishermen hand haul their daily catch and witnessed the most beautiful sunsets.

Sunsets are special aren't they? Very romantic, mesmerising and tranquilising, they make you feel that no matter what, everything is going to be okay.

22nd–25th November

Travelled forty-two kilometres further south today, it took just under two hours to reach Betalbatim, and the Jasmin Hotel.

This hotel has beautiful gardens and two swimming pools, but very little else. No bar and a tiny restaurant.

We decided to have dinner at the hotel — big mistake.

We chose off the menu instead of opting for the open buffet, but after about an hour our food still hadn't arrived. We had ordered wine, one bottle of white and one bottle of red, but halfway through drinking it the waiter tried to take it off us saying he had served us the dearer one, not the bottles we had ordered!

We negotiated, and kept our wine at a discounted price but with the long wait for food, and the mix-up with the wine, our evening was marred.

Again, not much to see or do here, apart from the lovely beach.

The hotel provided a shuttle bus service, so we spent the next few days on the beach reading, snorkelling and listening to music.

O — OMD
P — Peter Tosh
Q — Queen (of course)
R — REM
S — Style Council
T — Tears for Fears
U — U2
V — Van Morrison
W — Wham
X — X-Ray Specs
Y — Yazoo
Z — Ziggy Stardust (aka Bowie)

We both love listening to music and have similar taste. We have never been fanatical about going to concerts but over the years we have seen many artists live.

Once we went to see U2 at Wembley, we went several years on the trot with a dear lifelong friend of ours called Ray.

One particular year we had terrible seats so Ray's sister Christine pretended to be pregnant and reported to an official that she couldn't possibly sit high up in the 'gods' due to her incessant morning sickness. Ha-ha, so funny, moments later we were moved right down the front, almost in the VIP section.

Another occasion I was at work, on the children's ward at the time, when a young couple came in with their son who was suffering from acute appendicitis.

Unfortunately for them they had tickets to go and see

Michael Jackson that very same day. The father of the child asked if anyone would like the tickets free of charge, and after pulling straws I was the lucky recipient.

I quickly phoned Sawbridgeworth football club where Lou was playing his usual Saturday afternoon football game, his manager subbed him off the pitch at half-time, and off we went to see MJ in concert.

Madonna was such a great performer live, as was Kylie.

We've also seen many other artists such as David Bowie, Jamiroquai, Dolly Parton, Coldplay, Spandau Ballet (where I danced in the aisle with Shirley), Michael McDonald, Erasure, Take That, Tears for Fears, Robbie Williams, Michael Bublé, Simply Red, Alexandra O'Neill, and we once went to Ronnie Scott's to see the legendary George Benson.

Our great friend Andre is a member there, and it was an up close and personal performance, what a treat, only two hundred tickets, and we had two of them!

My absolute favourite though has to be the late, great George Michael. I loved him.

We found a great little beach shack 'Sea Waves' run by John and Neeta, a husband-and-wife duo who cooked the most exquisite luscious fresh food — we ate here every day.

25th–30th November

It's back to basics today, something I've always wanted to do, and now we are doing it!

Staying in a beach hut, on the beach, this place was recommended to us by one of the guests in Tajview Hotel, Agra.

Blue Corner beach huts in Benaulim, South Goa, are very

simple and uncomplicated, a hut, inside is a bed, a fan, a mosquito net, a loo, a cold tap and a bucket!

Should be a laugh, and it's literally thirty metres from the sea.

There is a restaurant and bar though, what else could you ask for, or need, when you are in paradise?

Again, we watched the most beautiful sunsets, and woke up every morning to the rhythmic sounds of the waves lapping the shore, not forgetting the sounds of the crows crowing, the cows mooing, the dogs barking, the trains horning, and the frogs croaking (we even had a resident family of them — frogs — living in the loo!).

Whilst in South Goa, we had also been recommended to visit Dudhsagar Falls, a four-tiered waterfall located on the Mandovi River not far from where we were staying.

It is the fifth highest waterfall in India at 1,017 feet and is a natural wonder.

Surrounded by deciduous trees we needed to trek a little way to reach it, crossing rocks and streams, and there it was in all its majestic glory.

Well worth the visit. I swam in the freshwater pool amongst the giant carp, saw monkeys steal someone's clothes they had left on the rocks, and another steal someone's glasses!

I managed to find a nice leather-bound notebook, so I wrote a message of thanks to Dale. I also found a nice silver 'Tiger's Eye' ring for Ju (the palmist had told her to wear one on the middle finger of her right hand for good luck)

A local man took me to the post office on the back of his moped whilst Lou waited in town. I managed to post them home, but who knows when and if they will arrive?

30th November

Next stop and last destination in India, Mumbai. Our flight was with Indigo Airlines, and in just under two hours we had travelled 440 kilometres as the crow flies.

Our flight was delayed due to severe smog in Delhi; they say that the air pollution is 'off the charts', they have soared to hazardous levels and the local government have declared a public health emergency. Schools have been closed, and many flights have been cancelled.

They have put the crisis down to human and environmental factors such as recent Diwali (fireworks) celebrations, agricultural crop burning and fumes from passenger and freight vehicles stating that Delhi has turned into a 'gas chamber'.

It was quite a long transfer from the airport and we arrived at the 'Hotel Elphinstone' in the dark.

First impressions are not great; I wouldn't even call it a hotel if I'm honest.

It was more like two back-to-back corridors with rooms each side, there is no communal seating area and the reception was a desk located on the first corridor.

Entry was via a very dingy and dark doorway, then up two flights of concrete steps that had a real menacing feel about them, almost scary.

Our 'superior' room is like a shoebox, it had two single beds with a gap in between so narrow that you have to turn sideways to walk along to get to the shower room at the end!

The location feels desperate too, in the middle of a

crossroads and littered with rubbish, trucks, and mopeds and there are people everywhere.

So disappointing.

We ventured out for a walk, but quickly turned back, it really wasn't a nice area.

Oh well, we managed to grab some food from a takeaway, ate in our room and retired to bed. Let's see what tomorrow brings.

1st December

Breakfast was served in the corridor! Basically, the choice was eggs or Indian.

We had seen that it was the first day of the season for the Mumbai turf races, so we decided to go.

It didn't look too far on the map so we decided to walk, and on the way, we stopped to watch a cricket match (well some of it anyway) and a groom arriving on the back of a horse in all his splendour ready for his wedding, that was nice.

The walk seemed never ending, and eventually we gave up and jumped in a tuktuk. A good job really, as it was a good 25 minutes by road.

The races were really great fun, a bit like the race tracks we have been to in the UK, parade ring, big screens, bookies trackside etc.

Lou came out winning and I broke even, so it paid for our day out and this evening's dinner.

A dismal evening looking for somewhere to eat but eventually we found an 'okayish' looking local hangout. It's funny because it was all men, all smoking and all drinking copious amounts of whisky!

As usual, we had too much food, so we bagged up what

we hadn't touched and took it to some local children who were extremely excited and appeared very grateful, so that felt good.

2ⁿᵈ December

Gateway of India was not far from the Hotel Elphinstone so after breakfast we went walking. My goodness, it is really filthy and still feels menacing.

It took about thirty minutes, but we made it!

We could only walk around it because it was cordoned off; they were setting up for naval celebrations that were due to be taking place over the next few days.

Still, this colossal archway monument overlooking the Mumbai harbour is one of India's most unique landmarks.

It is not that old, constructed in 1924 to commemorate the visit of King George V and Queen Mary to Bombay, it served as an entrance point to India for the British Viceroys. Years later, a horde of British troops left India through this gateway.

The monument has been subject to terrorist activity, notorious as the most visible target of the 2008 Mumbai attack alongside its neighbour the Taj Mahal Palace hotel.

The Taj Palace hotel is considered one of the finest hotels in the east, and has been frequented by presidents, captains, royalty and stars of show business. It is directly opposite, so we went to take a look and have a cocktail but unfortunately, we had terrible service. I waited forty minutes for my drink, Lou had already finished his by the time it arrived, and there were only eight people in the bar! Never mind.

On the way back we went to see the famous Victorian train terminal, 'Chhatrapati Shivaji Maharaj Terminus' a gothic-style monument in itself. It is hard to believe from the outside that this is a train station — imposing three-storeys high, with spires, turrets, domes, and all wonderfully carved with floral and animal patterns.

It was also a target in the 2008 terrorist attacks where fifty-eight people died.

The station serves more than three million of the city's residents per day.

It is also a UNESCO World Heritage Site

Mumbai is the economic powerhouse of India and is said to be the fastest-moving, most affluent and most industrialised city in India. It handles over 50% of the entire country's foreign trade yet once upon a time it was nothing more than a group of low-lying swamps and malarial mud flats.

From what we see it still has problems with the most enormous slums, overcrowding and poverty, super rich/abject poverty, gleaming high rises/desperate shanty towns, pollution like you have never seen before/opulence fit for an Emperor.

Plus, ALL the men seem to chew tobacco, and then spit out their saliva like a snake sticks out its tongue, it's disgusting, there is gob everywhere.

I can't stand it here for another night, we are going to move on a day early and head nearer to the airport.

We ate in the same local dive tonight (there really is nowhere else to go) I gave the street urchins some food, crisps and fruit; again, they were really happy which makes me happy.

3rd December

We checked out of the Elphinstone and booked an Uber to the 'Radisson Blu Plaza' yes, it was the best move ever. When we arrived, they had upgraded us to an executive suite which was more like it! (I had emailed them to say that it was our last night after five weeks' travelling India, and we wanted it to be really memorable).

The bed was gigantic, big enough for a three or four; we had windows full length two sides of room, a very large walk-in wet room big enough for a party.

There is a rooftop pool, a funky restaurant and cocktail bar too.

After the anxious feeling in Elphinstone we decided just to chill and stay in the hotel.

We had a swim, went for dinner on roof terrace, drank far too much wine, and played Scrabble.

4th December

Hung over this morning, we haven't drunk that much wine for ages, I guess we're not used to it any more LOL

We did get up for breakfast, but then went back to bed. The hotel let us have a late checkout for an extra £40, we could check out at seven p.m. which is perfect, as our flight to Bangkok is not until eleven thirty p.m.

We spent a few hours around the pool, washed (in the super-duper shower) and changed, then had dinner before checking out and heading to the airport.

We flew Thai airlines to Bangkok, had lovely complimentary food and drink, and watched *Rocketman* before trying to get a few hours sleep.

More films we have added to the list to watch on our return

home include

- *The Darkest Hour*
- *Hotel Mumbai*
- *Best Exotic Marigold Hotel*
- *Gandhi*
- *Slumdog Millionaire*
- *Lion*
- *Bombay*
- *Life of Pi*
- *Million Dollar Arm*
- *The Lunchbox*
- *Octopussy*

Chapter 8
Thailand

5th December

It was a great flight from Mumbai non-stop to Thailand touching down in Bangkok at 05:00 taking about seven hours to fly 4,770 kilometres.

I saw the most incredible stars out of the window on the way, different clusters, shapes and sizes shining bright, dazzling and intense, brilliant and vivid like diamonds in the sky. I wish I knew more about astronomy and space. I did have a telescope once but could never really work it properly. I do have an app on my phone for the International Space Station though, I've seen that quite a lot.

We decided to head straight off south, travelling down the east coast of Thailand, to Hua Hin. We will travel northern Thailand on the way home after exploring Far East Asia.

The shuttle bus leaves every hour, so we got tickets for the next available at 07:30, it took three hours to travel the 200 kilometres.

Arriving at 'Hotel Peony', again a little disappointed, I wouldn't call it a luxury twin room that's for sure. It has made me question some of the reviews on TripAdvisor and Bookings.com, some of the time it seems that they are referring to completely different places. You get what you pay for, I suppose.

Surprisingly it's very windy today and quite chilly too.

It's impossible to walk along the beach at the moment, the tide is right in and the waves are almighty.

It is a seaside resort on the Gulf of Thailand, once a quiet fishing village, but it grew into a fashionable holiday resort for residents of Bangkok when the royal family-built summer palaces here.

We went for a stroll to the night market, there are two here, and oh my, the Thai street food looks incredible, we are definitely going to be eating here. Awesome lobster, crab, shellfish, flat fish, prawns, squid — fish, fish, and more fish. You pick what you want; they cook it for you, simple.

Lou and I both love fish and seafood, it's never the same at home, is it? Unless you live in Cornwall or anywhere on the British coast, really. Gary and Mandy live in Mevagissey and are always buying the freshest fish from the Cornish coast at the quayside.

I spoke to Ju tonight, it's eight months now since Jeff died. Seems like five minutes, and yet it seems like a lifetime ago, too.

6th December

Had a lie-in today as tired from all the travelling, we dawdled around until midday and then went for a walk. Again, it is very windy today, but not cold.

Lunch was nice, I had katsu chicken with rice and Lou had duck with noodles.

On the way back we went to visit Hua Hin train station.

It is popular with tourists as it has been considered to be the most beautiful station in Thailand, of which the locals are very proud.

The royal family were Hua Hin's main visitors at the start of the twentieth century, but the place became popular when the railway opened making trips to the seaside much more viable.

It was built in 1910 for King Rama VI when he served as a commander so that he could have his own first class waiting area on the railway. It is beautifully decorated and carved in classic Chinese style. Made of half wood and half brick, it is influenced by Victorian architecture. It is well maintained and has won awards for its preservation.

Still stuffed from our late lunch we skipped dinner, sat on the balcony, had some wine and played Scrabble instead!

7th December

I was awake on and off most of last night, Lou's legs were dancing, jerking and playing football for England, I am sure he has got 'restless leg syndrome'.

We decided to hire pushbikes for the day and cycle to the bus station in preparation for the next destination — Krabi.

At first, we went in the wrong direction, way off track, but eventually found it. The bus to Krabi is overnight and takes nine hours — argh.

My watch tells me we rode a total of 27.3 kilometres, my bum agrees, so sore.

Stopped off at a few temples, and went to see a Buddhist rock temple but we couldn't get across because of the tide.

We also cycled to see the Palace, the current King lives here most of the time, but it was closed to the public.

Dale, Michelle and Ju have been to the Wolseley for breakfast today, eggs benedict, kippers, kedgeree, crushed avocado with tomatoes, and the famous Arnold Bennett omelette — yummy.

They certainly made a day of it because it was Tate Modern next followed by Sushisamba for cocktails, then on to Dishoom in Shoreditch for an Indian.

How lovely, I wish I was there.

8th December

Relaxed today around the pool trying to soothe our bum aches and other bits!

Later we decided to go for a Sunday roast, there is an Irish bar called Father Teds, we saw it advertised the other day.

I had roast lamb, Lou had roast chicken, and it was lovely but nothing like home.

It's the one thing I am quite good at cooking, I always do all the trimmings, and in my opinion no Sunday roast is complete without cauliflower cheese!

We phoned lots of people, Mum and Dad, Pam, Dale and Ed, Lolly and Ian, my dear friend Tracy, John and Keeley, Jeff and Marion, Mandy (Gary wasn't in) Duchess and Leafy (no reply) Bunny and Ju.

There are loads of pictures on social media today of everyone decorating their Christmas trees.

9th December

Another lazy day today around the pool relaxing. It's breezy again so we figured there is no point going to the beach, the sea will be really choppy and the tide is always high.

Later we walked to the street food market — lobster, crab, prawns, sea bream, salmon, food glorious food, captivating the senses, all the different appealing aromas, the tastes, the textures, the succulent appearances are tantalising my taste buds (and making my mouth water big time)

Then there's the noodle — numerous shapes, colours and textures — they form the basis of most Asian speciality dishes — round, dried, flat, glass, spicy, fried, egg, thin, wide — the choice is just phenomenal

Well it was so overwhelming we 'bottled it' a bit and settled for Thai steamed rice, mixed vegetable stir-fry noodles, sweet and sour pork and crispy chicken with cashew nuts, peppers, onion and carrot.

Just scrumptious.

10th December

We got up for breakfast, like in India, when they have Indian for breakfast, Thailand has Thai for breakfast too. It's weird trying to eat noodles and rice first thing in the morning.

We went for a walk along the pier and sat watching the fishermen for a while.

They were using rods, which had about ten hooks along the line; they were casting out and reeling in almost straight away.

Lots of fish but very small, they must be edible or why bother?

They have the most peculiar guest houses here, old squid piers on stilts strung along rickety wooden jetties. This was the hub of the original fishing village.

On the way back we walked along the beach, it's the first day we can; the sea has been restricting its access so far.

Stunning late lunch at a beach hut restaurant, steamed rice with sweet and sour prawns and chicken, they really do know how to cook the freshest, fast, piping hot and luscious food.

We sat on the beach until late, and then the worst happened! We went back to our hotel, the Peony for some drinks, got really drunk and stupidly decided it would be a good idea to go out at midnight, to watch Liverpool in the Champions League!

Liverpool won the game 2–0; we had far too many bevies but somehow found our way home at three a.m.

11th December

Neither of us woke up until one o'clock in the afternoon.

Hungover; the only term to describe us today.

Nothing more to do today except relax and rehydrate.

A few metres up the road from the Peony there was a little restaurant which was always packed with locals, so we went there for some dinner.

They had 'fried morning glory with crispy pork' on the menu, it made me laugh, I didn't try it although I am sure it is really tasty.

12th December

Today the Conservative Party, led by Boris Johnson, won the general election.

Please somebody help me, Lou has 'man-flu', snivelling and sneezing all over the place. I am not sexist but why is it a man with a cold is twice as poorly as a woman with one? And why is everything so severely exaggerated?

The cough, oh the painful, hacking 100 decibel wet and spluttering cough, the sneeze, like a semiautomatic convulsive explosion from the mouth and the nostrils with added sound effects, followed by the sniffing up or blowing out of the copious amounts of snot and the inevitable adoption of the totally helpless role.

Apparently, there is some science to suggest that a man's immune system may be weaker than a woman's. It's to do with oestrogen and testosterone, oestrogen increases the number of antibodies needed to fight a virus, but... there is very little evidence to suggest 'man-flu' actually exists.

We did go to the beach, hired a couple of sunbeds, and ate lunch at the same shack as the other day. I didn't go in the sea as there was a jellyfish warning!

No going out tonight as Lou is 'too poorly' so I went out and picked up a pizza takeaway, we sat on the balcony playing Scrabble.

13th December

Dylan, our great-nephew is sixteen today. Where do the years go?

Lou still has 'man-flu' so we have spent our last day in Hau Hin around the pool.

It was very hot today, so frequent dips in and out of the pool, a bit of reading, listened to some music and relaxed.

We ate dinner at the hotel too, before heading off to the bus station for our overnight transfer to Krabi.

The bus was a little delayed, but we had VIP seats in the lower deck of the bus (there were only seven seats — all recliners — but only me, Lou and one other passenger).

I guess it is like business class on a flight, only on a bus, we even got given a soft drink, cake, biscuits and coffee.

14th December

After a long night with little sleep for me we arrived in Krabi, a province on the east coast of Thailand.

We had travelled eight hours, further south for 586 kilometres.

Krabi is said to have shimmering beaches, clear calm seas and is a world class Mecca for rock climbers. You can see why, some of the province presents landscapes which have been shaped over thousands of years, amazing rock formations. If you close your eyes, you can imagine the pterodactyl flying high above just like in the film *Jurassic Park*.

'Cozy Place' is a family-run hotel, it's nice enough, the rooms are spacious and we are ground floor right next to the pool.

Because we booked for the travel night we could unpack straight away and have breakfast (otherwise we would have had to wait until check-in at two p.m.)

We went for a walk along the riverside, it was clean and pretty, it had lots of sculptures and unique fancy and elaborate lamp posts, mostly animals or sea creatures in traditional Thai style, lining the streets and adorning the traffic lights.

My favourite sculpture, is The monument of Black Crabs, it represents respect for the mangrove forests which are the natural habitat of the black crab.

The hotel let us borrow their bikes this afternoon, so we went for a ride to get some provisions. We found a little wine and beer shop, so we stocked up before heading back out to a local bar to watch this evening's Liverpool game.

I brought the children of the hoteliers some sweeties.

The cocktails were BOGOF, so they went down a treat.

On the way home we walked through the street food market to have something to eat. However, we had lost track of time, it was ten p.m. and all the stalls were closed!

No dinner for us tonight. Never mind, we were tired anyway so we just went to bed.

15th December

Up this morning nice and early for breakfast, eggs and bacon, toast and jam, fresh fruit and cake — not Thai noodles and rice.

We decided to sit around the pool, listen to music and read, it was lovely until it started to rain!

I don't think we have seen any rain since the torrential storms in Venice.

It didn't rain for long.

Later we went to the night market, but earlier than we went last night — so much tempting food on the menus but some not so tempting such as barbequed crocodile or scorpion skewers.

It was really funny because there was entertainment in the square. Some Thai singers singing English Christmas carols, a small kids' band, dancing to music, and a little girl in the most elaborate traditional costume, making graceful body movements, which was very engaging, especially her make-up, and very long brass nail extensions.

Later we sat on the balcony, watched the sunset and played Scrabble. I am getting quite a grand master at it now, I

might even consider applying for *Countdown*
when I'm home, I am that good at it.

16th December
Seeing as we have had a few lazy days we decided to head to the beach today so we caught the local bus to Ao Nang. It took around forty-five minutes.

Ao Nang is Krabi's vibrant tourist centre known for its long Adaman coast, turquoise waters and long-tail boat tours.

The waters used to be a hideout for Asian pirates due to its abundance of jungle and limestone islands and sea caves, now the only 'pirates' here are developers who 'steal' islands for luxury accommodation.

This area is heavily populated with the tourist in mind, hotels, resorts, clubs, bars, restaurants, supermarkets, street food markets and much more.

Tsunami warnings are everywhere and there are signs with directions to the nearest evacuation point all the way along the beachfront.

It is much livelier than where we are staying.

We sat on the beach for a while, and I did venture into the sea, but not very far… it's not very blue, or clear come to that, jellyfish alert radar would not work in these waters.

After a beer we caught the bus back. It is really easy to do so, we just stood at the side of the road where the buses that are like a big tuktuk cruise along and pick up passengers.

I went out to a local street food vendor and picked us up some takeaway dinner, fried rice with chicken, flat noodles with beef and four fried chicken pieces and we sat on our balcony to eat it.

It really is quite tiring doing nothing much at all.

I spoke to Mum and Dad on the phone, I also spoke to Ju and Dale.

17th December

We hung around the pool all day today although the weather was not so good, cloudy but still hot.

I had a swim; I've been getting back into it now.

At home I would get up at six, be in the pool by six thirty, and swim 1000 metres (just over half a mile) most days.

Of course I have given up my membership at the gym whilst I am away, but I'll renew it when I get home, I love swimming.

I often think how my swimming friends are getting on? There is a group of five of us that would be there in the mornings; Terry, Jan, Nicola, Val and me.

Before I left, I wanted to get them all something so that they didn't forget me LOL. The choice of gift was a plant, a variety of lily, called *Alstroemeria*, I wonder if they bloomed in summer?

We had a great dinner again this evening, I had steamed rice with chicken and cashew nuts, my new favourite, and Lou had Thai green curry — very tasty.

We sat on the balcony and played Scrabble again, there's not much else to do!

18th December

Had a lie-in, missed breakfast, it's ridiculously early here anyway, seven to nine a.m.

We decided to look at booking some forthcoming flights for the remainder of the trip and found one Bangkok to Heathrow on 16th April 2020.

It seems really weird that we are already planning our journey home.

We also booked flights from Singapore to Philippines and from Philippines to Vietnam.

It's a good job we stayed at the hotel today as I had a phone call from the Lloyd's fraud squad! My card has been cloned and used at Sainsbury's in Finchley Road, London twice!

Both transactions were for £156.36, thieving buggers. Luckily Lloyds recognised the dodgy transactions and stopped the payments but I have to destroy my card and they have cancelled it — a flipping inconvenience, but hats off to Lloyds.

Lou had a chat with Bunny today; it's his dad Len's funeral.

We went out for a walk and look around the fruit market and decided to have dinner at a 'pop up' street food place we had seen earlier.

Great fun, you pick your raw ingredients; we chose Chinese cabbage, green beans, mushrooms, chicken, prawns, pork steak and sticky rice, they bring it to your table all cut and portioned up, then they stick a great big terracotta pot onto burning coal in the middle of your table that has stock in it, then you cook it yourself — wow, so simple, fresh and luscious.

We had a nightcap on the balcony and guess what? Played Scrabble and I totally thrashed Lou!

It was kind of spooky, but I had hung my wet swim towel on the rail, and the way it was drooping you could see an apparition; a face which looked eerily like my twin brother John! I WhatsApp-ed him, he saw Marc Almond!

19th December

We made breakfast today and then sat around the pool for a bit, it was really hot.

I had a swim, 1000m again, my watch tells me so.

The hotel has a washing machine so I washed and dried all of our clothes in preparation for our next move tomorrow.

Just down the street was the Wat Kaew Temple, a Buddhist temple, one of the largest in Krabi so we decided to go and take a look.

It was nice enough, nestled on top of a hill; the entry staircase was pretty impressive with golden snakes slithering down the balustrades.

Inside the temple the walls are covered in murals which depict traditional scenes, then in the centre the large golden Buddha is eye-catching. It was pleasant but I have seen better.

20th December

We got up for breakfast as we are moving on again today, to Phuket.

The hotel lady (I didn't get her name) gave me a shoulder bag and a scarf as a gift, which was lovely.

One hundred and sixty-three kilometres and three hours later, we arrived at Hotel Phoenix Grand.

Phuket/Patong is the most famous beach resort in Thailand.

With its wide variety of activities and nightlife it is a place to party and play night and day.

The town has a notorious bustling nightlife which includes hundreds of open façade beer bars, restaurants, clubs and go-go bars on the Bangla Road.

The hotel is okay, it has a rooftop infinity pool, a bit of a view of the sea, and the location is central.

We have a balcony but there is no furniture to sit on — what's that all about?

Memories took us for a walk down Bangla Walking Street, it's earlyish still, so not as packed as we imagined, we sat and had a drink whilst watching the passing crowds.

It seems very different from last time, hardly any lady-boys, there were perhaps half a dozen, if that, who were demanding money if you were seen taking their photos.

I do remember the beer bar being fun and friendly, everyone played Jenga or Connect 4, and then there was this game that we played where you have to hit a nail into a piece of tree trunk using the thin side of the hammer head; whoever hit their nail in flush first was the winner.

Then there were the girls dancing on the bar and performing all sorts of acrobatics up and down the poles; there are still a few, but the girls 'performing' look miserable, lacking in enthusiasm, lacklustre and dull, barely swaying forwards and backwards.

21st December

Today we decided to go in to Phuket town so we could get

our bus ticket in preparation for the next part of our journey. The local bus dropped us off in the town, but then we had to walk to the main bus terminal.

Well, we walked and we walked and we walked a bit more. It was exhausting in the heat, my watch told me it was six miles! I was not happy at all.

I think I had heat exhaustion, my body was boiling, I felt nausea, dizzy and my legs were cramping… then I fell over! I didn't 'collapse' I just tripped on an exposed tree root.

At first, I was disorientated and couldn't get up, I was winded and for a moment I thought I had fractured both of my wrists. Then I felt a trickle down my right lower leg (don't worry I hadn't wet myself LOL).

I had a really deep abrasion just below my knee, you know the type you get when you're a kid and fall off your pushbike, we called them kiddie grazes, yes just like that.

I am no drama queen by any stretch of the imagination but right then I wanted to cry, not because I had suffered a severely painful injury, but because I felt physically unable to walk another step… we got the bus back!

Just up the road from our hotel there was the street food market, we went there for dinner tonight. Again, so much amazing food to choose from, we plumped for noodles, prawns with bean-shoots and a whole freshly grilled mackerel to share… oh, I love street food.

Whilst eating we noticed a large police presence and they appeared to be stopping all the traffic. Then, a few moments later along came a police motorcade, followed by a precession of blacked-out window limousines. It turned out it was the Princess of Thailand who had come to watch the finals of the

National Thai Boxing competition in the stadium literally a few metres up the street. We went to watch it (from behind a barricade).

22nd December

Pool day today, I'm still suffering from heat exhaustion I think, but the good news is Lou is free of man flu.

We didn't do much else at all today although Lou had a Sunday roast, it was a carvery and his plate was piled high. I had sausage and mash. It made a nice change, actually.

23rd December

We stayed by the pool most of the day again today.

Lou got us some spring rolls with sweet chilli sauce for lunch, street food for dinner.

We brought a T-shirt each to wear on Christmas Day, just to get in the spirit of things, but it doesn't seem right — I am missing home.

24th December

It's Christmas Eve.

We moved hotels today, we decided to splash out a bit and book ourselves in to 'Nicky's Handlebar' hotel.

It's supposed to be 4.5 star — it's not!

Quirky yes, each room is decorated with unique features relating to Harley Davidson, elaborate sculptures made from exhaust pipes etc, and bathroom, wash basin, and dressing table area are themed in the same fashion, but the pool area requires attention, it's shabby — numerous tiles are missing and the grouting is dirty, there is no space to sit outside, one lounger per room, and that only fits lengthways, adjacent to the patio door entrance of the room. When we checked in a family of four were sitting on it right outside our door.

Very disappointing again — I wish people writing reviews would be honest — our room was advertised as 'pool access room' and it really isn't.

I am feeling even more homesick now.

We always make a big deal of Christmas at home. I have never been away from home at this time of year.

Christmas Eve is spent picking up the fresh turkey, gammon and fillet of beef from Smithfield Market.

When we get home, we have an all-day, indoor picnic of sausage rolls, pork pie, pickles, cheese and biscuits, wine and port while playing Christmas songs on the i-Pod. One year Lou ate a whole jar of pickled gherkins to himself!

My favourite Christmas song is *'Chestnuts Roasting on an Open Fire'* by Nat King Cole (the Michael Bublé version is fabulous too) closely followed by, *Last Christmas* by Wham.

Oh, that's just reminded me… when George Michael died on Christmas Day 2016.

He was my absolute favourite solo artist.

Bunny has his birthday on 25th December so Lou and I always pop round there after the day's celebrations with our family, it's tradition. We are usually 'well on our way' by then though.

In 2016 as customary, we arrived about ten-ish, wished him happy birthday and continued drinking and partying.

Bunny was playing his music through the TV when suddenly, one of us (I think it was Ed) received a text or tweet to break the devastating news. The music channel was turned on to the TV channel at 23:01 precisely, and there it was

'Breaking News' George Michael had been found dead at his home in Goring-on-Thames, Oxfordshire, aged fifty-three.

What a shock, disbelief set in immediately, followed by uncontrollable crying, inability to speak and total body shaking. Unable to comfort or alleviate my state of upset, I had to be taken home.

25th December

It's Christmas Day but it doesn't feel like it.

Santa has been to visit and left me a sack, it had a lovely bag and purse with some coins inside.

It's boiling hot today too, feels weird.

We went to the beach for the day, it is like any other day here. All the street vendors are out, the tourists are shopping and drinking, the buses are running, even the refuse collectors are clearing the remnants of last night's activities. We even saw some children in school uniform.

It is what it is... when in Phuket and all that!

We changed into our Christmas T-shirts, had some photos taken with the girls at the hotel and headed off out for Christmas dinner.

No turkey, gammon, beef and all the trimmings for us, oh no.

We had lobster, oysters and mussels — weird.

Obviously, we phoned family and friends, FaceTimed most of them so we could see them too, most of the family are at Michelle and Ashley's today, it is very emotional, we miss being at home at Christmas. Never again.

26th December

Boxing Day.

We had a walk just to check out the bus times ready for our transfer tomorrow.

It's really hot again today, we had a drink in the bar, popped into the shopping centre, had a swim in the pool and later went out for dinner — street food again but I don't think I'll ever get bored of it, in fact you could eat more than adequately without ever entering a restaurant here. The street vendors, especially the ones that either have a queue, or are surrounded by locals provide some of the best lip-smacking feasts I have tasted. I think I love it so much because it is so fresh, takes minutes to cook, is so very tasty, and you know that it's not sloppy leftovers or yesterday's produce.

We WhatsApped Dale, who was at Mum and Dad's with Ju, John, Keeley, Miles and Rory.

Phuket has changed a lot since we first came here over twenty-odd years ago, it's very commercialised and pricey too!

Of course everyone remembers it was devastated by the Boxing Day Tsunami, in 2004. The Thai government reported 5,395 confirmed deaths, and 8,457 injured in this southern province facing the Andaman Sea alone.

Redevelopment was swift and sadly everywhere you look there is Starbucks, KFC, Burger King etc.

Bangla Road is not as much fun either, nor as friendly, competition for punters is fierce, everyone wants money, the music is very loud — each bar competing to outdo the next.

We must be getting 'past-it', we much preferred the pad Thai to the ping-pong. LOL.

27th December

We checked out of 'Nicky's Handlebar' and made our way

224

to the bus station. It was due at 10.15, however. When it didn't arrive, we asked at the information desk who told us that it had been cancelled, the next one wasn't due until 12.15.

Lou is really not very happy. I quickly had to find access to wi-fi as the hotel we are going to stated that reception would be closed at eight p.m.

The distance between Phuket and Satun is 232 kilometres and should take seven to eight hours.

We need to get there to catch the ferry to the Malaysian Island of Langkawi tomorrow!

We finally got on the bus, but goodness me, what a mammoth journey, horrendous, it must have stopped at least thirty times. As well as the bus service it appears it was DHL, FedEx and Royal Mail service too!

We eventually arrived in Satun at 21:30, the bus terminal had long shut, so the bus just dropped us off on the street, we were the last passengers!

It was pitch black and we had no idea of where we were. Luckily, Lou had taken a screenshot picture of the hotel and we found it quite easily.

A dear little old lady and her grandson were there — still waiting for us on reception — bless her.

They took us to our room where we just had a drink and went to bed. We have to get up early for the ferry tomorrow.

We have had nothing to eat today apart from some cheese and crackers, which luckily, we brought for the journey, just in case.

Didn't get a chance to see anything of Satun.

Chapter 9
Malaysia

28th December

Had to wake up early as our ferry to Langkawi was leaving at nine a.m., so we left the hotel and headed for the bus station.

A local tuktuk driver stopped and wanted to charge us 100 baht each, but the bus was only thirty! A local man helped us out, telling us what bus to get on.

We arrived at the port, queued and purchased our ticket and got on the ferry almost straight away.

The trip took just over an hour; we hopped in a taxi and on to the hotel.

The Western Hotel in Pantai Chenang, oh dear, another complete disappointment — tiny room, nowhere to put our bags let alone our clothes, no window and a toilet/shower room that you couldn't swing a cat in!

We walked into town along the beach, which is beautiful, and got some provisions.

There doesn't appear to be much to see or do here. We have found a nice little place called Billie's, dinner was lovely.

We will make the most of it, I'm sure.

Langkawi means island of the reddish-brown eagle, Lang (eagle) Kawi (a red chalk stone). It is part of an archipelago of ninety-nine islands surrounded by sparkling emerald waters and powder-fine sandy beaches.

The island is only 15.5 miles from north to south and a little more from east to west.

29th December

Breakfast; well, it's the worst breakfast you will ever be subjected to.

Consisting of fried eggs or omelette that must have been batch cooked hours ago, stone cold, between two plastic (and very stained) plates, same with the toast, a large greasy tub of margarine and jam, coffee so strong that you could stand your spoon up in it — yuk — disgusting.

We went to the beach for the day, but no swimming in the sea, there are loads of jellyfish! They do have the nets but the little blighters still manage to escape.

30th December

As you can imagine we didn't bother with breakfast today, we just stopped off at the bakers on the way to the beach and brought a quiche.

We have decided to stay in Langkawi for longer than planned; it's duty free here, so we'll save a little money and just chill out. We have booked to move to the south of the island next week.

31st December

It's New Year's Eve so we have decided to have a day out to the SkyCab and skybridge today.

We tried to hire a scooter, but so had everyone else .it seemed... not a single place had any left, so we went back to the hotel to plan something else when the hotelier started talking to us. When we told him about the scooter he went off, got a second crash helmet, gave us the keys, and told us to borrow his for the day.

The scooter ride was enjoyable, I think Lou misses his motorbike; it was his pride and joy, his dream bike, Honda Africa Twin, which he had got from new and kept it in immaculate condition… until some scumbag stole it from right outside the house.

The SkyCab is basically a cable car that takes you right to the top of Machinchang Mountain that has a 125 metre curved single pylon suspension bridge 660 metre above sea level.

When you get to the top you have to walk back down through the natural forest, watch the monkeys in the trees, climb down some very steep steps, then you reach the bridge.

The views are spectacular, and on a clear day you can see neighbouring Thailand.

There are a few glass panels on the floor of the bridge where you can see directly down in to the dense rain forest too.

It was fun, but you have to be fit. Climbing back up to the SkyCab in the blistering heat is not easy.

We also visited the 3D art gallery; we took some really funny photos which made us look like we were inside the artwork.

On the way home we stocked up on some booze for NYE tonight on the beach.

We took our towels to sit on and our provisions and went to the beach. There were lots of other people there and some fireworks, but not as many as expected and no sky lanterns either. I had imagined there would be hundreds of them, but no.

Lou was very, very drunk — 'Mr Spaghetti legs' again.

It took me about an hour and a half to walk him ten minutes home!

Happy New Year.

1st January

It's New Year's Day and what a better way to spend it than on the beach?

There's not much else to do here, so we stayed for the day, went home and got washed and changed, then came back to watch the stunning sunset.

Both of us had a haircut and we spoke to most of the family again via FaceTime.

They're all good — I miss them.

2nd January

We left the Western Hotel this morning and travelled to the main town Kuah.

The Greenish Hotel is much bigger, and they gave us the choice of rooms, both are similar but one had two large beds, so we picked that one.

Kuah is the capital of Langkawi and the administrative headquarters.

As mentioned, it is duty free here, so very cheap. If you're not an alcoholic, then you're a chocoholic here, it's everywhere, and they buy bagsful of the stuff.

The jetty is here too, and serves as the main ferry terminal for boats/ferries that ply between Langkawi, the mainland and many other nearby islands.

It is also a birdwatcher's paradise.

There are no beaches this end of the island; it is pretty quiet too, not many bars or nightlife.

Oddly, in Langkawi there is no public transport either — bus/trains etc, it's a taxi or hire a scooter.

We went for a long walk, into town and got some tourist information. It felt a long way in the heat to Eagle Square (Dataran Lang) one of Langkawi's best-known man-made attractions, a large eagle poised to take flight. It's the first thing you see when you arrive on the ferry, a twelve-metre-high statue at the port.

It's a nice spot to take some photos and look out across the harbour.

Later we had some street food, duck noodles, lemon chicken and sticky rice.

3rd–5th January

We stayed at the hotel for the next few days, dipped in and out of the pool; I swam my 1000 metre each morning.

The gardens around the pool are pretty; they have lots of exotic flowers and fresh coconuts and bananas growing on the trees.

Lou shouted at me to take a look, and there just crossing the grassland was a massive, and I mean massive lizard, literally the size of a small child, I reckon about four feet long or so. It looked like a Komodo dragon with its long neck, huge claws, powerful tails and very muscular limbs.

The waiter in the hotel said it's called a monitor lizard and that attacks from these lizards on humans are rare, but they are carnivorous and will eat small animals, snakes, mammals and birds. They eat their prey whole and have been known to pick up small babies if left unattended.

Malay food is as good as Thai; the street food here again excels any restaurant, especially the night market. We ate at the street food market, a different stall each evening, a little more spicy that Thai food but we have not had a bad meal yet, or a dodgy tummy!

6th January

We went out for the day today. We booked a jet-ski tour of some of the islands that we had seen advertised, it was pricey, but when in Rome. The reviews were good too.

The reception ordered us a taxi which took us back to Pantai Cenang where we met our guide, Patrick. There were three other couples, so five jet-skis in total.

It was really great fun.

First, we stopped off at Beras Basah Island, the only other island in the archipelago that is inhabited.

It looked like paradise with its expansive sandy beach, palm trees and crystal-clear turquoise waters. There is an old wooden pier where the boats moor up, a rustic stall selling drinks and snacks, wild native monkeys, and that's about it.

We then headed to Singa Besar, home to the eagles. Our guide threw some raw chicken into the air and we watched as they swooped, hundreds of them, white-bellied fish eagles and kite eagles, to catch their lunch.

This island is untouched by humans so is a natural haven for wildlife.

Then it was on to the 'Lake of the Pregnant Maiden' so

called because the mountain ridge silhouette bends smoothly giving the appearance of a pregnant woman lying on her back. Some believe that the lake is a sacred place for couples with infertility, and that, if they take a swim in the lake, they will be blessed with a child.

It is a freshwater lake which Patrick explained was created when the mountain top collapsed, caving inwards and forming a large crater with mountains all around it. Over the hundreds of years this crater has filled with fresh rainwater.

To reach the lake is quite a challenge though, you have to climb a small precarious rock face, and then descend the other side before walking a rickety old boardwalk through the mangroves which really has seen better days.

The swim in the lake was refreshing; we sat and enjoyed the view with a nice cold drink.

On the way back Patrick took us to Kukos and Kukus Islands, so called because when we stopped our jet-skis in the waters between the two (they are very close together) and you call out your name it echoes between the two like a cuckoo, I suppose.

It was amusing and entertaining seeing who could call the loudest.

One of our group jumped in to the sea, Patrick was spinning around and using our phones to take pictures for us. I was just about to do the same (jump in that is) when I spotted a mahoosive jellyfish next to our jet ski. I mean it must have been at least four feet long, my shout then was definitely the loudest, and the group member enjoying his dip couldn't clamber on to his jet-ski quick enough!

We switched drivers for the last leg. Cutting through the waves of the Andaman Sea was thrilling and adrenaline was pumping, but blimey my arms ached from holding on so tight and my butt cheeks felt battered, bruised and beaten.

Tremendous day though and well worth the money.

7th January

We had a lazy day today, breakfast, followed by relaxing around the pool and the usual swim.

Later we had dinner, again street food but this time not great. I must have spoken too soon, I'm not sure what it was, but it sure resembled pedigree chum. (Other dog foods are also available) LOL.

8th January

We spent the whole day today researching and booking our next move.

We have discovered on this trip that sometimes it seems to take forever organising the next destination, hours and hours surfing the Internet, making sure we can get from A-B, how we are going to travel, how long it will take, how much will it cost, what there is to see and do, and where we will stay?

Of course we have a rough itinerary, but some places are nicer than others. Our next move is usually based on all of the aforementioned.

9th –12th January

We didn't do much for the next few days, just sat around the pool mainly; secretly I was hoping to see the monitor lizard again.

We walked into town (over eight kilometres there and back), Lou brought some new sandals and we found a shop that had Wolf Blass wine on offer.

We had drinks on the balcony and played more Scrabble.

There is nowhere around here to sit in a bar for a drink, the town is strictly Muslim, but we are quite happy with our own company.

We listened to some more music, and listened to some football on the radio.

We went out for more delicious food, locally they are known as hawker food stalls, I know I go on a bit about food here, yet the places are anything but posh, and certainly not fine dining, most food is served on stained melamine plates then the bowls and chopsticks are 'washed up' in huge buckets, the dirty dishwater is then spilled out into the streets. They are addictive, almost every mouthful is an explosion of flavour. The Malay staple is nasi lemak; soft fluffy rice cooked with coconut cream with pandan leaf, fried crispy anchovies and toasted peanuts, served alone as a snack or as a main with fish/chicken/duck etc. It has amazing quality, textures and flavours.

It is often eaten by the natives in the morning, the workers need a hearty meal first thing, carbs, oils, protein and natural sugars keeps them full for the day.

Having stayed in the north and the south it is evident that Langkawi has some beautiful places to visit, but there are developments everywhere, so it may be a place to come back to in the future. Or visit now before it becomes invaded.

We are moving on tomorrow, next stop George Town, Penang, which is on the peninsula of mainland Malaysia.

13th January

The ferry took three hours, a smooth journey across to Penang, an island off the north-west coast of Malaysia, we arrived at 13:30.

Formerly known as Prince of Wales Island its capital, George Town, was founded by the British East India Company in 1786. It once served as the capital of the Straits Settlements and it became a regional centre for spice production as well as a bustling harbour during its heyday under British rule.

The Japanese briefly occupied Penang during WW2 before surrendering the colony to the British when the war ended.

Malaysia gained its independence from the British in 1957.

We found 'WOW Hotel' easily enough using Google maps, but it is so hot walking in the midday sun for over half an hour with our backpacks.

It turns out that when we arrived there were two other couples that had been on our ferry. We could have all had a ride in a cab together!

The hotel is nice enough, new and modern in design, but our room is so small again, there is no balcony and only a tiny window.

However, its redemption lies in the lovely two rooftop jacuzzis.

We went straight out for a walk and we found Gearing Plaza shopping centre which had a Sephora.

It sells my favourite lip gloss, so I brought four (that's all they had) which should last me a while.

Oddly we stopped off for dinner before heading back, TGIF!

This evening I spoke to Mum and Dad, Dale, Ju and Michelle.

I am feeling better now about missing home.

14th January

A sightseeing day today.

First of all, we walked to take a look at the jetty houses on stilts. Originally, they were used for loading and unloading goods from the sampans and had no water or electricity, but development has seen them transformed into communal houses. Interestingly none of the residents pay any tax as they do not live on the land.

Next it was off to The Queen Victoria Clock house (aka Jubilee Clock Tower) which was built to commemorate her Silver Jubilee, and is a testament to Penang's royal connections. It stands sixty feet high, each foot represents a year of her reign, and the six steps us to the memorial represents the decades.

Then it was off to Fort Cornwallis, a preserved eighteenth century English fortress, unfortunately our look at the fortress was hindered by currently undergoing renovation and an archaeological dig project.

Just up the road we passed the Cenotaph, City Hall and Town Hall, located at Esplanade Road overlooking a historic parade ground, all had the most beautiful Edwardian architecture reflecting years of British presence on the Island.

Penang has one of the largest collections of pre-war buildings in south-east Asia.

St George's Church was next on the list. The oldest Anglican church in the Far East and an UNESCO World Heritage Site.

I chatted to a church warden there called Jacinta after spotting some cross-stitched prayer stools. They are the same as my dad has made for our local church back home, St Mary Magdalene.

Jacinta told me that only a few women were attracted to this skill, and it was also difficult for them to get the resources such as wool. She was amazed, very interested and impressed when I told her about Dad. I gave them a nice donation.

On the way back we saw another monitor lizard, not as big as the one we had seen around the pool, it was eating a fish on the rocks. They are really ugly and very terrifying.

15th January

We got up for breakfast but it was a total disaster! There was only one man on duty, taking orders, doing the 'cooking' and clearing the tables. The food was a mish-mash of Western and Asian food and it was all cold. I felt sorry for him.

Anyhow, we caught the local bus to go and see Chaiya Mangalaram Buddhist Temple. Its main attraction is the reclining Buddha statue. Its length and height (108 feet x 32 feet), make it the largest in Malaysia.

There are also about 30,000 Buddhist images in the hall representing Cambodia, Ceylon, Vietnam, Japan, Laos and Thailand.

I learnt that my Chinese year of birth is the Rabbit.

Rabbits have good social relationships, are popular, gentle, elegant, skilful, kind, patient, responsible and considerate. Albert Einstein, Michael Jordan, David Beckham and Lionel Messi are also rabbits!

Lou is the Ox and Dale is Monkey.

It is a really lovely place, kind of strange because it made me feel really calm and spiritual, like peace was in the air. There was an inscription on the wall, which read:

'Today is a very special day, because it will only happen once, these breaths will only happen once, it's a special day.'

We lit a lotus-shaped candle and said hi to loved ones who are no longer with us.

Later, on the way home we stopped off for some street food, crispy pork, mixed vegetable noodles and sticky rice — again mouth-wateringly luscious.

Apparently, Penang is one of the world's most popular foodies' destination, Assam laksa (noodles and fish broth) and char kota teow (flat noodles and prawns) are specialities.

16th January

Up early today, travelling on again by bus to Kuala Lumpur, (or KL as it is commonly known) a journey of 294 kilometres and five hours.

George Town is connected to mainland Malaysia by Penang Bridge, a 13.5 kilometres long structure modelled on San Francisco's Golden Gate. It crosses the straits of Malacca and is amazing. Prior to its construction the only way to get from Penang to the mainland was by ferry.

The only thing to see for virtually the entire journey was palm tree plantations, miles and miles and miles of them, as far as the eyes could see. Palm oil is one of Malaysia's main exports, along with coconut oil and petroleum.

We arrived in Kuala Lumpur central station and got on the monorail. About five stops later and a short walk we found our studio apartment — Mercu Summer Suite.

KL is a modern metropolis/mini-Manhattan, and the capital of Malaysia. It is recognised as one of the most vibrant cities in Asia.

We have a balcony, not much of a view, but on the seventeenth floor and fairly spacious, and there is also a gym and a pool here.

The plan was to go straight out and explore, but then the heavens opened and it absolutely poured with rain.

Luckily the complex had a small supermarket in the lobby so we went to buy some food. A bit of a concoction of spaghetti, saveloy, fresh tomato, onion and mushrooms all mushed in together, but surprisingly very tasty.

17th January

My favourite again today, the Kuala Lumpur hop-on and hop-off bus tour.

The ticket cost fifty-five ringett each (around £11) and gave us access to two separate routes, one being the city tour and the other the garden tour.

There are quite a few attractions to see in Kuala Lumpur. The city abounds with landscaped parks, heritage sites, pre-war buildings, places of worship, the world's largest free flight aviary, Chinatown, little India and architectural marvels such as the Petronas twin towers and the KL telecommunications tower.

We did both tours today.

The Petronas Twin Towers are very majestic. A gleaming structure of steel and glass, and the centrepiece of KLCC which houses a shopping mall, hotels, a park with dancing fountain, and a convention centre. You can go up inside and visit the skybridge and the viewing deck

We are both feeling really tired today, so last night's leftover pasta for tea followed by an early night.

18th January

We hopped back on the bus today (24hr ticket) to go to China Town. This place is crazy, buzzing with stalls and shops full of tut and 'real fake' sports gear, electricals, mobile phones, and handbags etc.

There are also lots of hawker food stalls in Petaling Street selling all kinds of the weirdest dishes such as fresh frog porridge, raw fish porridge and crispy innards porridge. No thanks.

We did buy a gizmo for the camera on the iPhone which magnifies and allows a wider shot, it's pretty cool.

Back on the bus to the Petronas Towers where we popped in to the shopping mall, they advertised a Marks and Spencer — we found it!

Yes, they had wine, buy one and get 50% off a second, so we brought some along with jacket potatoes, a cooked chicken, some sirloin steaks and a lovely fresh mixed salad from the salad bar.

19th January

We had a lazy day today and stayed in researching the internet, booking the next destination — Melaka.

We watched *Maleficent 2* on Netflix, and really enjoyed it.

We ate the steak, salad and jacket potatoes.

I spoke to Mum and Dad, Dale and Ju. They are all doing fine.

20th January

A trip out for the day today to see the famous Batu (rock) Caves.

It is set in a limestone hill and has three caverns; it is one of the most popular Hindu shrines outside of India.

At the entrance there is a huge statue of Lord Murugan the Hindu god of war, which is amazing, standing forty-three metres tall it is said to be the largest in the world.

To enter the caves, you have to climb 272 steps, not easy in the blistering heat, whilst being wary of the numerous long-tailed macaques that live on the cliff face.

Once inside there are several Hindu shrines, unfortunately the main one is closed today in preparation for a massive pilgrimage which happens on Chinese New Year; apparently over one million Hindus will visit to give offerings to the gods.

Then it was off to a batik silk scarf making demonstration. Fascinating. We watched as hot wax was applied to the silk to make the pattern using a tjanting tool, then dye is dropped onto the fabric, the wax acts as a barrier for the dye, then once the pattern is complete the wax is then melted off, finally fabric is then steamed to seal in the design.

Next stop was the Royal Selangor Visitor Centre, founded by a young pewter smith named Yong Koon, and now makers of the world's finest pewter.

We explored events of the tin rush in colonial Malaya in 1885, and learnt of the secrets of the pewtersmithing with demonstrations from the actual workers in the factory, handled a lucky teapot which saved a soldier in the trenches, viewed some bespoke trophies commemorating victorious moments of sporting events and stood beside the world's largest pewter tankard.

I wasn't really expecting much but this place was awesome.

We then headed home, washed and changed and walked to the Petronas Twin Towers to watch the fountains dancing to music and lights, it was really pretty.

We tried to get tickets to go up the towers in the morning, but unfortunately it was sold out, again we didn't even think to pre-book (like Alhambra Palace) and now we have missed out, never mind.

We stocked up on wine in M&S before stopping off at a nearby hawkers' market for dinner.

21st January

Moved on again today, travelled south down the west coast, 145 kilometres to Melaka by bus which took just under two hours. It's our penultimate stop in Malaysia.

We had to get a local bus from the main terminal to final destination but the bus driver was very helpful, and after a short walk, we found the apartment easily enough.

Were on the thirty-ninth floor this time, with great views right across the city, we can also see the sea!

After settling in we went for a short walk around the

block.

We stopped off at a local restaurant for dinner, sweet and sour pork balls, noodle soup, fried vegetable bean sprouts, special roasted spring chicken and steamed rice.

Yummy.

22nd January

Feeling exhausted today so we lounged around most of the day. We did go to the gym, and then went shopping for some provisions.

Lou cooked dinner and we watched a few films on Netflix.

23rd January

A very busy day today.

Melaka offers a rich mixture of history, culture and natural beauty.

It is located on the Malacca Straits, and was once an important trading empire.

It is compact, easy to navigate and a picturesque little town, an excellent window in to the history of the Portuguese, Dutch and British rule as well as being a quiet and very charming place to visit.

Remnants of its illustrious past can be seen everywhere.

We visited Red Square (Dutch) with its church and clock tower, and the Queen Victoria Fountain (British) which stands very elegantly, it is one of the last remaining traces of Britain's colonial era in Malaysia.

We also went up a very steep hill to St Paul's church; (Portuguese) built in 1521 by a nobleman giving thanks to the

Virgin Mary for saving his life during a storm at sea.

It is in ruins now and has no roof, but it's still interesting with lots of engraved burial stones. The tomb stones of five members of one family are there, they all died within twenty days of each other during the diphtheria epidemic of 1756.

The views from the hills are amazing.

We then went to the Proclamation of Independence Memorial — an old colonial mansion that houses permanent exhibits, photographs and manuscripts celebrating Malaysia's independence on 31st August 1957.

Jonker walk next, the Chinatown street of Melaka. It was once renowned for its antiques, and there are still some emporiums left, but now there are more clothing and craft outlets, with tasty hawker stalls in between.

There is not much going on today, but it is supposedly much livelier at night and at the weekend.

We did see some vibrant, elaborate, vivid and multicoloured dragon dancing costumes being prepared for the street parties for the Chinese New Year.

On the way home we stopped off at Kampung Kling Mosque, it was ancient, a historic mosque with ornate Asian, Portuguese- and Dutch-inspired architecture.

A lady spotted me taking a peek. The next thing I knew, I was dressed in a Muslim outfit, taken inside and given a guided tour.

The ablution fountain was beautiful, as was the graveyard, I asked the guide why all the headstones were painted white and she told me that it was because Allah is the light of the heavens and earth.

We have walked so far, my watch tells me 8.5 miles, but it's been a really good day, we ate the leftover pasta for dinner and watched a film. I had a long soak in the bath (which has a window overlooking out across the skyline). My legs feel like lead!

24th January
Today would have been Bill's birthday.

We decided to head to the post office in town to post some maps, receipts and my diaries home. I don't want to get rid of anything but they weigh quite a lot now and I am having to carry them around in my backpack, so after a swim and gym session we jumped on the free shuttle bus into town… just as we got to the door, they put up the closed sign, so we stayed on the shuttle bus and went back to the apartment, I couldn't carry the parcel around with me all evening!

It's Chinese New Year's Eve here today, so we treated ourselves to a river cruise.

It only took about forty-five minutes but it was delightful. We saw some vibrant and intricate street art, colourful bridges and were given some historical facts. The sun was just setting on the return journey and all the twinkling lights looked really pretty.

Jonker Street was very quiet this evening but it is NYE, maybe many locals are at home with their families, so we decided to grab something to eat and head back to our apartment armed with fizz to help them celebrate!

Wow, we sat on the balcony to watch the night unfold, and boy, oh boy… the most amazing fireworks we have ever seen, which went on almost all night long.

25th January

Gong hei fat choi! It's the year of the Rat.

Pool and gym for us today, trying to get fitter and slimmer LOL.

Later we had a walk to the Portuguese settlement, locally referred to as 'Little Lisbon'. They speak Cristao here, a dialect of Portuguese from sixteenth to seventeenth centuries.

The square is a culmination of colourful and splendid Portuguese custom during festivals and celebrations, but all year round it is famous for its restaurants serving spicy seafood dishes, and cultural performances where the dancers dress in traditional costume.

Tonight we were not disappointed; we ate the most delicious prawn tempura, sweet and sour chicken, beef and bean shoots and steamed rice, and were entertained by a traditional lion dance where live performers mimicked lion movements in costume, to the music of a beating drum, symbols and gongs to bring good luck and fortune.

Fascinating — until they pulled the claws from two very large live crabs!

There were lots more fireworks tonight too, and firecrackers absolutely everywhere.

26th January

It's our great nephew Finley's birthday today.

So, we stayed in all day today as we had a lot to sort out for the next leg of our journey (we're off to the Singapore next).

It's incredible how much 'screen time' you can spend surfing the Internet, we have both been on our tablet and phone all day.

We finally decided on everything — flights, buses, hotels etc at seven p.m. Exhausted, and with a headache from wearing reading glasses for the entire day we popped to the 'Porridge Restaurant' across the road for dinner.

Once again, scrumptious deep-fried crispy pork with sesame — cooked in Marmite! Fragrant jasmine rice and noodles with fresh oysters.

Sat on the balcony for the rest of the evening watching yet more fireworks lighting up the sky in a kaleidoscope array of colours.

I spoke to Ju, and twin John. Dale was busy with his friend Dawn so said he'd call us tomorrow.

27th January

After breakfast on the balcony, we set off into town in an attempt to post my parcel back home before our flight to Philippines, only to find that it was shut today due to the Chinese NY celebrations — whoops, didn't even think of that!

On the way back we saw a glass tank with live bullfrogs inside. You chose the one you liked the look of, then had it cooked any way you like; steamed, deep fried, grilled or boiled with garlic, ginger, onion, or chilli — I'll try most things, but this one I'm afraid doesn't appeal one little bit.

28th January

Travelling on today, so up and out early, it's our last stop after five weeks in Malaysia. The bus to Johor Bahru took us down the west coast to the most southern tip, 219 kilometres with a journey time of almost three hours, a lovely ride though along the coast line.

Johor Bahru sits at the strategic location between Kuala Lumpur and Singapore, on the southern tip of the Malay Peninsula, and with a causeway across the straits of Johor connecting it to Singapore, it is a gateway for exploration.

Traditionally it was a fertile site for agriculture, manufacturing and food processing but in recent years Johor's economy has increasingly come to rely on tourism and retail. The city is one of the fastest growing municipalities in Malaysia with high rise condominiums everywhere.

It's quite a good set up with most of the Airbnb we have booked. You are given a location to collect the keys, and a code to access, then you just let yourself in, it really is as easy as that.

Finding the apartment was straightforward enough again, this time on the twenty-ninth floor, but not much to look at, just a view of other apartment blocks. Cute though, and very modern, I think most of these places are owned by investors, it seems popular here.

We went for a walk, 14,512 steps to be precise (so my watch tells me) and stocked up at the local supermarket.

I cooked a Thai chicken curry for tea but it was really not nice! In fact, it was pretty damn awful... and I nearly set the place on fire. Maybe we will still go to the hawkers for dinner.

29th January

We decided to go to the train station to book our ticket to Singapore. It recommends that you do this in advance, as there is only certain number available each day. We booked it okay, in two days' time.

We had a little mooch around the shopping mall, it's enormous, six storeys high, and spotted an M&S; it was tiny though, and only sold biscuits/crisps etc.

On the way out of the mall we stumbled across a beautiful Hindu temple.

Arulmigu Rajamariamman Devasthanam, a typical south Indian Hindu temple smack bam in the middle of Johor Bahru.

There is a large and colourful Gopuram above the front door (a monumental entrance tower with ornate carvings).

It was established in 1911 by a community leader in Johor who wanted a place of worship for Hindus; it was built on a piece of land donated by the Sultan.

We were invited in by an employee at the gate, there was a ceremony going on, so after taking our shoes off and washing our feet we stood and watched, then we were blessed by a Hindu devotee.

It was interesting, the relief sculptures included explanatory notes about what was being depicted, and the sculptures of Hindu deities had their names printed below so we were able to identify the characters.

Anyone can practice Hinduism, there is no conversion required; it is the oldest religion in the world and one of the main glories of Hinduism is the wide range of divine manifestations it has conceived, the deities, who all represent the same Brahman, are pathways to salvation, but there is only one God.

After the temple we walked down to the old town but the heavens opened and it started tipping it down.

Lou took shelter in a barber shop and had his haircut, we then went into a small café, Lou had egg and chips, and we both had a coffee.

When it finally stopped raining, we ventured back to the apartment, I managed to post my parcel home; the cheapest way was by sea, but they said it could take up to four months!

We walked a lot again today, 14,571 steps.

Lou felt tired so he stayed in the apartment while I went for a swim.

I'm ashamed to say it but we had a Burger King takeaway for dinner.

30th January

Today it was off to find Arulmigu Sri Rajakaliamman Glass temple, reportedly the oldest Hindu temple in Malaysia.

Not easy to find, and we had to ask for directions quite a few times, but we made it.

From the outside it didn't look much, it had the typical south Indian-style Gopuram again, but once inside — wow.

The entire interior of this temple is completely covered in over 300,000 pieces of reflecting or coloured glass mosaic.

Founded on gifted land donated by the Sultan, it was a small shrine originally dedicated to goddess Kali.

It was not built with a glass interior, but during a trip to Bangkok by the temple chairman and chief priest, guru Bhagawan Sittar, he was inspired after catching a glint of light in a *Wat*.

The guru decided to cover his temple in glass to attract more devotees and visitors.

In 2008 work began; the glass tiles are from Thailand, Belgium, Nepal and Japan.

The gleaming makeover took two years to complete and

was funded partially by public donations.

With crystal chandeliers which light up the multicoloured glass mosaic the reflections make a dazzling festival of shimmering light throughout the sanctuary.

Besides its many Hindu deities the glass temple also displays statues of other faiths such as Jesus Christ and Mother Teresa.

An awesome temple, simply stunning.

It is listed in the 'Lonely Planet' secret marvels of the world.

I had a bag of clothes with me that I wanted to donate, so I asked the devotee if he knew of any refuge nearby. He gladly accepted the clothing for a women's refuge.

Chapter 10
Singapore

31st January

We checked out of our apartment this morning and walked across the pedestrian walkway to the train station.

I gave the last of our Malaysian ringgits to a homeless lady before getting onto the train to Singapore; a journey which took just four minutes!

On arrival at the train station, we were temperature checked before being allowed entry. There is news about a virus that may be spreading across the Far East, and Singapore is taking extra precautions.

Once in Singapore, we had to go through passport control and again we went through a heat sensor. There were medical staff present that were ready to isolate anyone who gave a reading above 37.5.

We travelled by local bus to the main train station, and then by train to our location.

Q Loft hotel seemed okay but the room they put us in was appalling, not at all what we had booked (again).

It was tiny with no space at all; you had to climb over the bed to reach the door to the 'balcony' and then step over a ledge to access it.

I went to reception to complain but they informed me that

there were no other rooms available.

I was really cross, so I went back to the room and searched on Booking.com... guess what? I found the room we had actually booked advertised as available.

i-Pad in hand I marched straight back down to reception to show them my findings. Red-faced and apologetic they moved us into the room. Still not brilliant but 100% better than the one we were in... I'm getting quite good at not being taken the P out of. Us Brits do not complain enough sometimes.

We decided to go straight out for a walk; Chinatown is just up the road, not far at all.

Then we headed to Merlion Square to see the fountain, Marina Bay Sands Hotel and its famous sky deck, and the Helix Bridge (aka DNA bridge).

The Merlion (meaning sea lion) Fountain is the first thing you see; it symbolises Singapore's humble beginnings as a fishing village and is now an iconic emblem for the Singapore tourist board. With its lion's head and fish body it sits on the mouth of the river to welcome visitors; its spurting water is seen as spitting money into a deep ocean of money — the Singapore River.

We then walked around the bay and over the Helix Bridge, so called because it is shaped like a double helix, or strand of DNA.

It joins the foreshore promenade with the bay, and is an incredible pedestrian bridge made of steel.

We sat for a while, and had a drink before heading off to the Singapore Flyer, basically a big wheel just like the London

Eye, and to see the F1 pit lane and track.

There was supposed to be a carnival on, but we couldn't find it, so we decided to head back to Chinatown as we felt hungry and tired.

On the way home we saw and heard several supercars passing by, and then we noticed loads of photographers standing on the kerb. There was a Lamborghini owner's convention taking place at the Mandarin Oriental Hotel.

So much walking again today, yes, my watch confirms, 23,270 steps, no wonder my legs ache!

We will do the red bus tour tomorrow.

1st February

Off to Chinatown first thing to get a ticket for the open-top bus tour, I cannot walk too much today as my whole body aches.

They have four different routes, red, yellow, green and blue, so we decided to smash it and try and do all four (average time length is six hours in total).

Well, we managed it, we have seen all of the sights, some repeated but hey-ho, we have been to Chinatown, Little India, Raffles Hospital, Raffles Hotel, the majestic Fullerton Hotel, Clarke Quay, the cricket ground, Parliament House, several shopping malls, Marina Bay Sands, Merlion Fountain, and the Singapore Flyer.

Singapore really is an incredible place, here are some fascinating facts that we learnt today:

- It is a new city but it still retains its colonial architecture with its balconies and balustrades built by the British in the nineteenth century.

- It gained its Independence from Britain in the 1960s.
- Spitting, smoking, drinking alcohol in public, jay walking, chewing gum, littering and forgetting to flush the loo are all illegal, and you can be arrested if caught doing any of the above.
- Surprisingly, its first spoken language is English, followed by Malay.
- It has over 5.5 million inhabitants.
- Singapore translates to 'Lion City'.
- It is only twenty-five kilometres by forty-three kilometres.
- National service is mandatory at the age of eighteen years, your service is for two years but you can be called up at any time until the age of fifty.
- $600 million a year is made in profit purely from medical tourism alone.
- Its national library holds nine million books.
- Reclaimed land along the shore increased its acreage by 25% adding an additional three kilometres to the city using sand imported from the Middle East.
- Sir Thomas Raffles was a British lieutenant who landed in Singapore in 1819. It was he who recognised the immense potential of the swamp-covered island and he helped to negotiate a treaty with the local rulers to establish modern Singapore.
- Last but not least, it is the birthplace of the Singapore sling!

Definitely recommended for the 'Book-it' list!

After such a busy day we decided to stay out and watch the light show at Marina Bay Sands which takes place every evening across the bay.

We sat in a bar opposite to watch and had some wine — it's much more expensive here, probably like London prices, two glasses of wine were £18. Never mind, we've earned it today.

On the way home we suddenly heard all this commotion, firecrackers and saw fireworks and when we turned the street corner there was a traditional wicker dragon dance in progress.

The difference between a lion dance and a dragon dance is that a lion dance has two performers, inside a silk lion costume and a dragon dance has ten to fifteen performers with a twenty-five foot long dragon controlled with long poles.

The whole street was out partying, and there were hundreds of incense sticks being waved, it was so loud and so colourful, as well as being very entertaining.

We have had a really good day today.

2nd February

Lou said that he didn't want to walk far today as he felt too tired… and guess what? we have managed a mammoth, almost record breaking 31.105 steps — that is thirteen miles, yes thirteen miles.

First, we visited a couple of (crappy) shopping malls, and then we went to an outdoor market. After that we went to Clarke Quay, which was lovely, we saw the statue of Lieutenant Thomas Raffles and next to him that of Sang Nila Utama, who was his interpreter.

Then we walked to Marina Bay Sands and through to 'The

Gardens by the Bay'.

Now what an incredible place this is; acres and acres of plant life from around the world, towering vertical gardens, super-trees, topiaries, sculptures, florist artistry, a cloud forest, a flower dome, a kingfisher lake and a dragonfly lake.

We learnt about the intricacies of plant life and immersed ourselves in the sights and sounds of the gardens; the air is so clean and fresh with the waft of scents from the orchids and sweet white blooms of the Daphne tree — it really does smell like pineapple!

Truly an outdoor treasure.

Whilst in the area it would be madness if we hadn't taken the opportunity to go up to the Marina Bay Sands SkyPark. I had seen images of this place before, and not long ago I watched a TV programme where couples had to race across the world on a limited budget only travelling over land — this was their final destination and whoever got here first won a monetary prize — I never thought that one day I would be here too!

Now this really is a massive feat of engineering. It sits perched on top of the three-pronged Marina Bay Sands Hotel (originally inspired by a deck of cards), is on the fifty-sixth floor and 200 metres above sea level.

It is a wooden decked area shaped like a cruise liner, with a cantilevered platform, and nothing but a sheet of glass and a few wires between you and the panoramic view across Singapore. We could see the super-tree grove and had a bird's eye view of the rest of the park we had just visited, as well as the Singapore Strait and all the shipping lanes that have built Singapore's rich multicultural history.

There is an infinity pool up there too; sadly, it is reserved for hotel guests only.

Guess what? More walking, this time to visit Raffles.

How very charming to plunge ourselves into this splendour, and as discerning travellers we have every right.

You cannot possibly visit Singapore without having a Singapore sling, and it just has to be from here — its birthplace!

The hotel opened in 1887 and is one of the few remaining great nineteenth century hotels in the world.

We sat in the (recently renovated) old school colonial 'Long Bar'.

Rudyard Kipling, Ernest Hemingway and Alfred Hitchcock all once favoured this watering hole.

Inspired by Malayan life in the twenties it has contemporary plantation motifs, palm tree leaf fans, woven rattan chairs, dark mahogany timbers, deep rich colours and lush greenery; it immediately transports you somewhere tropical.

I watched as the cocktail waiter prepared my drink — gin, pineapple juice, lime juice, curaçao, grenadine and cherry liquor. I sat and enjoyed every last sip of it whilst eating monkey nuts and throwing the shells on the floor!

Traditionally nutshells were used to keep the wooden floors clean and free from dirt and dust, they made it easier to sweep the floor with a broom — Raffles Long Bar has kept this tradition.

Yes, it's pricey at $35, but so are most indulgent things, eh? It felt quite wonderful.

On the walk back to the hotel we decided to go back to the Gardens by the Bay and watch the free evening light show; I'm so glad we did, it was awesome by day and even more spectacular at night; a garden rhapsody, a dazzling and magnificent sight of lights and music in the super-tree grove.

Finally, back to Chinatown for street dinner of duck, noodles, and hainanese chicken rice.

A brilliant day but we now feel properly knackered.

3rd February

It's our last day in Singapore, and we have suitably exhausted it, there is only one more thing left to do and that is to visit Sentosa — the state of fun!

After a short ride on the train to the harbour we walked over the foot link bridge to the island famous for its tropical beaches, luxurious hotels and theme park attraction Universal Studios.

We didn't bother with Universal Studios, we've been to numerous theme parks over the years, instead we went to take a look at Siloso Beach, the most south-eastern point in continental Asia.

Amazingly we saw another monitor lizard!

There is quite a lot to do here, as well as Universal Studios they have an underwater world, a cable car, a waterpark, a zip-line, a simulated freefall wind tunnel, a monorail, spas, lush rainforests, a butterfly and insect kingdom and resort-style hotels.

There is also a luge ride, so that's what we chose!

To get to the start of the luge track we had to ascend up

the mountain on a ski chairlift which gave us a nice scenic view of the island, Singapore city skyline and the South China Sea. Then we chose the 'dragon trail' to descend the hairpin corners, exhilarating tunnels and exciting downhill slopes.

I've always wanted to have a go for real, on the ice, they say it is one of the most dangerous sports in the Olympic Games with speeds up to ninety miles per hour, whilst sliding down face up and feet first — I quite fancied myself as an Olympic athlete in my youth.

Chapter 11
Philippines

Up and out early, to Changi Airport, one of the largest transportation hubs in Asia, and what a striking place. It's no surprise that it is voted the world's best airport. It has a butterfly garden, a cactus garden, a cinema and even a swimming pool.

Super clean and super-efficient; everything is automated, self-check-in, your baggage labels are dispensed, you tag your own bags, scan the barcode then place them on the baggage belt and off they go — just like that — easy peasy.

Our flight wasn't until four p.m. so we had lunch and relaxed in the cactus garden before flying 2394 kilometres to Manila.

We settled into our apartment, (again there are patrols on the main entrance checking everyone's temperature) and I sent a text message to our friend, Shaggy (aka Nick).

He lives here in Manila and is the executive chef at the Sofitel Plaza, an old schoolfriend that I have known since an infant, I probably haven't seen him for around ten years now, but we are meeting up tomorrow.

So exciting as he has a new wife, Isha, and a baby, Jack!

5th February

We walked to the Mall of Asia, a large shopping centre in Pasay where we have arranged to meet Shaggy et al.

Crikey, it's so lovely to see him, and to meet Isha and little cutie Jack.

We ended up sitting, chatting, laughing and drinking all day, I really don't know where the day went, but before we knew it, it was ten thirty at night.

We had to get a taxi home, Lou had his 'Mr Spaghetti' legs on again.

I rang Ju for a chat before collapsing to bed, she is doing fine.

6th February

Bizarrely, the apartment we are staying in only takes cash payment, so we had to walk into town to find a cashpoint.

On the way we saw Chinatown, the basilica and Rizal Park.

Poverty incidence amongst families here is more than 20% and average unemployment in depressed settlements located in Manila is nearly fifty per cent.

Although the Manila development authority has adopted programmes and projects for the rehabilitation and development of slums and blighted areas, waste, sewage and shelter it is evident that basic services are a big concern.

It reminds me of some places in India, hazardous unsanitary shanty towns and slums located next door to affluent wealth and opulence.

Had some lovely food on the way home, noodles, rice and pork adobo (pork marinated in vinegar/soy sauce/spices and garlic). Yummy.

My watch tells me we have done a lot of walking again today — 20,064 steps to be precise.

7th February

Went to Greenbelt (another large shopping mall) to meet Shaggy, Isha and Jack.

It pelted down with rain all day.

8th February

We have arranged to go and spend today at the Sofitel Plaza, as executive chef, Shaggy's guests for the day.

It is still raining on and off, and Shaggy is duty manager of the day, so he couldn't join us until the evening for dinner.

Lou and I sat around the pool, had some cocktails with lunch, watched a wedding and a glossy magazine photo shoot on the lawn and chilled out.

The Spiral Restaurant awaited — A foodie's heaven, this place redefines interactive dining with a gastronomic voyage of the world's finest dishes.

It has twenty-one ateliers (or workshops where the master creates) Filipino, Asian, Korean, Thai, Chinese, Peking, Japanese, Indian, Italian, French, Western, seafood, sushi, sashimi, rotisserie, churrasco, salads, appetisers, la patisserie, chocolaterie, and la boulangerie, all offering an enticing journey of taste delivered by its expert culinary artisans.

Who knew where to start? So the executive sous chef, helped us with our menu.

First, we were served an array of mixed sushi, sashimi, seafoods (oyster, salmon, prawn and crab) and foie gras which would have been enough delight for anyone.

Then we had a selection of meats, rack of lamb, rib eye steak etc. with vegetables, followed by tiny tasters of Indian and Thai dishes (now completely stuffed) but left just enough room for a bite-sized éclair and a small selection of cheeses.

I don't know how but Isha took Jack to bed whilst Shaggy, Lou and I sat in the bar drinking until three a.m.

9th February

We were not seeing Shaggy today so we had a lie-in and did some more research into next move, Boracay. It's a long way to travel by bus and ferry, but we decided it would be fun.

Later in the day we walked to find the bus station where we would be leaving from, and it's not very far at all so that's okay.

The streets are full of jeepneys, the most popular form of transport in the Philippines. They're great fun, overcrowded, kitsch, battered and iconic. There is a push to phase them out to ease congestion, but I can't help thinking it would be a shame not to see the customised fast and furious vehicles with their painted slogans, elaborate fonts and blaring music.

We picked up some food at a local takeaway. I don't know why but the street food doesn't look as deliciously appetising here, most of the stalls look grubby and have plastic bowls with filthy water in to wash their utensils/plates etc. and I've read that people do actually get sick from fermentation, which is common here.

They do have some weird foods though such as 'pork blood stew' and 'meat stewed in liver'.

Had a game of Scrabble tonight, I phoned Dale — no answer, but did manage to speak to Jeff and Mal and John and Keeley, which was lovely.

For some reason I can't get through to Gary and Mandy, they're not on WhatsApp so I have tried to call regularly, but I can never get connected?

10th February

We had another lie-in today and didn't get up until eleven thirty!

Lou did some washing and then we researched Ho Chi Min City formerly known as Saigon, we're so looking forward to going there.

We headed over to Sofitel Plaza for one last time to see Shaggy, Isha and Jack, just sitting in their apartment chatting, playing and drinking wine.

On the walk back home, we stopped off at 'Jollibee' for a takeaway.

It's a chain of fast-food restaurants out here, a bit like when we have McDonalds and Burger King back home.

Their signature dish is crispyliscious, juicylicious chicken served with rice and gravy (a bit like KFC) but they also serve 'Yum Burgers', 'Jolly Spaghetti' and 'palabok' (a traditional Filipino noodle dish covered in garlic sauce, crushed pork rind, shrimp and egg).

It was surprisingly delicious.

We packed up ready for our move tomorrow and went to bed.

11th February

We had a very long day/night ahead.

First, we had to walk to the bus terminal, then travel ninety-five kilometres on the bus to the ferry port in Batangas.

Our ferry wasn't until nine p.m., so we hung around for hours.

Lou went for a walk to get us some food, Jollibee again as it was the only thing available, and everything else was street food.

Waiting for the ferry was pretty dire, once through security there was nothing to do, just sit on top of each other; the departure lounge was absolutely packed.

Well, after standing single file in a line and sniffed by the drug/bomb sniffer dogs, then a pat down for every individual, we finally boarded the overnight ferry very late and set off over two hours behind schedule.

The ferry was an experience to say the least. There was a mad rush on as everyone made their way to the sleeping deck. It was a bit like one massive dormitory of bunk beds, two on the top bunk and two on the bottom bunk, rows and rows of them!

We managed to secure our bunk, both on the bottom row, next to each other on the corner, which I was glad about.

We settled down, drank some wine and ate our chicken and tried to get our heads down about midnight.

It didn't last long and we gave up trying to sleep at around four a.m.

Luckily there were showers on board, so we freshened up, changed our clothes and had some coffee.

12th February

Last night's 336 kilometres journey by ferry, took ten and a half hours, before we finally arrived in Caticlan at eight a.m.

266

To get onto Boracay Island you have to take another short ferry of about five minutes, so like sheep we all followed one another.

The Philippines as a whole is an archipelagic country rich with natural resources such as nickel, gold, silver and has a population of over 100 million, but is still poor and classed as a third world country.

Boracay is a small island within the archipelago known for its super beaches. Shaggy recommended it to us as we really couldn't choose where else to visit, and it is also known for being one of the world's top destinations to relax.

However, they had to close the island completely only last year due to environmental violations so they could clean it up after rapid development and pollution threatened its idyllic shores.

First impressions of the island are a bit disappointing for me. Yes, the beach is lovely, like being in paradise, but look beyond that and it is evident that to 'fix' things here is going to take years.

The roads are virtually non-existent, all dug up in an attempt to lay new pipe work and sewers. There are half-started building work and construction everywhere, improper waste management and reports of coliform bacteria in the waters at the beachfront.

On top of that the island was badly hit by a typhoon over Christmas, where it was brutally battered by winds and rain.

We had to get a tricycle to our apartment as it is far north of the island and impossible to get to otherwise.

We checked in okay and the apartment is nice — it overlooks a golf course. Again, it's one of those new condominiums probably owned by an investor, but for some reason it absolutely stinks of mothballs!

We had a quick swim but are both very tired, so we went shopping for supplies in the City Mall.

It wasn't a huge mall, but it has the largest supermarket on the island and bizarrely it asks you to 'Please deposit your firearm here on entry'. There are security guards everywhere, all with guns, but that's okay, at least it makes you feel a little safer.

Lou cooked dinner and we watched a film *Deep Blue Sea* before going to bed.

13th February

It's Mum and her twin sister, Pat's, birthday today, they are eighty-nine years young.

We both felt like we had a good sleep, so after breakfast of boiled eggs and soldiers we got on the free shuttle bus to the local private beach. It wasn't far, but an awkward journey because it was down a very steep an S-bend hill.

The beach is very nice and postcard picturesque although there is 'work in progress' all around.

The sea is crystal clear but wavy.

We watched as a local man climbed the palm trees around us, he was barefoot and carrying just a cleaver. There is no health and safety rules out here!

He scurried up the trees, hung on with one hand whilst chopping with the other, no harness or hardhat required. Amazing skill, but he's probably been doing it for years.

After spending a few hours on the beach, the shuttle bus came to pick us up; we had had enough sun by then.

We had a quick dip in the pool before dinner, and then we

researched and made some notes on Vietnam and Cambodia.

Dale took Mum and Dad, and Ju and Michelle for lunch today at Smiths, a local fish restaurant back home, for Mum's birthday.

I tried to call them but the Internet connection was poor — I'll try again tomorrow.

14th–19th February

I have had to catch up with my diary today as I haven't really been bothered to write every day.

We have stayed in or around the apartment and to be honest it has not been the most enjoyable stay. It's our fault really; the place is too remote, and too difficult to get anywhere without relying on the shuttle bus.

We have cooked every night, mostly chicken with rice or noodles as the street food still looks rank and inedible.

In fact, the other day we witnessed the grossest thing being eaten at the roadside, we had heard about it but not seen it until now. I'll try and explain.

It's called *Balut* and is a commonly sold street food in the Philippines. A delicacy that has been a staple in Filipino culture for over 200 years.

Basically, it is a fertilized and developing duck egg embryo which has been incubated for anywhere between fourteen and twenty-one days. The egg foetus is then boiled or steamed alive in the shell and the partially developed embryo is eaten, still warm from the shell.

This means that you are eating a cooked developing baby duck that is just a week away from hatching; thus far the embryo has feathers and a beak!

No, thank you!

We mainly went to the pool and the private beach twice. Lou had a haircut and I decided to dye my now grey hair blond — except it went very dark brown within about five minutes!

We have spoken to Mum and Dad, Ju, Dale, Jeff, John, Bunny, Lolly and Duchess this week.

Off to the south of the island tomorrow.

19th February

There was a power cut this morning and obviously there is no Internet, but really weirdly, all of my messages have been deleted from my mailbox?

Panic set in, because everything I had stored, all the info regarding tickets for onward flights and hotel bookings, had disappeared! Luckily Lou's phone is synched with mine and his is still working.

The shuttle bus took us to the south of the island for our next stop, station two just by D'Mall.

We arrived at hotel 'Grand Boracay Resort', and it's really not grand at all.

Again, very disappointed with description and reviews we had read on Tripadvisor, Booking.com etc.

The hotel entry/reception area is dark and dim, and our room is so dark you can hardly see. The bed sheets are tatty and almost threadbare, the shower is grimy and the pool is filthy and full of fallen leaves and twigs. The pathway through is littered with garden rubbish and old discarded furniture and there are numerous stray cats!

We had to change rooms immediately as they stuck us in one upstairs with no balcony.

The saving grace was that it is right in the livelier part of the island and only two minutes' walk to the beach.

Basically, this area is divided into three stations (1/2/3) and in a nutshell you don't really notice any separation between these as you walk along. It originates from the times when boats brought tourists directly to the beach and these stations were where the boats moored. (All boats/ferries now go to a main harbour).

Station 1 has a wider beach and the water is shallow, it is relatively quiet.

Station 2 is in the middle or 'epicentre' and is busier with bars and restaurants. It also has D'Mall — a shopping area.

Station 3 is home to the more budget and backpacker hotels, it is greener and very quiet with only a handful of bars.

The whole length between them is only around two kilometres.

So, we went for a walk along the entire length and then had a look around D'Mall.

It is a small open-air mall with a street market vibe. Lots of tasty snack shacks, souvenirs, fruit and veg stalls, and smoothie pit stops.

We found a small delicatessen that sold nice cheeses/pâté and wine, so we brought some tasty titbits, and headed back to chill out before the evening.

We decided on Mexican for dinner as Lou really fancied fajitas.

A very bad choice. He got three very small tortillas, three very strange-looking (and tasting) dips, and a plate of 'sizzling chicken' which resembled canned dog meat.

I had sweet and sour chicken and steamed rice, which was

nice.

Note to self... don't attempt to have Mexican in the Philippines, no more restaurant 'Tres Amigos' for us!

Over the last few weeks, I have developed a new liking for dark rum, probably due to the fact that buying wine is difficult and expensive. My favourite is Sanson, from Thailand, it's aromatic with a mellow flavour, and it's nice in coffee too.

So, we sat on the balcony, drank rum and coke and played Scrabble.

Spoke to Dale this evening; he is very busy with a project to make ten canvases which will eventually all become one painting.

20th February

I had a terrible sleep last night. it felt like there was sand in the bed but on waking and closer inspection it looked like larvae/eggs! YUK!

I called the chief maid in to show her and she insisted it wasn't insect eggs but debris that had fallen from the old wooden dado rail on the wall above my head... I am not sure myself, we'll see. Anyway, I made her change the sheets and vacuum, I'll sleep down the other end of the bed tonight!

Breakfast was rank, a few bain maries with rice and noodles, scrambled egg (cold) and some sort of cabbage — toast it was then.

We had a walk to the other side of the island today, Bulabog Beach is a kite surfer's paradise, so we thought we'd take a look.

Because Boracay is sandwiched between land masses it does not produce waves that make surfboarding possible, but it's all-year-round temperatures and reliable winds makes it ideal for the sport.

Goodness me; we watched the men and women launching themselves into the sky, navigating the kite downwind and upwind whilst getting a full body workout. They were all harnessed in which I imagine must relieve the tremendous strain on the back and shoulders, but my, the strength they must have, and the alertness — of other surfers — twisting and turning whilst flying literally twenty/thirty metres above the coastline.

I've tried to water-ski once or twice; it ended up with embarrassment, discomfort and frustration, truly a test of patience and perseverance which ultimately finished up in failure!

The sand and the sea are beautiful here, we went for a walk at sunset, and then further on to Station 1 to see 'Willy's Rock', arguably the most photographed landmark on the island.

It's essentially a volcanic rock formation, a rock plateau standing in shallow water, with a shrine on top dedicated to the Virgin Mary.

Some say its shape resembles a battleship and the shrine is its mast. It does look quite dramatic in the sunset as is becomes a darkening silhouette in the failing light.

On the way back we mooched down D'Mall and to the D'Talipa seafood market.

The unique thing about this place is that you buy your fish and then take it to any restaurant where they will cook it for you for a minimal fee!

We found an authentic tiny restaurant; it only had twelve chairs, and sat down for dinner.

We chose barbeque pork belly, creamy Filipino chicken, rice and mixed vegetable noodles, it was so delicious, but we couldn't finish it all.

Rum and coke on the balcony with a game of Scrabble before bed — upside down tonight LOL.

21st February

Oh no, it was raining when we woke up today, and forecast all day, but still very warm.

Oh well, we decided to go for a walk to a famous snorkelling beach called Tambisaan Beach where they have beautiful coral and loads of tropical fish.

It was a fair walk; 3.7 kilometres to be exact, through the poverty-stricken streets and shanty towns where the locals live and work.

There is construction going on everywhere, half started or half finished, but the homes were just decimated corrugated iron and wooden shacks, a blighted area of settlements, improvised buildings lacking in basic sanitation, water, electricity and street drainage.

When we arrived at the beach there were no crystal-clear blue waters today, just a murky swirl, a light wind and rain! On a normal day this beach is docked with fishing boats, snorkelling boats and visitors lapping in its shallow waters.

We did get to see 'Crocodile Island', an uninhabited island so called because of its distinctive resemblance to the shape of said reptile.

Washed up along the shoreline there were some very vivid

red and blue coral, so I am certain that if we could have snorkelled today it would have been fabulous, never mind.

We walked back to the hotel, stopped off at the supermarket for provisions, rum and coke LOL, not much else to do when it's pouring with rain; luckily, we borrowed the umbrella that was in the wardrobe.

We sat on the balcony and had a Jollibee takeaway for dinner, drank rum and played Scrabble. I don't feel too guilty as we have walked 12,258 steps today.

We had to go to bed early as there was a power cut, complete darkness and of course the hotel didn't have a generator.

I did manage to speak to Ju and it's a good job really, I woke her up, she had slept through her alarm and is off to Cornwall in a few hours.

22nd February

It's Laura's thirtieth birthday today.

We woke up at 08:30, although I had been awake for quite some time in the night when the electric came back on at 04:30 — didn't bother with breakfast, why would we?

It's still cloudy today, but not raining.

We had a late brunch of pâté, cheese and crackers that we brought from the lovely deli and then went to the beach for a few hours; it was very hot when the sun came out.

23rd February

We lazed around all day today, getting ready for the long journey tomorrow.

We did go to the beach to watch the most gorgeous sunset and took some photos before having dinner and drinks before bed.

I have mixed feelings of Boracay.

Beachside is like paradise, white powdery silky sand, lined with palm trees, bars and restaurants, panoramic views, coral reefs and a diverse marine life.

Beyond that all you see is extreme poverty, destruction, pollution, raw sewage, poor infrastructure and unregulated illegal construction.

An ecological catastrophe that they are trying hard to repair. I wouldn't expect a full restoration for many years — definitely a work in progress.

24th February

A very long day travelling today!

We were up early for the short ferry from Boracay to the mainland and Caticlan Airport. What a shambles, absolutely no organisation whatsoever, there were people everywhere; we finally got through to departures (we had our temperatures checked again — several times) and waited for the flight to Manila where we had to hang around for eight hours until the connecting flight to Vietnam, Ho Chi Minh City (HCMC).

During our time in the airport terminal, we saw a young man holding a placard and a bouquet of flowers waiting for his girlfriend at the arrivals gate.

'I love you, will you marry me?' It said.

She said YES and the whole terminal erupted with cheers, clapping and congratulations. It was lovely.

They did have a baggage store, so we deposited our backpacks and went for a walk outside of the airport but there was not much to do, the local area had a number of huge and very expensive 'resort hotels' in amongst the slums.

We checked in for the flight to HCMC, and then went for dinner, pasta for me, fish and chips for Lou.

The plane left on time and we arrived at our destination after travelling 1,671 kilometres at 01:30.

We had booked an airport hotel for the night as we knew it would be too late to find our way to the city, so after a short walk, and lots of hassle from a local driver who kept following us, we arrived at 'The Airport Hotel' which was lovely.

It's three a.m. now, so off to bed for a few hours.

Chapter 12
Vietnam

Good Morning Vietnam

Sorry, I can't resist the famous quote from the brilliant Adrian Cronauer, a disc jockey in the film of the same name, working for the Armed Forces Radio Service, played by the late Robin Williams, one of the best improvisational comedians of all time.

It's so exciting to be here as we have a lot planned. Our friend Bunny will be joining us in two days' time, he was supposed to come and visit whilst we were in the Philippines, but circumstances changed and he rescheduled.

The breakfast at the Airport Hotel was lovely, poached eggs, toast and marmalade.

The staff there helped us with our onward journey this morning and told us what bus to catch.

It only took about twenty minutes; we were staying in District 4, Gold View apartments, another new condominium alongside the river that had shops, restaurants, a cinema, swimming pool and a gym.

We are on the twentieth floor, so have quite a view

overlooking the city. The apartment is big with two bedrooms, two bathrooms and a large open plan kitchen/diner/living area. There is also an ample balcony and a utility room with washing machine.

HCMC was formerly known as Saigon, it changed its name in honour of the revolutionary communist leader to celebrate the reunification of north and south at the end of the Vietnam War.

It has twenty-four districts in total, but the seven numbered districts are where you will find most of the city's cultural and historical attractions. District 1 is city central, and although we are a little way out it is easily walkable.

We are feeling tired so just settled in, did some washing, got some supplies from the supermarket and cooked dinner.

26th February

It's a beautiful day and very hot 33°c.

I had been told by Shaggy that it is easy to get Grab cabs here, (same as Uber) and really cheap, so I downloaded the app to try it out.

He was right, a ten-minute journey to Ben Thanh Market for £1:40.

What a great place, Ben Thanh Market is one of the earliest survivors in Saigon, built in 1914, it has a main clock tower and belfry. It is an iconic destination for both locals and tourists from all around the world.

It is a large rectangular structure of 13,000 square metres and serves as a historical site, a landmark, a rendezvous point and a background for beautiful photo opportunities.

The market and surrounding area are buzzing.

Everything that is commonly eaten or worn is available

here, vegetables, meat, fish, spices, sweets, nuts, clothing, hardware, and of course souvenirs.

It was great fun; we ended up at the street food area for lunch.

Banh Xeo pancakes for me, a delicious creamy rice batter and coconut cream pancake filled with prawns and beanshoots, rolled and served with a sweet chilli dip and fresh leaves. Oh my, my mouth is watering — it was simply delectable.

Lou had the famous *Banh Mi*, a French-Vietnamese hybrid baguette filled with homemade pate, cold cut meats and sour pickled vegetables.

We have already booked surprise trips to Mekong River and Cu Chi Tunnels while we are here, so we walked to make sure we knew where the meeting point is.

We also checked out the bus ticket and visa requirements for Cambodia.

On the way back to the apartment I spotted a party shop, so I brought a helium balloon to take to the airport tomorrow when we meet Bunny.

I got Lou to write 'Good Morning Vietnam' in Vietnamese on the balloon using Google translate — excited.

27th February

We got up well early this morning (05:30) to get to the airport and meet Bunny.

He arrived bang on time, he loved the balloon!

We took him back to the apartment on the local bus so he could see some of the streets and sights, and settled him in to his en-suite room.

After a couple of beers, he went for a catnap, so Lou and

I went for a walk to the local wet market.

Strange/weird/terrifying/fascinating/offensive/powerful/gross... but normal daily life for the locals.

There were women (mostly) gutting and scaling fish and butchering meat, there are tanks and bowls full of live fish thrusting their bodies using lateral movements of their muscles in a bid to escape and skinned-alive frogs, some desperately still breathing from the thorax/throat because they had their heads cut off.

Some stalls slaughtering live animal to order — chickens, fish, shellfish and others, a smorgasbord of illegal and legal wildlife trading appears to be flourishing here.

We quickly moved on to see Bui Vien Walking Street, a narrow walking promenade in District 1 city centre. It's packed with bars and restaurants and supposedly very lively at night.

There is no better place to grab a seat and a cold beer, and people watch so that's exactly what we did.

Bunny woke up early afternoon, so straight back out to Walking Street. I had read a review on TripAdvisor about a nice rooftop terrace bar for pre-dinner cocktails called Banana Mama so that's where we headed; a nice modern bar with great décor and chilled vibes, the views were amazing, the sun was just setting over the Saigon skyline, as was the 'Pink Explosion' cocktail.

We stopped off at a street food joint for a Vietnamese dinner; *Cao Lau* (rice noodles with roast pork) *Mi Quang* (yellow noodles with fish broth, chicken and roasted peanuts) and *Com tam* (broken rice).

28th February

We were up and out early today for a trip to the Cu Chi Tunnels. Lou and I booked it a few days ago, VIP on a speedboat!

So, we met our guide David at the harbour, where another couple joined us, and boarded the speedboat to travel down the Saigon River.

On the way we had refreshments and pastries whilst taking in the sights.

The river itself was a tricky feat for the driver, it was amass with water hyacinth which is beautiful yet invasive and destructive, its purpose is to control and conserve environmental conditions by absorbing metals and mineral like copper and leads but it is highly invasive. It grows and reproduces causing dense mats that choke the river and make some areas impassable.

Several times we had to stop for the skipper to thrust the engine into reverse gear to clear the outboard motor of debris. It never fazed him; he obviously has had years of guiding his vessel through.

The journey took an hour and a half and on arrival we had a delicious lunch before heading to the tunnels; a whole grilled fish, sticky rice, yellow noodles, mixed vegetable broth and sweet and sour chicken.

The Cu Chi Tunnels are fascinating, David took us to the site, an immense network of underground tunnels that were used by the Viet Cong soldiers as hiding spots during the Vietnamese war. As well as serving as communication and supply routes, weapons cache and living quarters, they were also used as booby-traps and to mount surprise attacks on the enemy.

The tunnels here are approximately 123 kilometres long,

but with other areas they cover a distance of 250 kilometres; they are on three levels, with a depth of around twelve metres. They were dug in the late forties, often by hand and in heavily bombed areas and were where people spent much of their time underground.

Some of the tunnels have been widened to accommodate tourists, so we climbed down the steps and crawled along following our guide. Crikey, even though they have been modified they are still tiny — and pitch black.

We had a demonstration of the booby traps which were lethal, and then Bunny and I had a go in the rifle range; a few rounds with an AK-47.

We got back to the apartment around six p.m., so after a shower, change and a few drinks on the balcony we headed out for dinner.

There was a local street food place just up the road. We sat in the street on tiny blue plastic chairs and ate more yummy food; mixed seafood rice, crispy sweet and sour pork, Singapore noodles and deep-fried morning glory!

All in all, a great day.

29th February

Up and about early again today, I ordered a Grab and we went to the War Remnants Museum. Thank goodness for Grab, it's the best app I have downloaded, the cab was outside the apartment within minutes, and they are so cheap!

The museum has collected and conserved exhibits of war crimes and the consequences that were inflicted on the Vietnamese people by foreign forces.

Torture techniques against Vietnamese prisoners are listed

• Forcing the prisoner to roll on a hooked iron grill.

• Beating the prisoner with a pestle — mainly ankles, knees, elbows and shoulder blades.

• Beating the prisoner with a cane.

• Beating prisoners with a ray-tail whip, then rub salt or chilli powder into the wounds.

• Disembodying prisoner's teeth.

• Removal of prisoner's finger- and toenails.

• Using a radiating light to cause blindness.

• Holding of prisoners in a 'tiger's cage' woven from barbed wire.

• Burning of prisoner's sex organs.

• Burning of prisoner's mouths.

• Piercing prisoner's nails.

• Breaking the prisoner's kneecaps off.

• The soaking of prisoners in a boiling water pan.

• The pressing of wooden planks to the front and back of prisoners chests.

• Burying the prisoners alive.

It is set on three levels, and an open-air exhibition of planes, tanks and armoury.

There was lots of propaganda material and exhibits from the American war in Vietnam, and it is very one-sided but interesting for me, to think it was still going on when I was a child.

I didn't really know much about it before coming to Vietnam, but after yesterday at Cu Chi I would like to know more.

Particularly harrowing today was finding out about the

use of Agent Orange. From my understanding it was a chemical weapon widely used by the US military during the Vietnamese war.

It was sprayed by US army helicopters over agricultural land where it was believed the insurgents were concealed; its intent was also to target food crops and defoliate forest land.

The side effect to humans was devastating, the increase in birth defects of the children of military personnel was particularly disturbing; cleft palate, hydrocephalus, blindness, extra digits, dwarfism, limbs missing, co-joined foetuses — there are photographs of these and many more.

There is also sufficient evidence over the years directly linking Agent Orange to many different forms of cancers.

The chemicals used in Agent Orange can remain toxic in the soil for decades and the transgenerational health effects to its exposure can still be seen today.

Shocking.

Therefore, to lighten our moods back up we stopped for a few drinks on the way home before getting ready for tonight's shenanigans.

Ha-ha, so funny, Bunny thought we were taking him out for dinner, little did he know he had to cook it himself!

Yes, I had booked us all in for a Vietnamese cookery class.

• First course — fresh spring rolls using pork mince, prawns, herbs and fresh rice noodles.

• Second course — banana blossom salad with chicken and herbs.

- Third course — my favourite dish, *Banh Xeo*, a crispy creamy pancake with pork and prawns wrapped with fresh vegetables and served with a dipping sauce.

Great fun, a demonstration first then we cooked and ate each course before moving onto the next. At the end we were given recipe cards so we can try the dishes back home.

1st March

Pinch punch first day of the month — I get Lou every time and today was no exception.

We were all pretty tired this morning but up and out again, this time the open top Red Bus city tour.

We visited the Notre Dame, Central Post Office, Vietnamese History Museum, War Remnants Museum, Bui Vien (Walking) Street, Independence Palace, Zoo and Botanical Gardens, Ben Thanh Market, Bitexco Tower, Financial district, City Hall, Opera House and Jade Emperor Palace.

The bus stopped for a break at the Post Office, so we hopped off and had a look inside. Designed and built by a French architect in 1891 it is now mainly a tourist attraction with a western-style structure and eastern-influenced decoration.

It still has all its original features and the floor tiles are amazing.

I sent Mum and Dad a postcard, and Bunny sent one to his friends at work.

We couldn't go in the Notre Dame (a reproduction of the one in Paris) which is just across the street, as it's currently closed for refurbishment — impressive building though.

Just outside there was the 'Saigon La Poste' café where we had ice cold beer and a Scooby snack.

We'll go back and visit some of the other places in the next few days.

The evening was spent at a local eatery we had seen just up the road from our apartment. It was always packed with locals, every time we had walked by, so it must be good, eh?

YUK!

The first four dishes that came out were okay, then came the 'pièce de résistance'

Pho is a soft rice noodle soup in a broth prepared with beef or chicken which comes with a plate of leaves — fresh herbs, mint, coriander — and served with chilli sauce.

Well, seeing as it's a recommended local dish we had ordered a beef one to share.

It came out on a hot plate with the noodles and leaves on the side; you had to add them as required to the beef and broth.

I'm telling you now, there was no such thing as 'beef' in that pot!

Lung — yes.

Bowel — yes.

Testicles — yes.

Tripe — yes.

Liver — yes.

Kidney — yes.

The boys attempted to eat it, even tempting me saying it was tasty, no thank you.

2nd March

It's brother Jeff and sister-in-law Keeley's birthday.

Mekong Delta River trip today, so we had to get up really early.

We booked an organised trip some days ago and the coach was bang on time at 07:30. It was a comfortable ride with our guide Tu who drip fed us lots of interesting information on the way; we had a laugh trying to learn some Vietnamese words.

The Mekong is the longest river in South-east Asia — it extends from Tibet to the South China Sea.

A substantial majority of the people who live along the Mekong are involved in agriculture — mainly rice but also corn, tobacco and beans, or are fishermen.

The guestimation is, that here there are more freshwater fish per capita, than anywhere else on the planet, and that there are more than 500 known species of fish in the Mekong; these have sustained millions of people through droughts, deluges and even the genocide Cambodian regime of Pol Pot.

We visited a floating market on the river where we clambered from our boat onto a fruit and veg stall, where we were educated by the lady proprietor about the tropical fruits of Vietnam; we also got to taste them; pineapple, mango, papaya, bananas and durian.

Now durian is a notorious Asian fruit that some Asians are addicted to it. It contains an essential amino acid also found in chocolate. They call it the king of the fruits — like Marmite, love it or hate it.

Banned in some places because it is considered the smelliest fruit in the world, to me it absolutely stinks, and in my opinion tastes just as revolting as it smells.

Other boats were selling flowers, fish, nuts, beer, soft drinks and even wine, each of them hanging a stick displaying samples of their goods 'advertising' what produce they are selling.

Everyone is wearing a conical hat, commonly known as an Asian rice hat; they're made from leaves and bamboo to help farmers in the fields keep cool.

They are also an important accessory traditionally worn to honour a women's beauty. I've seen them loads of times on the TV; they are circular, cone shaped and taper smoothly from the base to the apex. I wish I could buy one but I'd have to carry it everywhere on the rest of our travels.

After the market we stopped off for a rice-paper-making and corn-popping demonstration — I had a go at it. Here we also got to taste the rice wine; some of the bottles had snakes in them!

Then it was back on the boat to cruise further along the river where we stopped off for some kayaking which was fun.

Back on land we had a brief cookery lesson and made some *Banh Xeo* for our lunch, (amongst other dishes) again absolutely delicious.

Last but not least Tu took us on a bike ride through the fruit orchards and back/forth over some bridges over the Mekong.

On the journey home we saw literally hundreds of graves, some on their own and some in clusters on paddy fields, the countryside is a patchwork of tiny plots.

Tu told me that when someone dies in a rural area the body is cleaned, placed in a coffin and buried above the ground on their land, usually in the middle of the rice field because it signifies harmony with its surroundings. This ensures that the deceased is respected at all times, and tended to daily.

Tu also said that landowners buy their own coffins at a young age, ahead of their time, and keep them in the house with the belief that they may live longer, but they also believe it is bad misfortune to die away from home, when death occurs the coffin is there ready.

We had dinner at the street food market — after last night's disaster we all picked our own dish, I chose barbeque pork and rice and it was bloody lovely.

A super fun day out today, more of that in store for tomorrow hopefully.

3rd March

We decided to go to Ben Thanh Market today so that Bunny could buy some souvenirs to take home.

It was a lot of fun haggling with the stallholders, and managed to get a handbag for Laura, down from $95 to $35, a real fake designer bag!

He also brought some lacquered dishes and some lovely chopsticks.

Then we walked to the Mariamman Hindu Temple (but it was shut) a temple dedicated to the goddess of rain, Mariamman. Apparently, it is known to have miraculous powers giving luck and wealth to anyone who visits.

It also has dedications to other gods such as Vishnu, Brahma and Ganesha.

We then walked to Ho Chi Minh City Museum. It was only a pound each to get in, so we had a look around, it's a lovely building, it used to be a palace, it tells the story of the city and its struggle with independence.

There was a wedding magazine photo shoot going on whilst we were there, several 'bride and grooms' posing on the window sills and on the sweeping staircase, they looked magnificent, like real life princesses, elegant, radiant, dazzling and glamorous, even in this stifling heat.

Next we walked to Nguyen Pedestrian Street to see the statue of Ho Chi Minh, the People's Committee Building and the Opera House.

It's a lovely area, like a boulevard — traffic free, and surrounded by beautiful French colonial buildings.

Bunny wanted to find the Vietnamese Airlines office and upgrade his flight home, which he managed to do for only £200 so he is well happy.

Whilst waiting I had a *Pretty Woman* moment! I was busting for the loo so I asked the security guard where the toilets were, he pointed me in the right direction and off I went. Unable to find them I asked again at the concierge desk and a young lady looked me up and down and then replied, 'We do not have any toilets here' (I was wearing shorts and a T-shirt, so certainly not glam).

I returned to find Bunny and Lou when the security guard spotted me — obviously he realised I hadn't found the toilet (I had been too quick) and asked me what was wrong. I told him what had happened and he promptly asked me to follow him. He escorted me to the toilets and instructed the young Vietnamese lady from the concierge desk to let me in; they were just behind her! Bitch!

Bitexco Financial Tower was next on the list. It reminded me of The Shard in London, its shape is similar and it has a sky-deck.

Seeing as Bunny loves Heineken we decided to go on 'The World of Heineken' tour that they are currently promoting. It was okay, though a little rushed. The tour guide was very sweet and enthusiastic, telling us all about the history of the Dutch lager.

We got to sample the lager and pour our own glass from the tap. The skydeck gave us fabulous views of the Saigon River and at the end we all received a personalised commemorative bottle of Heineken.

We got a Grab back to the apartment to wash and change before dinner, Bunny wanted to try the Pho (noodle soup) again, but it was still rank! Lou had beef which he said was okay, Bunny and I chose pork but it was full of fat, gristle and who knows what else?

On the way back to the apartment we stopped off in Bui Vien Street but it was crazy loud, the music was blaring from speakers and DJs were in every bar, all trying to outdo one another, there were street performers too, and lots of beggars.

4th March

It is Lolly's birthday today.

We went to Ben Thanh Market to grab a bite to eat, it was delicious.

We had some spring rolls, tempura prawns; roasted pork ribs and some chicken wrapped around a sugar cane with brown sugar and crushed nuts.

Bunny is not feeling too great today; I think Lou and I have 'burnt' him out LOL, so we went back to the apartment for the rest of the day.

Me and Lou popped to the supermarket and brought some pasta for tea, then we watched a film on Netflix and played Scrabble.

5th March

Bunny felt better today so we jumped in a Grab cab to go to the Chinese quarter. There was a big indoor market, Binh Tay, probably three times the size of Ben Thanh with hundreds of stalls, but it was mostly wholesale, okay if you wanted to buy fifty bras, 100 baseball caps, or 200 pairs of Crocs.

It's certainly a very busy and bustling place. The surrounding area is buzzing too.

We caught the bus back, a lady vendor selling drinks at the roadside helped us get on the right one after we brought a drink from her stall, so that was kind.

This evening we went to see the Starlight Bridge; it's a tourist attraction which comes alive at night with beautiful rainbow illuminations and a cascading waterfall. It was a nice spot to have dinner with lots of upscale Vietnamese, Korean and Japanese restaurants. Lou chose a burger, I had parmesan chicken cordon bleu and Bunny had Malaysian chicken with sticky rice.

6th March

Grab taxi again to Thien Hau Temple, a Buddhist temple, this one dedicated to the Chinese sea goddess Mazu.

The belief is that Mazu protects and rescues ships and fishermen by flying around those in trouble on a cloud! How dreamy and absolutely fairytale is that? I'm surprised that nobody has made a Disney film about her.

On the ceiling of the temple there are hundreds of very large hanging incense cones burning, when the cone is burnt right to the top and extinguishes then the soul of the person it has been lit for is freed.

We caught the bus back into district 1 to visit the Independence Palace, I am glad we made the effort; this was a really cool place to visit.

Once serving as the seat of the French colonial government it has witnessed many dramatic episodes in the rise and fall of the government.

You get an eerie feeling as you walk in; its halls are deserted, as are all the rooms, but you can just imagine the goings-on within the walls.

Situated on four floors it has an airy, spacious and open atmosphere.

It has four conference rooms, presidential offices, living quarters, games room, cinema, and a dance hall but the most impressive, interesting and ghostly is the basement where you can see the telecommunications room, secret bunker tunnels, an emergency bedroom for the President and his wife and the huge kitchens still fully equipped as they would have been over forty years ago.

This place has literally stood still in time; remaining just how it was when Saigon gained independence in 1975.

On the way back we stopped off in Bue Vien for one last time, it was early evening so not as loud.

We saw a little lady, about four feet tall who looked around a century old, in a crash helmet getting onto the back of a scooter, her very large bosom was swinging braless at her waist, they looked like she had smuggled a pair of coconuts down her top.

We also saw another 'ancient' lady wearing a conical hat, pushing a disabled man in his chair (begging to the crowds) waving his arms in the air and singing; I'm sure it was 'Who let the dogs out'.

There was a cocktail bar I had read about called 'The View', another rooftop terrace bar popular with tourists and locals.

It was okay, twinkly lights and pretty multicoloured lanterns set on three tiers but the view was not amazing as it was only ten storeys high. The staff were slow but the cocktails were delicious. We stayed for a couple before heading back to change for dinner.

It was our friend, Bunny's choice, as it's his last night, a place he had read about called 'MaM 148', it was a small little place not far from the apartment. The menu was explained to us and we were given recommendations for the western palate. The service was quick and the food was delicious, mixed spring rolls to start with sweet chilli dip and Pho chicken and beef noodles for main.

It did lack a little in atmosphere and could have done with some background music, maybe? But all in all, a great end to Bunny's stay in Vietnam.

Then it was back to the apartment, Bunny showered and got changed for his journey home, I ordered him a Grab to the airport and after waving him farewell Lou and I had a few drinks and watched a film on Netflix.

7th and 8th March

We are hearing more and more about the outbreak of Covid-19 now, it appears that the Foreign Office has advised against all travel to China's Hubei province and to Wuhan where the outbreak has been located.

British Airways have suspended all flights to China, and on the 28th February Britain had reported its first death from the disease which is apparently becoming a pandemic, confirmed as being present in many countries across Europe as well as the USA.

Lou and I spent these two days researching our next move to Cambodia, booking flights, buses and hotels etc.

We did all of our washing and tidied the apartment.

We're off to Phnom Penh in the morning.

Chapter 13
Cambodia

9th March

The Foreign Office has advised against all travel to Italy now; due to a massive rise in Covid-19 cases the country has gone into 'lockdown'.

Up nice and early, we had a long day ahead.

First of all we caught a Grab to the bus station, our bus was due at eight a.m. but on arrival we discovered it had been delayed until 09:45, apparently due to a problem with the Cambodia border crossing.

The bus took seven and a half hours, it wasn't really a complex journey, we had a guide with us on the bus who took all our passports to help us pass through the Moc Bai-Bavet border crossing; we travelled 213 kilometres.

On the way the bus broke down, its air con packed up so we all had to get off for about an hour. Luckily the driver and the driver's mate managed to fix it using several items of improvised spares which included an old discarded flip-flop!

We finally arrived in Phnom Penh around 18:30, we were swamped with tuktuk drivers, but after speaking to an English woman (who lived here), she helped us choose the right fare for the journey to our hotel.

Mr Thearea was his name, he was really funny, he spoke very good English as well as bursting into cockney rhyming slang every other sentence!

The 'Okay Boutique Hotel' was lovely, right in the centre of the historic city, really traditional décor with rich colours and textures representing traditional Cambodia arts and architecture.

We swapped rooms straight away after check-in, because we were allocated on the second floor, after a quick discussion with reception (not what we booked etc) we were reallocated to the sixth floor which was much better.

The rooftop had a pool and dining terrace, so after a quick spruce up that's where we headed for dinner and wine.

I spoke to Dale, he said things were getting serious at home with the virus outbreak; some folk are going crazy with bulk-buying and stockpiling fearing an uncontrollable situation and pending doom.

Apparently, the supermarket shelves are bare of pasta and loo roll!

The FTSE index is also plummeting at the concerns over the spread of Covid-19.

I spoke to John too; the horse he has shares in is running tomorrow at the Cheltenham Festival — good luck Pentland Hills.

10th March

We didn't have a great sleep, either of us. It sounded like there was building work going on for most of the night; who

298

knows, out here anything is possible.

After breakfast we set off to see the first attraction on our list, the Wat Phnom Temple.

It's free to get in for all Asians, but foreigners have to pay 1USD.

According to legend it was erected to house statues of Buddha which were washed up here from the Mekong River.

It is quite elaborate; its entrance is via a grand set of steps guarded by lions and snakes. Lots of worshippers were bringing offerings of fruit and flowers to the gods, as well as lighting incense sticks and praying.

Outside there were beggars, street urchins and women selling birds from cages.

The purpose of this is to give life, earn forgiveness and cleanse any previous sins. There are literally hundreds of the small birds, the women set cages by the riverbank each evening, trap the birds and then sell them to the worshippers who ceremoniously release them (only to be caught again probably!).

Next stop was the old market, it was absolutely crowded, crammed full of fruit and veg, clothing, religious souvenirs, massage parlours, beauticians, hairdressers, textiles, home appliances, still alive and flapping fish and every type of meat including innards and offal (which looked very unhygienic).

A walk along the riverfront took us to The Wat Ounalom Temple, the headquarters of Buddhism in Cambodia where the head of the country's brotherhood lives with the monks.

It was sabotaged by the Khmer Rouge in the seventies and many of its valuable artefacts were destroyed but this sacred and religious site is still beautiful and calming. Apparently, it contains what is believed to be an eyebrow hair of Buddha; it's really strange how these places make you feel.

Last of the day was a visit to the Independence Monument, built to celebrate Cambodia's independence from foreign rule and commemorate those who died for their country.

It's really fitting, styled on the shape of a lotus and surrounded by a big open park, flower beds and fountains that are immaculate.

We walked a lot today, 8.8 miles to be exact, so we went for dinner at a nearby street food market, one street food stall had BBQ frogs on the menu, but we plumped for chicken and cashew nuts, noodles and rice.

Pentland Hills lost in the horse race, by the way.

11th March

We felt tired this morning, so sat around the pool, had a swim and recharged batteries before heading out in the afternoon.

Just up the road from our hotel was the Royal Palace. It is an absolutely magnificent complex of buildings which serves as the royal residence of the king of Cambodia.

It is divided into four compounds and is a grand example of Khmer architecture. It includes a throne hall, a temple for the Emerald Buddha, a silver pagoda, and the royal palace; again, how on earth they built these structures (some in the early nineteenth century) is beyond comprehension.

My favourite thing here, was the Emerald Buddha, which is reported to be made from Baccarat crystal, it's tiny but priceless.

My second favourite thing was a life-size model of Maitreya Buddha which is encrusted with almost 10,000 diamonds.

On the way home there was a street vendor who had a queue. I went to take a look and I am not kidding, she had trays full of deep fried wiggedy grubs, locusts, lizards, and spiders the size of tarantulas — YUK!

Off to bed pretty early tonight as we have planned a busy day tomorrow.

Goodnight.

12th March

It's Rory's birthday.

Six people in the UK have now died from Covid-19.

We were up early today; we hired a tuktuk to take us to The Choeung Ek Genocide Centre; AKA 'The Killing Fields'.

• On the 17/4/1975 the Khmer Rouge, led by Pol Pot who was once a teacher then a dictator of the Communist regime, took over Cambodia.

• He ordered the closure of schools, hospitals and shops taking all tradespersons, professionals, and foreigners, those who wore glasses, a wristwatch or any other form of modern technology, or those with soft hands as his prisoners.

• His intention was to have a classless communist community transforming the country into his vision of an agrarian utopia.

- Within three days every city in Cambodia was deserted.
- City dwellers were considered greedy.
- Over two million people were murdered.
- This site was chosen for the massacre as it was 'out of the way'.
- Music was played loudly to cover the screams of those being slaughtered.
- DDT (chemicals) was showered over the bodies thrown into the mass graves, both to kill the stench and secondly to 'finish off' those who were not quite dead.
- There are over 129 mass graves.
- The prisoners were beaten and hacked to death using the dried peeled bark of the palm trees which were sharp and ragged. Bullets were too expensive.
- Soldiers who defected from the Khmer Rouge were executed as traitors here, their penalty was beheading.
- Children and babies were killed by swinging them by their legs and smashing their skulls against 'the killing tree'.
- All religion was forbidden.
- 300 prisoners were killed every day.
- Pot believed it was better to kill the innocent by mistake, than to spare an enemy by mistake.

This place is shocking. The audio guide takes visitors around in almost complete silence, giving respect to all of the innocent humans who lost their lives here; you witness the executioner's office, the mass graves, the killing tools, bone, teeth and clothing fragments, the killing tree and much more.

There are over 300 killing fields throughout Cambodia.

Pol Pot was later put on trial in the hope he would stand trial for his crimes against humanity but he died whilst under house arrest in 1998.

As dreadfully sad, completely devastating and beyond your understanding this place is it's a definite for your 'book-it' list.

Our tuktuk driver then took us to Tuol Sleng; aka S21, where for most, the terrifying ordeal began. Here there was a secret centre of a network of nearly 200 prisoners at a time who were tortured by the Khmer Rouge before being sent to the Killing Fields.

Over short space of time between 12,000 and 20,000 people were imprisoned at S21; there were only twelve confirmed survivors.

Again, an audio guide, in almost complete silence, takes you around the site where employees of Pol Pot were forced to torture and murder the prisoners.

It was formerly a school, the classrooms on the ground and first floor were divided into cells, all the windows and doors were boarded up, prisoners were shackled, stripped naked and starved. The list of rules for the prison guards to the prisoners was as follows.

- You must answer accordingly to my questions — do not turn them away.
- Do not try to hide the facts by making pretexts of this and that. You are strictly prohibited to contest me.
- Don't be a fool for you are a chap who dares to thwart the revolution.
- You must immediately answer my questions without wasting time to reflect.

- Do not tell me either about your immoralities or the essence of the revolution.
- While receiving lashes or electrocution you must not cry at all.
- Do nothing, sit still and wait for my orders. If there is no order keep quiet. When I ask you to do something you must do it right away without protesting.
- Do not make pretext about Kampuchea Krom in order to hide your secret or traitor.
- If you don't follow the above rules, you shall get many lashes of electric wire.
- If you disobey any point of my regulations, you shall get either ten lashes or five shocks of electrical discharge.

In the gallows prisoners were roped at the ankles, hung upside down and their heads lowered then dunked into pots containing human urine and excrement until they passed out, when they came round, they were dunked again and so on until their death.

There is so much evidence on show here proving the atrocities of Pol Pot's rule, instruments of torture, gallows, dossiers and documents, mugshots of victims with their names, photographs of the tortured and dead, paintings and clothing and belongings.

The Vietnamese invasion of Cambodia finally ended the genocide when troops seized Phnom Penh toppling and defeating the brutal Pol Pot and the Khmer Rouge in January 1979.

There remains two of the twelve confirmed survivors still alive today, and we were lucky enough to meet one of them in person, Bou Meng, who was there doing a book signing.

It was painting that saved him. He was an artist and was put to work by Pol Pot to paint personal portraits of Pot and other communist leaders; you can still see them here today.

Although his wife and two children were killed here and profound grief dominates his life, his memory has become a tool in search of truth and justice.

I brought the book — why wouldn't I?

Wow, what a day, emotional, very thought-provoking and unbelievable really to think that all this happened in our lifetime.

Our hotel offered a free sunset river cruise which we had booked onto for this evening. Of course nothing is 'free' and you were expected to order food and drink to have on the ride.

It was a very nice end to the day, chicken noodles, vegetable fried rice and BBQ pork ribs whilst cruising the river and watching the magnificent sunset.

We were then transported back to the hotel where we had a nightcap on the balcony before bed.

Since we met up with our old school friend Shaggy, his wife Isha and new baby Jack things have changed rapidly for them. His contract as executive chef at the Sofitel Plaza in Manila came to an end and two days ago they moved to the Sofitel Phnom Penh here in Cambodia.

We are going to see them again tomorrow — who would

have thought it?

13th March

Apparently, the Chief Medical Officer from the UK has raised the risk of a pandemic for Covid-19 from moderate to high. There have been more UK deaths and the number of confirmed cases has risen to over 1,000 and reports say that the death toll is now twenty.

This morning we were up and out early, off to visit the National Museum of Cambodia, it was just up the street from our hotel so only a ten-minute walk.

The museum houses mainly Khmer artefacts such as statues, pottery, ceramics and bronzes.

It is a beautiful terracotta-coloured building built in 1917 and it is set around a really pretty courtyard filled with plants, trees and fish ponds.

Most of the exhibits are similar, and the audio guide was essential to know what you were looking at. Most of the carvings and sandstone statues were from the Ankor Wat era, some as old as sixth century, but sadly lots of the antiquities have unknown provenance as many objects were damaged or stolen due to the evacuation and abandonment of Phnom Penh during Pol Pot's reign.

Phsar Thmei (Central Market) next, a beautiful art deco building from 1937, shaped in the form of a cross with a large central dome and it was absolutely huge. Whatever I may have wanted to buy, I am sure I could have got it here. Sadly, there is no room in my backpack to take stuff home.

Gold, silver, jewellery, real fake watches, silks, stationary, household items, cleaning products, electrical items, flowers, food, and the list goes on and on.

After a quick wash and change we headed over to Sofitel to meet Shaggy and family. He bunked off work for the evening so we all headed out for dinner.

I tried frog, it was just like chicken really but a bit softer, we all shared some 'morning glory' too. It was a really nice evening.

14th March

It says in the news that UK retailers have urged UK customers to stop panic buying of products as most supermarket shelves have now sold out of pasta, hand gel and toilet roll! What on earth is going on?

This morning we had a nice lay-in and then lounged around the pool for a few hours before getting ready to go and see Shaggy, Isha and Jack for the last time for who knows how long?

They have moved into their new apartment today, it is really lovely.

I took Jack for a swim in their pool, he seemed to really love it giggling and splashing around.

We had a few rum and cokes, and a lovely chat before heading back home in a tuktuk. Shaggy has a wedding to cater for tomorrow for 600 guests.

15th March

The Foreign Office have advised against all but essential travel to Spain and the USA and the Health Secretary has warned that every UK resident over the age of seventy will be advised within the coming weeks to self-isolate to shield them from Covid-19.

Seeing as it is our last day in Phnom Penh, we have decided to go for a drink in Raffles Hotel Le Royal. The one in Singapore was so fabulous, they also have one in Siem Reap and that's our next destination.

The Elephant bar is not as lush and distinctive the Long Bar in Singapore but indulgent all the same. Jacqueline Kennedy stayed here once.

I had their signature cocktail, the Phnom Penh sling, a mix of Seekers gin, lychee liqueur, Cointreau and pink guava juice. I'm afraid we declined a bar snack of chongret rotie — Kampong Thom province fried crickets with crispy lime leaves and lemongrass salt.

16th March

Off to Siem Reap today so up early for our transfer to the bus station and onward journey.

As we were boarding the bus we had a temperature check, we were relieved that we were both okay. Although neither of us have been ill at all throughout our entire trip (touch wood).

Things seem to be getting worse by the day. The UK death toll is now fifty-five and the prime minister has advised all UK citizens to avoid travelling abroad to try and curb the spread of the virus.

People are also being advised to work from home where possible.

We left at 09:00 and arrived in Siem Reap at 15:00, after

travelling 317 kilometres.

The roads seemed very dry and the land barren. There was the occasional herd of cattle and we saw lots of the houses along the way were made of wood and were on stilts. Lou says this is to protect them from the floods in the monsoon season.

The family's livestock and scooters along with children's play area and laundry lines were underneath, and nearly every house had a large haystack at the front of it.

After taking a short tuktuk ride we arrived at Angkor Holiday Hotel where once again they tried to put us in a room with no balcony. I have learnt now not to be so 'British' and after complaining (again) we were moved to a much nicer room as we had booked.

It is quite strange here because for the first time it is quite noticeable that there is a distinct lack of tourists.

It is really quiet, even down 'Pub Street' where it is reported to be like Blackpool or Benidorm and even Bangla Road with partying around the clock by backpackers, and flashpackers both young and old.

There is absolutely no evidence of the debauchery, loud pumping live music or dancing.

I feel sorry for the locals who tell me that everything stopped a few weeks ago when news of the coronavirus spread and the tourists stopped coming.

Later I spoke to Mum and Dad, Dale and Ju who tell me things are desperate at home.

The shops are empty and there is a real fear of impending doom.

Lou and I had a long conversation about the situation as we are both starting to feel really anxious about our family (even though we are absolutely fine they are frantically concerned about us).

We may need to rethink, and change our plans?

17th March

We didn't do much today, just chilled by the pool but we only saw two other guests.

I had a text from Lloyds Bank to check my account, and when I did it turned out that I had received a pension adjustment and a tax rebate, so that was a nice little surprise, happy days!

Later we went to the gym before walking towards Pub Street for some dinner.

We had handmade wood-fired pizza, it was quite a pleasant change from rice or noodles, and really quite tasty.

18th March

Everyone is getting uneasy and fearful back home.

The UK death toll from coronavirus now exceeds 100, and the government has announced that all schools will shut at the end of the week.

Princess Beatrice has postponed her wedding, Glastonbury festival has been cancelled, and all BBC filming is suspended until further notice.

Lots of countries across the world are closing their borders.

Lou and I had a long chat at breakfast this morning.

Cambodia has restrictions on flights to the UK, and all

flights are indirect, meaning you have to have a connecting flight from elsewhere in South-east or East Asia.

Sadly, we came to a decision that we would leave Siem Reap eight days earlier than planned, and at least if we get to Bangkok in Thailand, we would be more likely to able to get home from there, should we need to, if Cambodia closes its borders.

We already had a flight booked with Air Asia so we walked to their offices to try bring the flight forwards.

So did lots of other travellers so it seemed. There was a queue of people from all over; Germany, Sweden, France trying to do the exact same thing.

They wanted another £46 each to change the flight, or we could cancel and rebook.

I went online and managed to book new flights for 21st March, we will have to cancel the original flight booked for the 28th at a later date.

Feeling a little deflated and gloomy it was time to cheer ourselves up, so we got dressed up and headed off to find Raffles Grand Hotel d'Angkor.

It wasn't far, another opulent property like the last two we have visited. It's described as an oasis in the heart of Siem Reap.

Here the famous bar is called 'Elephant Bar' and of course no visit to Raffles for me would be complete without having the signature cocktail!

This time called Airavata; it's named after a multi-headed elephant from Hindu mythology; a delicious concoction of rum, coconut passion, lime, crème de banana, pineapple and coconut juice — all served up in a ceramic cocktail mug in the shape of the elephant god.

We then walked to find the oldest temple in town that I had read about but it was really disappointing, very run-down and appeared deserted. I almost trod on an almighty dead bat. At first I thought it was a black umbrella that had blown inside out and buckled by a fierce gust, but no, it was definitely a dead bat!

On the way home outside the Royal Palace, we stopped off to see the flying fruit bats that come out to feed at dusk. There were hundreds if not thousands of them colonised in the trees, they have a wing span of up to 1.5 metres. Wow, a fascinating spectacle watching them soar above foraging for their food source, but I'm glad these mega-bats are not interested in humans!

It was back to street food tonight, we had seen a small stall earlier with all their fresh ingredients on show, locals were eating their too so we figured it must be good.

We weren't let down, beef noodles, mixed vegetable fried rice and lamb skewers before heading off to bed, we have an early start tomorrow.

19th March

I have been so looking forward to today for so long.

We were off to see the magnificent Temples of Angkor.

Every article I have read says you must go before sunrise or at sunset to experience the beauty of this UNESCO World Heritage Site, once the capital city of the Khmer Empire, so it was up by alarm for us today.

Amazingly the Khmer Rouge spared Angkor as a symbol of past national glory.

Briefly (you would need a whole book on its own otherwise) Angkor is one of the most important archaeological sites in the world and contains scores of temples.

It is one of the world's most popular tourist spots, and without a doubt is on everyone's 'Book-it' list.

The complex is huge and covers over 150 hectares.

Incredibly it was built in the twelfth century as a city and temple complex, initially Hindu and then Buddhist.

It was home to the most impressive and advanced city in the world at the time, until it was abandoned by its residents (some say by flooding, others say due to a change in religion) and taken over by the surrounding jungle.

I am sure that you have all seen images of Angkor Wat, its emblazoned on the national flag for one, and it really needs no introduction but I am telling you nothing prepares you for the moment you actually physically see it for yourself.

At five a.m. we hired a tuktuk driver to take us to the ticket office; they have moved it out of town to prevent fraud and fake vendors, and now this is the only legitimate place to buy your pass.

Having purchased our ID passes we excitedly entered the world heritage site to find our spot (as recommended by all the reviews) to watch the sunrise over Angkor Wat.

Angkor Wat is the most famous of the temples here, and truly a feast for the eyes, a Hindu temple and the largest religious monument in the world.

It's dedicated to the god Vishnu and was built in the twelfth century.

The sunrise was breathtaking; we sat in front of the lake and felt truly spellbound by its tremendous beauty.

Honestly, words cannot describe it. It felt like we were in a film set, lots of blockbuster movies have been shot here; *Lara Croft Tomb Raider*, is probably the most well-known to us.

It is crammed full of intricate and grand bas-relief (raised) carvings and female deities which depict stories about the beginning of time and the creation of the universe. They are so detailed and surprisingly well preserved — gods, demons, heaven, hell, kings, warriors, animals, demons, nymphs, and much more.

We decided to hire a tuktuk driver to take us around the rest of the site, and boy oh boy, it was the right decision. For $25 we spent the next four hours with him driving us to all the major attractions in this unbelievably incredible place.

• Banteay Kdei — Enchanting and tranquil, a citadel of chambers, previously a monastery decorated with Buddhist bas-reliefs and very spiritual.

• Ta Prohm — A Buddhist temple that is almost crumbling and choked by the embrace of the banyan and kapok tree roots which stranglehold around its walls, it's slowly being eaten up by the jungle. Quite haunting, yet charming and fairy-tale like here — where trees rise from the ruins — incredible.

• Ta Keo — aka Temple tower, built entirely from

sandstone and with the absence of decoration, it is over seventy feet high, with five towers, and terrifying to climb up to the top, but worth it for the view across Angkor.

• Thommanon and Chau Say Tevoda — a pair of small and elegant Hindu temples dedicated to Hindu gods Shiva and Vishnu both have some well-preserved devatas (heavenly and divine) carvings.

• Victoria Gate — one of five gates which guarded the ancient city of Angkor. It is carved with the heads of both gods and demons facing in the four cardinal directions.

• Bayon — a mesmerising temple of Cambodia's most celebrated King Jayavarman VII. It is richly decorated by fifty-four gothic towers, 216 giant smiley faces, and has over 11,000 figures. It stands in the exact centre of the ancient city.

• Elephant Terrace — so called because of the elephant carvings, this was used as a giant viewing platform for the King to greet his returning victorious army. It is also decorated with life-sized garuda (a mythical bird) and lions.

If you ever do come to Cambodia, you really must visit Angkor — it really is the most wonderful, mesmeric and entrancing place I have ever been.

Our driver took us back to the hotel in his tuktuk, he only wanted $14 but we gave him $25, he was over the moon.

What a day.

20th March

The Prime Minister has ordered all cafes, restaurants and pubs to close, as well as nightclubs, theatres, cinemas, gyms and leisure centres.

UK workers are being furloughed (granted leave of absence from their workplaces); the government will pay 80% of the wages for employees unable to work due to coronavirus.

We had a walk in to town today, it is almost completely deserted now, the poor market vendors are desperate for a sale.

I brought some silk scarves for the girls at work and a few bits for the children at home. I tried to get my hair cut too, but we couldn't find a barber shop.

Apart from the lack of tourists everything else is as normal, the supermarkets are full, restaurants are open and it is business as usual.

Dinner was delicious again. I had chicken amok, a mouth-watering creamy coconut curry dish served on a banana leaf, Lou had Lok Lak, sautéed cube-shaped beef marinated in fish sauce, soy sauce, crushed kampot pepper, sugar and oil, served on a bed of lettuce, tomatoes and cucumber with jasmine rice.

21st March

Sadly, we had to leave Siem Reap early this morning due to events unfolding all over the world with Coronavirus.

We had booked a tuktuk driver to transport us to the airport; he was waiting outside as arranged.

Our journey to Siem Reap Airport took about fifteen minutes, the check-in was smooth and easy enough, we had to show confirmation of our onward flight to the UK (which we booked in December). Shockingly ours was the only flight on the departure board that didn't have CANCELLED displayed in big red capital letters.

The flight to Bangkok was lovely, we were served a complimentary breakfast of sausage and scrambled eggs, and the flight only took forty-five minutes!

On arrival in Bangkok, we had to fill out a health declaration form and walk through a heat sensor. It was rather chaotic and no one really knew what was going on, but eventually we passed through customs and collected our bags.

We had already decided to go to Thai Airlines office in an attempt to bring our flight to the UK forward; we were due to fly home on 16th April, but at no extra cost and with very little issue our tickets were changed and reissued for the 27th March.

I did feel some sense of relief, but at the same time sadness — at least we were now in a safer place (in terms of getting home), but the finale of our dream trip was somewhat marred by this awful pandemic.

We had a room booked for tonight, in Bangkok before heading to Pattaya tomorrow.

The 'Quarter Hotel' is modern, has a nice pool and gym. I managed to get my hair cut and then we had room service for dinner; Lou had fish and chips, I had Pad Thai.

There is not much we can do about it except enjoy our last few days, so we have booked a six-star hotel in Pattaya for the last five days and we are going to make the most of it.

Before bed we heard that Air Asia has cancelled all international flights throughout Asia until further notice. We felt so lucky that we flew to Thailand today, being in lockdown in Cambodia would have been a real problem.

Chapter 14
Thailand

22nd March

It's Mother's Day today.

The Environment Secretary has urged shoppers to stop panic buying. Tesco, Aldi, Asda and Lidl are struggling to keep up with demand.

All driving tests are cancelled.

Up early this morning and checked out of the Quarter Hotel before heading back to Bangkok Airport for the bus to Pattaya.

We were heat sensor tested throughout the airport, and before travelling on the bus to Hotel Siam Bayshore, a journey of 150 kilometres, taking just under two hours.

Pattaya was the only place we could get to really, given the circumstances.

Affectionately known locally as 'Patsy' it is a beach resort south-east of Bangkok.

It was once a fishing village and was a popular visiting spot for GIs based in Nakhon.

Lacking in culture it is famous for its nightlife, and sex industry, that it why it is aka Sin City, loud, frenzied and full of ladyboys.

We had been here before and found it quite sleazy, and I was not keen to come back, but we had to make the best of a bad situation.

Lou was pick-pocketed last time we came. We were walking along the street back to our hotel, it wasn't really late but it was very dark and all of a sudden, a ladyboy came at him and was trying to caress him. He pushed her away; he jumped over a small wall and got straight onto a waiting moped before speeding off.

And that was that, within seconds he realised his wallet was gone, the bitch had stolen it and fled.

We do have one really funny memory of the place though. One night we were sitting in a bar having a drink, there was a man walking up and down the bustling street selling the most beautiful and fragrant garlands.

The garlands were made by stringing various flower combinations together to create these symbols of luck and respect.

They are often hung in vehicles, offered to the gods and worn in ceremonies, as well as obviously sold to us tourists tempted by their beauty and smell.

I went to buy one and got chatting to the seller, of course I had had a few drinks by this time and the next thing I know I had three of the things draped around my neck whilst sitting on the back of an elephant and parading down the middle of the street laughing my head off calling to Lou to take a look at me... his eyes nearly popped out of his head, it was hilarious.

The hotel is gorgeous, set in some gardens it has two swimming pools, tennis courts, a gym, two lovely restaurants a bar and a piano room.

We have decided to try and forget about things and embrace the short time we have left but it is so sad.

'Walking Street' is a tourist attraction which draws hundreds of tourists and locals primarily for its nightlife. It is supposed to be pumping with live bands, discos, girly bars, beer bars and the busiest and biggest 'hotspot' in the whole of Thailand.

It is not as we remembered. Gone are the girly bars, ladyboys and tourists. The beaches are empty too, and swimming in the sea is currently banned.

This evening it is virtually deserted, like a ghost town, with the last few stragglers of travellers wondering around aimlessly, and the locals desperate for trade — those who are left, anyway.

I spoke to Dale tonight, and then to the two mums; we told them we were coming home and you could actually feel the sense of relief in their voices.

23rd March

The hotel really is lovely, breakfast is like a feast, buffet style that includes Asian and Western cuisine, I had poached eggs this morning, followed by toast and jam.

It's a scorching day, so we sat around the pool to enjoy a swim and the sunshine.

We listened to some music on the iPod; working our way through the alphabet as usual, today's list was;

A — Aztec Camera

B — Brand New Heavies
C — The Calling
D — David Cassidy
E — Echo and the Bunnymen
F — Frank Sinatra
G — George Benson
H — Herbie Hancock
J — Joe Cocker
K — Karyn White
L — Leo Sayer
M — Meatloaf
N — New Order
O — OMD
P — Pointer Sisters
R — Roxy Music
S — Stylistics
T — Talking Heads
U — Ultravox
V — Visage
W — Whitney Houston

Later we went for a walk to the pier and along. We found a nice seafood restaurant and sat on the veranda overlooking the Gulf of Thailand. Lou had oysters to start, then we shared crispy belly pork with pak choi, grilled jumbo prawns in tamarind sauce, and spicy fried noodles with chicken; I really think that Thai food is my favourite.

We spoke to Mum and Dad, just to reassure them and confirm that we would be home at the end of the week.

24th March

In a televised address the Prime Minister has ordered the British public to lockdown, which means that people must stay at home, except for limited purposes such as shopping, exercise and medical need.

The Secretary for Health has warned all British Citizens currently abroad to 'GET HOME NOW'.

That's the message, so we decided to go to the Thai Airways office in town to ask the questions.

We found it easy enough, and so did hundreds of others!

We were number 163 in the queue.

There was lots of anxiety and speculation amongst the crowds; holidaymakers of all nationalities were uneasy, worried, and troubled by the unfolding events.

Lots of rumours were being spread around; flights cancelled, need a Covid test in the form of a medical certificate issued with seventy-two hours of travelling etc… but we waited our turn and were reassured that our flight as arranged for three days' time is safe, and that we wouldn't require a Covid medical certificate to leave Thailand (you only need one if you are travelling through).

All Thai Airlines flights would continue until 31st March, but after this date they would likely be cancelled.

We now feel less fretful and could breathe a sigh of relief.

Even with all that is going on, we are determined to enjoy our last few days.

We spent the afternoon round the pool and then went out for dinner at a local street market place.

We had beef with spinach, duck and noodles, jasmine rice and some rum and coke!

25th March

Breakfast was lovely again, cereal and strawberry yoghurt, poached eggs, toast, jam and marmalade.

We went to the beachside pool and for the majority of the morning we were the only ones there, so we had several dips in and out of the pool and topped up on our tans for one last time.

A delicious dinner again tonight, sweet and sour chicken, satay chicken, duck and pork noodles… and rum!

On the way home we walked through 'Walking Street' and the place was deserted, almost every single bar, club and restaurant was closed with chains securing their entrances and signs explaining 'due to the pandemic of Covid-19 we are closed until further notice'.

It was a really relaxing day today, and as sad and gloomy as it is we have to obey the rules, we are going home tomorrow — SAD.

We have booked a car to take us to the airport as there are now rumours that Thailand may have a curfew on travelling through towns after eight p.m. which will start tomorrow.

26th March

Well, this is it, our very last day of almost a year travelling.

We had breakfast, followed by a swim in the pool.

When we checked out at midday the lady on reception said that there were only twenty guests left in the hotel and that they had no more bookings, so would likely close within the next two weeks.

Our ride to the airport took just over an hour so it was really fast, we were really early as our flight is not due until 00:15, so we had to sit around for hours in anticipation hoping that our flight would not be cancelled.

As we watched the departures board, flight after flight were being cancelled, there were hundreds of irate passengers from Germany, as the only two flights scheduled for the day were announced as cancelled. Hamburg and Frankfurt were the destinations, and now all of those passengers congregated at the stand-by flight counter 'fighting' each-other for a place on any plane out of Bangkok to any destination available in Europe.

We talked about other films we need to put on the list to watch when we get home. There is going to be lots of time because we have to quarantine for two weeks as we are returning from Asia, and then who knows how long lockdown will last?

Ju has been getting some essential supplies for us, and Jess will still be in the house.

- *Good Morning Vietnam*
- *The Gate*
- *S21 The Khmer Rouge*
- *City of Ghosts*
- *The Killing Fields*
- *Platoon*
- *First they Killed my Father*

There are several screening points within Bangkok Airport including thermal imaging, and the wearing of a facemask is mandatory. Each time you pass in or out you are checked and a sticker is applied to your T-shirt which means you are OK.

Finally, our flight appeared on the departures board, flight TG910 from Bangkok to Heathrow was go, go, go!

We checked in our luggage, it's a shame because my bag only weighed 14.3 kilograms and I had a baggage allowance of thirty kilograms, but there had been no time for shopping.

Still, we had our boarding cards in our hands and knew now that our flight was confirmed.

27th March

We took off from Bangkok almost an hour late, but at least we were on our way.

The cabin crew served dinner and wine almost straight away it seemed.

I don't know about you but I love in-flight catering, it's so exciting when you get your little compartmented tray with fruit, a roll and butter, a desert of some sorts, and then you open your foil dish with dinner inside.

Today it was Thai green curry — of course, why wouldn't it be?

I couldn't sleep so I watched three films;
- *Judy* — a film about the life of Judy Garland played by the amazingly talented Rene Zellwegger
- *Charlie's Angels*
- *A Beautiful Day in the Neighbourhood* — starring Tom Hanks, very weird but surprisingly watchable.

An hour or so before landing we were served breakfast of omelette, sausage mushrooms and tomatoes, croissant and jam, orange juice and coffee.

The flight landed ahead of schedule and we touched down at London Heathrow airport at 06:20 on the morning of Friday 27th March.

Bunny was waiting for us, and would drive us home.

So, after 327 days, eighteen countries, ninety-nine towns and cities, and roughly 29,700 miles later, we were home safe and sound.

It sure has been an incredible journey even though not quite the homecoming we were expecting, but we are so lucky to have been able to fulfil our dreams, visiting many places on our 'book-it' list, experiencing some unbelievable customs and cultures and making the grandest of memories.

Probably the best year of our life!

Epilogue

Since coming home, like everyone else we have endured months of lockdown, self-isolation and social distancing.

I have been kept busy writing this book and cataloguing all of our photographs, I have been making photo albums with the best ones, and it is quite difficult as there are over 12,000 to choose from.

So far, I have completed India, Singapore, Malaysia, Cambodia, Vietnam, Philippines, Gallipoli, Troy and Istanbul.

Jess stayed with us for a while as her flat rental was severely delayed due to Covid, but she has now moved out and enjoying her own place.

I started to do some volunteering; I have been busy as an NHS responder for the Royal Voluntary Service.

It is mainly a check in and chat role, or prescription collection and delivery, I sometimes do some shopping, or make a collection and drop off from the local food bank.

I am one of an army of volunteers who stepped up to support vulnerable people who are most at risk in this pandemic and I have spoken to and met so many wonderful people who are lonely, distressed and emotional.

The whole experience has been incredibly humbling, to me it is just a small act, but for those who are not able to leave their house it is life changing and everyone I am helping is so grateful for the support.

I can honestly say that I love being a volunteer during this difficult time. We think of ourselves far too much and sometimes do not realise how lucky we have been to have had such a wonderful gap year, it has given me so much joy and made me feel that I am giving something back, however small it is.

I even have a few 'regulars' now.

Lou returned to work, his firm gave him a year sabbatical I guess you call it.

They employed someone on a year's contract whilst we were away, and on our return, he went back to his job as a driver.

How did this trip impact on life? Well of course you are never too old to travel like we have, but if you are going to do it by yourself it is important to have good health and be reasonably fit. Lou and I pinch ourselves sometimes, thankfully we are and have had relatively good fortune stowed upon us, but as we all know things in life can alter rapidly and sadly some peoples plans never come to fruition.

Some folk go through life always wanting more, like a state-of-the-art kitchen, a better car, a bigger house, maybe with a swimming pool and gym, I don't know.

Lou and I have never been really materialistic, but we do like nice things like eating out, the theatre, weekends away etc... And sometimes we take these for granted.

Sure, I missed going to The Wolseley for some fine dining, but some of the places we have seen and people we have encountered are so poor they do not even have basic food, let alone clothing, shelter or amenities, they are economically denied of basic necessities ... Are they happy? Well, my feeling is that the majority of them appeared so, that's just how it is and all they know.

Lessons learnt and how we have changed as individuals on analysis is really interesting — in the greater scheme of things objects and items, such as a frayed carpet (which we have on the landing), a chink on the enamel in the bath, a new pair of trainers, an ultra-smart TV or a chip on a plate of your dinner service suddenly do not matter.

Neither of us has brought a single item of new clothing since returning home, and previously items that we may have 'needed' are no longer essential.

We are lucky to have a roof over our heads, food in our bellies, central heating, a car, running water and sanitation, our health, the best son in the universe, and a wonderful family and friends.

We don't have to rely on government handouts and food-banks. We don't have a constant stream of hospital appointments. Financially we are not rich but we are comfortable.

We enjoy our little house, it is ours and paid for by us, we enjoy fine dining, we enjoy entertainment and driving our car, we enjoy seeing our family and socialising with our friends.

Lou and I have had the most amazing time together and will cherish the memories.

Would we do it again? There are still a few things on the 'book-it' list.

Here's to the next chapter, whatever that may be.

Printed in Great Britain
by Amazon

84504911R00192